Labour Economics

Other books by J. E. King

The Political Economy of Marx (with M. C. Howard)
The Economics of Marx (edited, with M. C. Howard)
Relative Income Shares (with P. Regan)
Readings in Labour Economics (editor)
Ten Per Cent and No Surrender: The Preston Strike 1853–4
    (with H. I. Dutton)
Economic Exiles
A History of Marxian Economics: Volume 1, 1883–1929 (with
    M. C. Howard)
Marxian Economics (editor)

Labour Economics
Second Edition

J. E. King

MACMILLAN

First edition 1972
Reprinted 1983
Second edition 1990

Published by
MACMILLAN EDUCATION LTD
Houndmills, Basingstoke, Hampshire RG21 2XS
and London
Companies and representatives
throughout the world

Typeset by Latimer Trend & Company Ltd
Plymouth

Printed in Hong Kong

British Library Cataloguing in Publication Data
King, J. E. (John Edward), 1947–
Labour economics.— 2nd ed.
1. Employment. Labour
I. Title
331
ISBN 0–333–48315–4 (hardcover)
ISBN 0–333–48316–2 (paperback)

Contents

v

Preface

This is a completely rewritten and greatly expanded version of a text which was first published in 1972. I am grateful for the helpful comments of Mike Howard, Russell Rimmer, Sheila Rimmer, John Singleton and Jim Taylor, to whom the usual disclaimer applies; and for typing by Maree Hartigan, Monica Hodgkinson, Rosemary Moore and Jenny Sifonios.

J. E. KING

1

Alternative Approaches to Labour Economics

1 Introduction

Economists are notorious for disagreeing amongst themselves, and labour economists are no less fractious than the rest. The controversies involve much more than straightforward differences over matters of fact which can in principle – if not always in practice – be settled by careful observation and painstaking empirical research. When schools of thought come into conflict with each other in economics, much broader issues are, almost inevitably, involved. What is at stake, in the most serious arguments among economists, is precisely what is to count as a (scientifically relevant) fact, how such facts are to be interpreted, and what generalisations can be made from them. Not just theory but also methodology is in dispute. This is why economic arguments are often so difficult to resolve (King, 1988, ch. 1; Woodbury, 1979).

In labour economics, as elsewhere in the discipline, there are competing schools of thought which can be separated, more or less clearly, in every one of these dimensions. That is, they use contrasting conceptual frameworks, cite different types of evidence, and often reveal conflicting moral and political presuppositions. This is not to deny that the rival schools share some common ground, nor that on particular questions the distinctions between them are often rather blurred. But much less harm will be done by emphasising

1

their differences than by ignoring them, or by presuming that one school is correct and the others are all fundamentally mistaken. Thus throughout this book we shall distinguish *neoclassical, post-Keynesian, institutionalist, radical-Marxian* and *green* approaches to the study of labour markets.

2   Neoclassical economics

A large majority of academic economists belong to the neoclassical or orthodox stream of thought (these two terms are used interchangeably here). As orthodox theorists have internal differences of their own, any brief definition is likely to prove unsatisfactory, but there would probably be general agreement on four basic points. The first is the central role of maximising behaviour on the part of economic agents – individuals, households and firms – subject to well-defined technological and budget constraints. Second, there is a deep suspicion of explanations which run in terms of habit and custom, collective as against individual decision-making, or the idiosyncrasies of human institutions. These suspicions are derived from the philosophical position known as *methodological individualism*, which assigns logical priority to microeconomic analysis over macroeconomics, and requires that statements about aggregate phenomena be grounded in a rigorous theory of individual behaviour. Some of the most interesting developments in neoclassical economics in recent decades have involved the application of methodological individualism to collective, institutional and other ostensibly 'non-economic' issues (Becker, 1957; Williamson, 1975; see Chapters 4 and 6 below).

Third is the principle of substitution. Individuals and households are supposed to choose from a wide range of commodities and to allocate their time between many different activities. Firms select techniques of production and levels of input usage from the large number which are available, while workers optimise in their choice of jobs, work and leisure. Fourth, and finally, most orthodox economists assume that there is a strong tendency for markets to clear, and for economic agents to be in, or rapidly approaching, equilibrium.

It must be repeated that not everyone would agree on these four propositions, and certainly not on their precise implications. Within the neoclassical camp there are, in fact, several more or less distinct sub-schools. *New classical* economists, for example, are much more confident about the forces which generate equilibrium than the *neo-Keynesians*, as is evident in their treatment of unemployment (see Chapter 10 below). *Austrian* theorists, for their part, reject any precise mathematical formulation of maximising behaviour and the equilibria to which it is expected to lead (Klamer, 1983). For all their differences, however, the various factions share enough common ground for there to be a clearly recognisable neoclassical perspective on almost every major problem in labour economics. As we shall see, this gives orthodox analysis a definite advantage over its theoretical rivals.

3 Post-Keynesian theory

The intellectual legacy of John Maynard Keynes has proved to be profoundly ambiguous. For many economists his ideas are fully reconcilable with the first three tenets of neoclassical analysis, requiring only certain modifications to the fourth to allow for the evident failure to clear of some markets (especially those for labour). In effect those neo-Keynesians, as we have termed them, constructed a synthesis of neoclassicism and Keynes's *General Theory*, the earliest and most important component of which was J. R. Hicks's IS–LM analysis (Hicks, 1937). At the microeconomic level, orthodox analysis survived without serious challenge.

For Michał Kalecki, John Robinson, Sidney Weintraub and other *post-Keynesian* theorists, this neoclassical interpretation of Keynes is entirely mistaken. It represents merely a 'bastard Keynesianism' (Robinson, 1965), in which the significant innovations which are explicit or implicit in the General Theory have been suppressed. The post-Keynesians argue that a genuinely Keynesian economics must be built on non-neoclassical foundations, as regards both micro and macro theory and methodology (Eichner, 1979).

In their microeconomic analysis the post-Keynesians attach very little importance to the behaviour of individuals, whether as workers or consumers. Individual decisions are more effectively constrained by macroeconomic factors, and by their lack of any real economic power, than by orthodox budget constraints, while workers obtain real influence only when they combine in trade unions. Much more emphasis is placed on the firm, by which the post-Keynesians mean large corporations rather than small owner-managed businesses. They claim that neoclassical marginalist equilibrium theory is irrelevant to the modern corporation, which is typically an oligopolist. Owing to perceived interdependence between the price and output decisions of competing oligopolists, there are no determinate demand or marginal revenue functions. Moreover, long-run cost curves are downward-sloping rather than U-shaped, and, in the short run, average variable and marginal costs are constant over a wide range of output. Prices do not reflect the impersonal forces of market supply and demand, but are set by the firm itself through the application of a fixed percentage mark-up to its variable costs of production. Prices vary with costs but not, as a general rule, with demand.

Post-Keynesians claim that there is a high probability of macroeconomic disequilibrium in an economy made up of large oligopolistic corporations. Taken together with the wage-setting ability of large trade unions, the corporations' mark-up pricing generates chronic inflation. Excess capacity is the normal state of affairs, and failures of effective aggregate demand give rise to mass unemployment. Neoclassical market-clearing models are as inappropriate here as they are at the micro level.

Although post-Keynesians consider their theory of the firm to be consistent with their conception of the macro economy, they repudiate any logical priority for microeconomic analysis. The direction of causation runs both ways, and the influence of economic aggregates upon individuals is, if anything, the stronger. Post-Keynesian analysis highlights the behaviour of broad social classes – in particular the differences in their savings propensities – in a way which neoclassical theorists find difficult to comprehend (see Chapter 9 below). Thus the post-Keynesian break with orthodoxy involves methodology as well as questions of substantive theory. They offer a quite distinct conceptual framework, albeit one which remains to be fully articulated.

4   Institutionalism

Institutionalism first took shape in the United States at the end of the nineteenth century, as a reaction against what was seen as the narrowness and spurious precision of the new neoclassical economics. Among its best-known advocates were Thorstein Veblen and John R. Commons, who was also a prominent early labour economist. The institutionalists were never more than a small minority among North American economists, but they continue to assert themselves on the margin of the profession through the *Journal of Economic Issues*. The Nobel laureate John Kenneth Galbraith is by far the most famous of modern institutionalists (though he also has strong links with the post-Keynesians).

Precisely because the institutionalists reject the elegant theoretical system of orthodox economics, their own thinking is less easy to pin down. An aversion to formal modelling is certainly one pronounced feature, which has developed in recent decades into a rejection of econometric techniques in favour of more informal literary modes of thought and expression. Institutionalists sometimes describe themselves as 'evolutionary economists', highlighting a second major element in their ideas. They maintain that economics is not a body of immutable and timeless truths, but is necessarily socially and historically relative: different periods, and different forms of society, require different types of economic analyses. This distinguishes the institutionalists very clearly from neoclassical economists, and is also one theme which they share with the radical-Marxian school.

The third and most obvious characteristic of institutional economics is its emphasis on habit, custom and collective behaviour, and its insistence that these phenomena cannot be reduced to the maximising behaviour of isolated, calculating individuals. Thus institutionalists refuse to take for granted the existence of markets, but ask how, where, when and why regular patterns of market exchange appear – and fail to appear. They also reject the neoclassical treatment of individuals' tastes as non-economic data. For the institutionalists the social formation of consumers' and workers' preferences is among the most important of all economic issues.

This points to a fourth feature of institutionalist thought, which is its close affinity with sociology and politics and its repudiation both of any sharp demarcation between economics and other social sciences, and of the neoclassical claim to sovereignty over them. Its multidisciplinary perspective helps to explain why institutionalism has always been influential among labour economists, who from the nature of their subject-matter are inherently more conscious than their colleagues in other branches of the discipline of the social and institutional framework which underpins market behaviour.

Traditionally, too, many labour economists moved into the area from industrial relations and became impatient with, or entirely oblivious to, the boundaries between the two subjects. In the US, J. R. Commons inspired a whole generation of 'neorealist' or 'post-institutionalist' labour economists, including Clark Kerr, Lloyd Reynolds, Arthur Ross and Richard Lester (Kerr, 1983; Segal, 1986); in Britain E. H. Phelps Brown was the most eminent representative of a similar stream of thought. During the heyday of human capital theory in the 1960s (see Chapter 3 below), neoclassical theory seemed to have overwhelmed the institutionalists, but there has since been a powerful reaction against it. The institutionalist revival has been spearheaded by Michael Piore (1973) and Lester Thurow (1976), whose writings have proved increasingly influential also in Britain (Turk, 1983; Marsden, 1986). Rather like post-Keynesian economics, however, institutionalism is not yet at the stage where it offers a fully convincing and comprehensive challenge to orthodox labour economics; it is still less coherent, less rigorous, less fully elaborated. As we shall see in later chapters, it remains open to the accusation that the practices it describes are nothing other than neoclassical maximising behaviour in disguise.

5 Radical-Marxian political economy

Over a century after his death, the influence of Karl Marx remains very substantial. In Britain and Western Europe his followers generally describe themselves as 'Marxist' or 'socialist' economists, and tend to be rather more punctilious in their adherence to the letter of his writings. North American Marxism is more open-ended and flexible, paying less attention to textual accuracy than to the spirit of Marx's ideas, and preferring the label 'radical'.

All agree on the importance and fundamental characteristics of Marx's central organising concept, *capitalism*. This is an economic system in which the means of production (machines, buildings, raw materials, land) are owned by a minority class who employ the propertyless, producing class as wage labourers. As in any class society, the producers perform *surplus labour*: that is, they work longer than would be necessary for them collectively to produce the goods that they themselves require. In capitalism goods are produced for sale on the market, as *commodities*. The working class, too, sells the only commodity which it possesses, its capacity to work, which Marx termed its *labour power*. The surplus labour which is performed assumes a monetary form as *surplus value*. Capitalists aim to extract as much surplus value as possible from their workers and accumulate the greater part of it, to enable them to survive in the relentless rivalry with their competitors. More fundamental even than conflict between capitalists is the *class struggle* between capitalists and workers, which colours every aspect of the employment relationship (Howard and King, 1985).

On almost every count radical-Marxian theory is opposed to neoclassical economics. Its most significant economic agents are social classes rather than the individuals of which they are composed. It also places much greater stress on non-market, production relations than on market exchanges. A 'pure theory of exchange' with nothing to say about the organisation of production (with which neoclassicals often begin their analysis) would, for radical-Marxian economists, be an utterly futile exercise. They take very little heed of substitution possibilities; it is capitalist decisions which provide the system's motive power, so that the behaviour of individual workers and consumers is of little importance, and capitalists themselves have much more serious matters to attend to than marginal adjustments to methods of production as input prices vary with given technology. Finally, radical-Marxian theorists set little store by market-clearing equilibria. They regard capitalism as dynamically unstable, given to erratic bursts of growth but also prone to increasingly severe crises of failing profitability and over-production. And they see the constant pressure of mass unemployment as a vital factor in keeping real wages sufficiently low to permit the continuing production of surplus value.

Radical-Marxian economists are less consistently hostile to post-Keynesian and institutional theory. They share the post-Keynesians' methodological claim for the priority of macroeconomic analysis, and the institutionalists' socio-historical relativism, their stress on collective behaviour, and their multi-disciplinary inclinations. All three schools reject marginalist equilibrium analysis, both as a theory of the individual productive unit and at the level of the entire economy. In fact on some significant questions in labour economics – most obviously in the controversies surrounding dual and segmented labour market theory (see Chapter 7, section 6, below) – a very high degree of cross-fertilisation is apparent between the radical-Marxian, post-Keynesian and institutional approaches. On other issues – the importance of class conflict, the role of formal model-building, the eventual fate of the capitalist mode of production and the potential for socialism – the differences are more apparent.

There are also deep-rooted theoretical conflicts within the radical-Marxian school itself (Howard and King, 1991). One long-standing source of disagreement is the status of Marx's theory of value and the permissibility of reformulating his analysis of capitalism, which is stated in terms of labour values and surplus values, in price and profit magnitudes. Related to this is uncertainty concerning the value of labour power, a 'commodity' which, unlike all others, is not produced under capitalist control for profit. In consequence there is nothing approaching a single, generally acceptable radical-Marxian theory of wages. A third area of difficulty is the theory of crisis and the part (if any) played by class struggles in production and conflicts over wage rates in the tendency for the rate of profit to fall.

Finally there is a serious methodological debate, as yet unconcluded. Marxists often use functionalist explanations of economic phenomena, along the lines that 'X occurs because it is necessary to the survival (or beneficial to the prosperity) of capitalism that it does occur'. Precisely how this functional imperative is translated into individual action is unclear, and a small but growing number of radical-Marxian theorists are urging that it be replaced by motivational statements of the form 'X occurs because the individual economic agents who make it occur believe it to be in their best interests that it should do so'. This *rational choice Marxism* has evident affinities with orthodox methodological individualism, and this is quite enough to damn it in the eyes of more traditionally-minded Marxists. The problem is, of course, that no radical-Marxian economist would deny that in some sense capitalists do seek to maximise their profits. This, indeed, is one crucial proposition which they share with their neoclassical adversaries.

6   Green economics

Green economics is of much more recent origin than the schools of thought considered so far in this chapter. It grew out of the environmentalist movement of the 1960s and early 1970s, owing much to the work of E. F. Schumacher, who died in 1977. Schumacher's early writings were as an energy economist, but his interests soon encompassed the problems of Third World development and the interplay between work, technology and human organisation in the rich countries. He became a stern critic of orthodox economics, which, he argued, focused upon short-run concerns, exaggerated the value of market relationships at the expense of deeper social ties, and neglected humanity's duty to protect the 'free goods' offered by the natural environment. Schumacher advocated both an alternative economics and an alternative life-style based upon small-scale organisation, 'intermediate technology', and the restriction of resource usage to levels which could be maintained indefinitely (Wood, 1984; King, 1988, chapter 10; Ekins, 1986).

Three aspects of Schumacher's thinking are of direct relevance to labour economics. The first is his insistence that work should be viewed positively, as an end in itself, and not merely negatively, as the sacrifice of time to provide an input into the production of material commodities. Work alters the worker's personality and character, and its effect upon the individual should be treated as a joint product along with output. Such joint products are frequently bads, like pollution. They are ignored, Schumacher suggests, by orthodox measures of social welfare like GNP, which cannot therefore be taken seriously (Schumacher, 1979). Here green economics has much in common with the radical-Marxian analysis of alienation (see Chapters 3–4 below).

Second, Schumacher stressed the need for economic activity to be permanently sustainable. Since resources are finite this requires acceptance that there are natural limits to growth. Green economists place a higher value on increased leisure time – or, more accurately, upon the time available for non-market activities – and correspondingly devalue the continued expansion of material production. As will be seen in Chapter 3, this has important consequences for the analysis of work-leisure choices.

Finally, green economists regard the related questions of the organisational and technical scale of production as basic to human well-being. *Small Is Beautiful*, the title of Schumacher's best-selling book, epitomises the green position. Large hierarchical organisations stifle human creativity, and mass production techniques destroy established craft skills and degrade the physical and intellectual capacities of those enslaved by them. For green economists modern economic institutions are inherently elitist, wasteful and violent. They must be replaced by small-scale production units, controlled co-operatively and supplying local needs by the use of technology which stimulates rather than stunting the mental and moral development of the human beings involved.

There are many issues of great interest to labour economists on which the greens have, as yet, little or nothing to contribute. Clearly, however, green economics is at odds with neoclassical theory on fundamental questions, including the specification and measurement of social welfare, and the time-horizon to which economic analysis must relate. On some issues the greens are much closer to the institutionalists, especially in what they have to say about the socio-technical organisation of work, and they also tend to agree with radical-Marxian views on this subject.

There are also grounds for mutual suspicion between greens and radical-Marxian theorists. The greens oppose both the enthusiasm which many Marxists still display for large-scale technology and the neglect of environmental factors in radical-Marxist criticisms of the capitalist mode of production. Nor is class conflict a central problem for Schumacher and his followers. The green perspective does not rule out the emergence of a 'capitalism with a human face'. Many radical-Marxians, for their part, would agree with the neoclassical charge that 'small is stupid' in dismissing the many advantages offered by the social division of labour and attendant economics of scale (Beckerman, 1979).

7   Conclusion

To recapitulate: there is no one 'correct' approach to the study of labour markets. There are a number of competing schools of thought, but the boundaries between them are frequently untidy or ill-defined. Each is stronger on some questions than on others, and on particular issues it is often difficult to distinguish one from another. No simple resort to 'the facts', no single critical experiment, can be expected ever to vindicate one approach against all the others, since they differ on methodological as well as on substantive issues. In the remainder of this book neoclassical, post-Keynesian, institutionalist, radical-Marxian and green thinking is distinguished as far and as fully as is practicable. Economics is – or should be – pluralistic, open and critical, aware of the differences between competing theoretical frameworks and always searching for new ways of assessing their respective merits.

2

The Demand for Labour

1 Neoclassical theory: the short run

Neoclassical economics offers by far the most ambitious and fully-developed account of the demand for labour. Other schools make serious criticisms of orthodox analysis but – with the partial exception of institutionalism and post-Keynesian theory – very little by way of positive replacement. For this reason the bulk of the present chapter is devoted to neoclassical theory.

We begin with the fundamental postulate of marginalist equilibrium theory, that the firm is a profit-maximiser, and add to this two simplifying assumptions which will be removed later on. First, we are dealing only with the short run, in which the quantity of other inputs (in particular capital equipment) is fixed. Second, labour is an entirely variable cost.

Profit maximisation requires that labour be employed up to the point where an extra unit adds as much to the firm's revenue as to its costs. *Marginal revenue productivity* (*MRPL*) must equal *marginal labour cost* (*MLC*). *MRPL* measures the effect of each additional unit of labour employed on the firm's total revenue. It is easy to show that $MRPL = MPPL \times MR$, where $MPPL$ is the marginal physical productivity of labour, derived from the firm's production function, and MR is marginal revenue, given by its product demand curve.[1]

As the employment of labour increases, $MRPL$ must eventually decline (though it may increase at first). This follows from the *law of variable proportions* (also known as the *law of diminishing returns*), which states that the marginal physical productivity of any input must after some point decline as more of that input is employed, holding constant the amounts of other inputs which are in use. This is generally regarded by neoclassical theorists as self-evident, since one could not – in the limiting case – grow the world's food supplies in a flower-pot.

This conclusion is reinforced by a second consideration. Marginal revenue cannot rise with output. In most circumstances it will fall as an increasing quantity of output is sold. Two cases must be distinguished here. If the firm is a perfect competitor in its product market it faces a perfectly elastic product demand curve, and price is equal to marginal revenue ($P = MR$). Here, and only here, $MRPL = VMPL$, where $VMPL$ denotes the *value of the marginal product* of labour and is defined as $MPPL \times P$ (marginal physical product times price). If, however, the firm is a monopolist, monopolistic competitor, or an oligopolist, facing a downward-sloping product demand curve, its marginal revenue will be less than price

---

[1] The firm's demand function is $P = F(Q)$, and its production function is $Q = G(K,L)$; in the short run, K is constant. The total revenue productivity of labour is $TRPL = P \cdot Q$, and marginal revenue productivity is

$$MRPL = \frac{\partial}{\partial L}(P \cdot Q) = Q \cdot \frac{\partial P}{\partial L} + P \frac{\partial Q}{\partial L}.$$

Since, by the function-of-a-function rule,

$$\frac{\partial P}{\partial L} = \frac{dP}{dQ} \cdot \frac{\partial Q}{\partial L},$$

we can write:

$$\frac{\partial}{\partial L}(P \cdot Q) = Q \cdot \frac{dP}{dQ} \cdot \frac{\partial Q}{\partial L} + P \cdot \frac{\partial Q}{\partial L}$$

$$= \frac{\partial Q}{\partial L}(P + \frac{dP}{dQ} \cdot Q)$$

$$= MPPL \times MR$$

where $MPPL$ is the marginal physical product of labour, and MR is marginal revenue (as can be seen by differentiating $P \cdot Q$ with respect to Q).

($MR < P$), so that $MRPL < VMPL$. In this case the concept of $VMPL$ is no longer relevant to the firm's decisions.

There are, to recapitulate, two reasons why $MRPL$ declines as the employment of labour increases. One operates in production, since $MPPL$ declines in accordance with the law of variable proportions. The other works through the product market, reflecting the decline in marginal revenue because (outside perfect competition) increasing sales depress the product price.

The shape of the firm's marginal labour cost curve also depends upon the type of competition which it confronts, but this time it is the nature of the labour market which is important. In a perfectly competitive labour market the firm faces an infinitely elastic labour supply curve, since it is too small to affect the market wage rate, no matter how much labour it demands. The labour supply curve is identical with the firm's average labour cost (ALC) curve. Under perfect competition in the labour market, $ALC = MLC$, and both are invariant with respect to the firm's employment of labour.

Alternatively, the firm may be large enough for its actions to affect the market wage. This will be the case if it is a *monopsonist* (sole buyer), *oligopsonist* (one buyer among few), or *monopsonistic competitor* (one buyer among many, but not enough to constitute a perfectly competitive labour market). In these markets the labour supply curve faced by the firm will be upward-sloping, since each increase in its demand for labour will increase the market wage. Its MLC will now exceed the ALC because – assuming that it cannot discriminate between its employees – the firm must pay its existing workers the higher rates of pay required to attract the marginal units of labour.[2]

Figures 2.1 and 2.2 illustrate the equilibrium of the firm in perfectly competitive and imperfectly competitive markets. Its revenue productivity curves are the same in each case, with $MRPL$ first rising with increased employment and then declining. The associated *average revenue productivity* ($ARPL$) curves have a similar slope, and for the same reasons. In Figure 2.1 the ALC and MLC curves are identical horizontal lines, as already explained, while in Figure 2.2

---

[2] The firm's labour supply is $L = L(W)$, where $W = ALC$ (average labour cost). Total labour cost is $TLC = W \cdot L$, so that marginal labour cost $= MLC = \mathrm{d}/(\mathrm{d}L)\,(W \cdot L)$ $= W + (\mathrm{d}W/\mathrm{d}L) \cdot L$. Hence $MLC = ALC$ where $\mathrm{d}W/\mathrm{d}L = 0$, and $MLC > ALC$, where $\mathrm{d}W/\mathrm{d}L > 0$. The first case corresponds to an infinitely elastic (horizontal) labour supply curve, the second to a less than infinitely elastic (upward-sloping) curve.

15

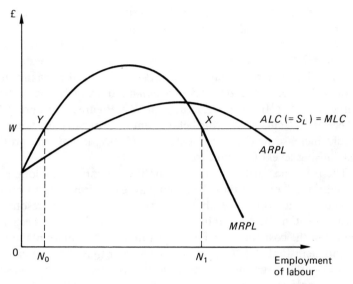

Figure 2.1

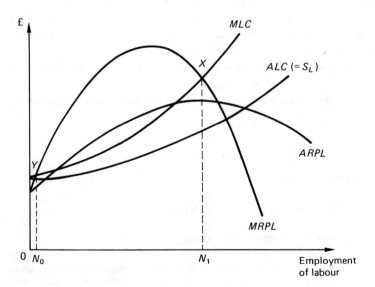

Figure 2.2

both *ALC* and *MLC* are upward-sloping, the latter being higher and increasing more rapidly as employment grows.

To arrive at its equilibrium level of employment the firm must equate *MRPL* and *MLC*. This, however, is only part of the story. It is, in technical terms, only a *first-order condition* for maximising profits. The related *second-order condition* requires that the *MRPL* curve cuts *MLC* from above, as at point X in Figure 2.1. At point Y, where *MRPL* cuts *MLC* from below, continued expansion of output would increase profits. Thus ON_1 is, and ON_0 is not, the profit-maximising level of output.[3]

There is one further condition for the attainment of long-run equilibrium. The firm must be making at least *normal profits* on its capital, or it will leave the industry and deploy its resources elsewhere. On the assumption that normal profits have been in-cluded in the cost curves in Figures 2.1 and 2.2, this amounts to the requirement that *ARPL* is equal to or greater than *ALC*. It can be seen from the diagrams that this condition is satisfied, in both cases, at the employment level ON_1. Both firms, in fact, make *abnormal profits*, since *ARPL* is greater than *ALC*. If *ARPL* had been less than *ALC* the industry would have contracted as firms moved out, pushing up the product price and shifting outwards the *ARPL* and *MRPL* curves of those which remained. Depending on the elasticity of labour supply to the industry as a whole, labour may also have become cheaper (lowering the *ALC* and *MLC* curves) as the number of firms competing for it declined.

The situation depicted in Figures 2.1 and 2.2 is one of long-run

---

[3] Profits (Π) are defined as the difference between *TRPL* and *TLC* (ignoring non-labour costs and normal profits). Thus $\Pi = TRPL - TLC = (P \cdot Q) - (W \cdot L)$. The maximisation of profits requires:

(i) $\dfrac{\partial \Pi}{\partial L} = 0$, that is $\dfrac{\partial}{\partial L}(P \cdot Q) - \dfrac{\partial}{\partial L}(W \cdot L) = 0$

    so that $MRPL = MLC$

(ii) $\dfrac{\partial^2 \Pi}{\partial L^2} < 0$, that is $\dfrac{\partial}{\partial L}(MRPL) - \dfrac{\partial}{\partial L}(MLC) < 0$,

    that is, $\dfrac{\partial}{\partial L}(MRPL) < \dfrac{\partial}{\partial L}(MLC)$.

Since *MLC* is either constant or rises as employment increases, a sufficient condition for (ii) is that *MRPL* is downward-sloping. This is the *second-order condition* for a maximum.

equilibrium, however, only if the product markets concerned are not perfectly competitive. If there is free entry into the industry, any abnormal profits will be competed away by a process which is the reverse of that which has been described. The number of firms will expand, the product price will fall, and the firms' revenue productivity curves will shift downwards. If the industry's labour supply is less than infinitely elastic, *ALC* and *MLC* will also move up. The eventual outcome of the process of competition is for *MRPL* to equal *MLC* at a level of employment where *ARPL* equals *ALC*. This is shown in Figures 2.3 and 2.4 for perfectly and imperfectly competitive labour markets.

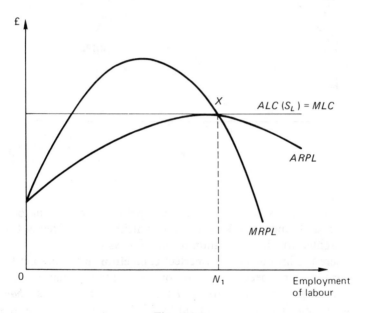

Figure 2.3

Note that there is no necessary reason why the degree of competition in the labour market should correspond with that in the product market. The most powerful multinational oligopolist will enjoy little or no market power when hiring secretarial or clerical staff in central London, while a Norfolk wheat farmer who faces a perfectly elastic product demand curve may well be something of a monopsonist in the rural labour market. Neoclassical writers tend to assume,

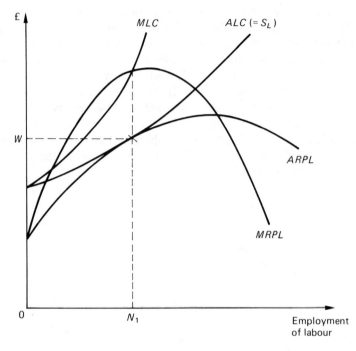

Figure 2.4

somewhat carelessly, that perfect competition prevails in both product and labour markets, but this is neither self-evidently true nor essential for the application of their analysis.

Where the firm is indeed a perfect competitor in the market for labour – and irrespective of conditions in its product market – the downward-sloping part of its *MRPL* curve also serves as its *labour demand curve*. That is, it traces out the profit-maximising quantities of employment corresponding to each level of the wage rate. This is illustrated in Figures 2.5 (for the industry) and 2.6 (for the individual firm); note that the scale of the horizontal axis is different in the two diagrams. In Figure 2.5 successive shifts in the industry's labour supply curve increase the market-clearing wage from OW_1 to OW_2 and then to OW_3. They are reflected, in Figure 2.6, in shifts in the firm's perfectly elastic labour supply curve and related reductions in the quantity of labour employed, from ON_1 to ON_2 and then to ON_3. For simplicity the *ARPL* curve has been omitted from Figures 2.5

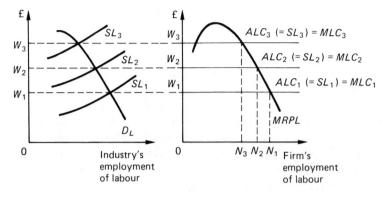

Figure 2.5   Figure 2.6

and 2.6, and the relationship between *ARPL* and *ACL* has been ignored.

For each wage rate there is, as can be seen, one and only one profit-maximising level of employment for the firm. This may be read off from its *MRPL* curve, which can therefore be regarded as its labour demand curve. This is why neoclassical theorists consider it so important that *MRPL* is negatively sloped, since this establishes the fact that the *law of demand* applies to labour as well as to its products. Higher wages mean lower employment: this is the golden rule of the orthodox theory of labour demand. It applies both to the firm and to the industry, and is often extended (with much less justification) to the economy as a whole. As we shall see in later chapters, this principle has major implications for the neoclassical analysis of wage differentials, trade unions, income distribution and unemployment.

2 An important qualification

The principle is, however, applicable only to perfectly competitive labour markets. In all other markets the firm has no labour demand curve, and no monotonically decreasing relationship between wages and employment can be established. Compare Figures 2.1 and 2.3 with Figures 2.2 and 2.4. In the former, the firm is in equilibrium where the wage rate is equal to the marginal revenue product of labour, since the wage = *ALC* = *MLC* = *MRPL*. In the latter, equilibrium occurs with the wage rate less than the marginal revenue product, since the wage $= ALC < MLC = MRPL$. The firm is off its $MRPL$ curve.

If the elasticity of labour supply changes, altering the position and/or the shape of the ALC and MLC curves, the same wage may be associated with a different equilibrium employment level, and vice versa. Hence there is no unique negative relationship between the wage rate and employment, as there was in the case of the perfectly competitive labour market, and no labour demand curve for the firm. The reasoning is identical to that which shows that the product market monopolist has no supply curve, since in equilibrium it is off its marginal cost curve.[4]

One extreme but revealing example is illustrated in Figure 2.7, which depicts the introduction of a trade union or statutory minimum wage in a hitherto imperfectly competitive market. Originally the firm was in equilibrium at C, hiring ON_1 units of labour at a wage rate of OW_1 and making abnormal profits of $ON_1 \times AB$, where AB is the gap between $ARPL$ and ALC (that is, abnormal profits per unit of labour). Note that there is also a gap of AC between the wage $(= ALC)$ and $MRPL$.

The minimum wage prohibits the payment of a wage below OW_2. But it also guarantees the firm a perfectly elastic supply of labour at OW_2 up to an employment level of ON_3, beyond which the suppliers of additional labour begin to hold out for more. The new equi-

---

[4] The elasticity of labour supply is

$$n_L = \frac{\mathrm{d}L}{\mathrm{d}W} \cdot \frac{W}{L},$$

so that

$$\frac{1}{n_L} = \frac{\mathrm{d}W}{\mathrm{d}L} \cdot \frac{L}{W}, \quad \text{and} \quad \frac{\mathrm{d}W}{\mathrm{d}L} \cdot L = \frac{W}{n_L}.$$

Hence $MLC = W + \dfrac{\mathrm{d}W}{\mathrm{d}L} \cdot L$ (see note 2 above)

$$= W + \frac{W}{n_L}$$

$$= W(1 + \frac{1}{n_L})$$

Thus   if $n_L \to \infty$, $MLC = W$
       if $n_L < \infty$, any change in n_L means that each W is associated with a different MLC from that prevailing previously.

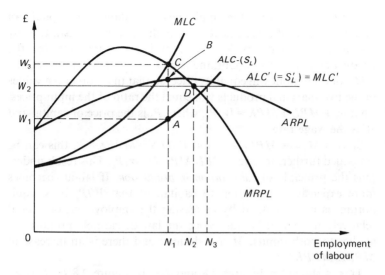

Figure 2.7

librium is at *D*. Here the higher wage OW_2, which is now equal to *MRPL*, is associated with increased employment ($ON_2 > ON_1$). In fact any minimum wage below OW_3 would involve a level of employment greater than ON_1.

This particular outcome can occur only once. As soon as the firm's labour market power has been destroyed, and it has been forced onto its *MRPL* curve, further wage increases must be at the expense of reduced employment. But the general point remains valid: except where there is perfect competition in the labour market the firm has no labour demand curve, and the central theorem in the neoclassical analysis of the demand for labour cannot be relied upon.

3   Neoclassical theory: the long run

We now relax the first assumption with which we began, and allow the firm to vary the quantity of capital in response to changes in its price relatively to that of labour. Profit maximisation requires the minimisation of costs; and cost-minimisation requires that the same rule be applied to capital as to labour: marginal revenue productivity must equal marginal cost.

The implications for the employment of labour and capital can best be seen if the argument is simplified, rather drastically, by assuming perfect competition to prevail in all markets, for the product as well as for labour and capital. Then, in equilibrium, the *VMP* of each input will equal its price, so that the ratio of the values of the two marginal products will equal the ratio of the input prices. That is, $VMPL/VMPK = W/P_k$, where P_k is the price of capital and W is the wage rate.

Since $VMPL = MPPL \times P$ and $VMPK = MPPK \times P$, this can be simplified further, to give $MPPL/MPPK = W/P_k$. This result underpins the principle of *substitution in production*. If labour becomes more expensive, in relation to capital, so that W/P_k rises, equilibrium is re-established by increasing the employment of capital relatively to that of labour. Since the law of variable proportions applies to both inputs, *MPPK* declines and there is an increase in *MPPL/MPPK*.

This is shown in Figures 2.8 and 2.9. In Figure 2.8 Q_0Q_0 is an *isoquant*, derived from the firm's production function and tracing

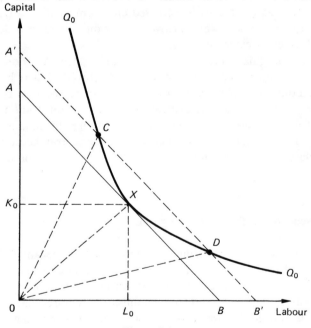

Figure 2.8

out all the combinations of capital and labour which are capable of producing one particular volume of output. There is an infinite number of isoquants, one for each output level. The slope of the isoquant at any point reveals the increase in labour input needed to compensate for a reduction of one unit in the usage of capital. This is the *marginal rate of substitution* of capital for labour. Disregarding the negative sign, it is equal to the ratio of the marginal physical products, $MPPL/MPPK$.[5]

The *isocost* line AXB shows all the combinations of the two inputs which the firm can purchase for a given outlay. The steeper its slope, the more capital can be bought relative to labour; the higher, therefore is the relative price of labour. The slope of the isocost line thus measures the ratio of the two input prices, W/P_k.[6]

The firm minimises costs by selecting that combination of capital and labour inputs which places it on the lowest available isocost line for any given output. X is a cost-minimising combination. Here the slope of the isoquant Q_0Q_0 is equal to that of the isocost line AXB, and $MPPL/\text{MPPK} = W/P_k$. It involves the employment of OL_0 units of labour and OK_0 units of labour, with a *capital–labour ratio* of OK_0/OL_0 (this can also be measured by the slope of the ray OX from

---

[5] Totally differentiating the production function $Q = G(K,L)$, we have:

$$dQ = dK \cdot \frac{\partial Q}{\partial K} + dL \cdot \frac{\partial Q}{\partial L}$$

Along an isoquant $dQ = 0$, so that

$$-dK \cdot \frac{\partial Q}{\partial K} = dL \cdot \frac{\partial Q}{\partial L}, \quad \text{and} \quad -\frac{dK}{dL} = \frac{\partial Q}{\partial L} \Big/ \frac{\partial Q}{\partial K}$$

Here, the left-hand side is the slope of the isoquant, and the right-hand side is the ratio of $MPPL$ to $MPPK$.

[6] The isocost function is defined as $\bar{C} = W \cdot L + P_K \cdot K$, where W and P_K are given to the firm, and $\bar{C}$ is a constant. Hence

$$K = \frac{1}{P_K}(\bar{C} - W \cdot L)$$

and the slope of the isocost function is

$$\frac{dK}{dL} = -\frac{W}{P_K}$$

This is the ratio of the two input prices. Since both are assumed to be in perfectly elastic supply to the firm, this ratio is constant.

the origin to X). Both a more capital-intensive method of production, at C, and a more labour-intensive technique, shown by D, are inferior to this since they involve the higher isocost line $A'B'$, and hence greater costs of production.

In Figure 2.9 the isoquant Q_0Q_0 is as before, but there are now two isocost lines with different slopes. AXB is the same as in Figure 2.8, but DYE illustrates a higher wage, relatively to the price of capital. The firm responds to the higher price of labour by moving to point Y, using a new and higher capital–labour ratio OK_1/OL_1 (which is equal to the slope of the ray OY). Its employment of capital has risen by K_0K_1 units, and employment of labour has fallen by L_1L_0. Relatively cheaper capital has been substituted for relatively more expensive labour.

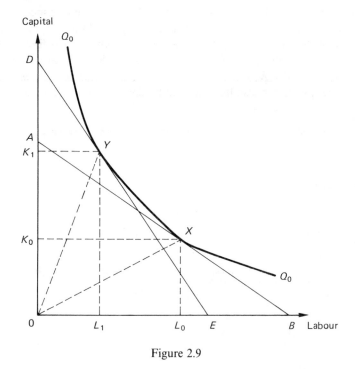

Figure 2.9

The degree to which substitution is technically possible depends upon the curvature of the isoquant Q_0Q_0. In more technical terms, it is governed by the *elasticity of substitution* (σ), where

$$\sigma = \frac{\text{proportionate change in } K/L}{\text{proportionate change in } w/P_k}.$$

The elasticity of substitution links the proportionate change in the relative quantities of the two inputs to the proportionate change in their relative prices. In Figure 2.9, for example, the first of these changes is shown by the relationship between K_1/L_1 and K_0/L_0, while the second is reflected in the increased slope of the isocost line DYE by comparison with AXB.

There is a considerable range of possible values for the elasticity of substitution, ranging from *infinite* when the isoquants are straight lines, meaning that the two inputs are perfect substitutes and, since there is no discernible difference between them, the firm simply employs the cheaper of the two; *positive but finite*, as in Figure 2.9; and *zero*, as shown by Figure 2.10, where there is only one cost-minimising combination of capital and labour, whatever their relative prices may be. The L-shaped isoquant Q_0XQ_0 in Figure 2.10 illustrates this special case of fixed technical coefficients of production, with a capital–labour ratio OK_0/OL_0 (equal to the slope of the ray OX) which is unchanged whether labour is relatively expensive (as shown by the isocost line DXE) or relatively cheap (isocost line AXB).

In a later chapter we shall see that the elasticity of substitution plays a major role in the neoclassical theory of relative income shares. Here it is of greatest significance as one of the four *Marshallian conditions* (Marshall, 1920, Book V, Chapter 6) governing the elasticity of labour demand, that is, the degree to which employment declines as the wage rate rises.

The four Marshallian conditions are:

(i)   the elasticity of substitution;
(ii)   the elasticity of supply of other inputs;
(iii)   the elasticity of demand for the product; and
(iv)   the proportion of labour costs to the total costs of production.

The first and second conditions concern the ease of substitution in production. The higher the elasticity of production the greater, *ceteris paribus*, is the elasticity of labour demand. This can be seen by comparing Figure 2.9 (where $\sigma > 0$ and employment of labour falls by L_0L_1) with Figure 2.10 (where $\sigma = 0$ and the employment of labour is unchanged when the wage rate increases).

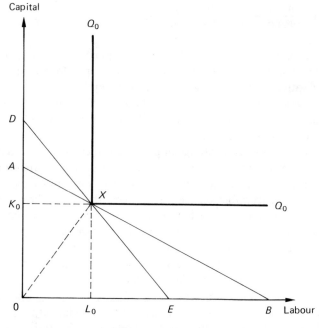

Figure 2.10

Both figures presuppose an infinitely elastic supply of both capital and labour to the firm; this was assumed at the beginning of this section, in order to obtain linear isocost functions. If, however, the supply of capital is relatively inelastic, the isocost 'line' will be curved.[7] The firm's increased demand for capital will push up its

---

[7] If labour is in imperfectly elastic supply, while the supply of capital remains perfectly elastic, we have $W = W(L)$ and the formula in note 6 for the isocost line is modified to:

$$\bar{C} = W(L) \cdot L + P_K \cdot K$$

Its slope is:

$$\frac{\mathrm{d}K}{\mathrm{d}L} = -\frac{1}{P_K} \{W(L) + L \cdot \frac{\mathrm{d}W}{\mathrm{d}L}\} < 0 \quad \text{since} \quad \frac{\mathrm{d}W}{\mathrm{d}L} > 0$$

The curvature of the isocost function depends upon

$$\frac{\mathrm{d}^2 K}{\mathrm{d}L^2} = -\frac{1}{P_K} \{2 \frac{\mathrm{d}W}{\mathrm{d}L} + L \frac{\mathrm{d}^2 W}{\mathrm{d}L^2}\}$$

which is < 0 unless $\mathrm{d}^2 W/\mathrm{d}L^2$ is strongly negative.

price and retard its substitution for labour, again reducing the elasticity of labour demand. This is the meaning of the second Marshallian condition.

The remaining conditions deal with substitution by consumers, in the product market. The argument runs as follows. A higher wage rate will raise unit costs and increase the product price. The more elastic is product demand, the greater will be the fall in the quantity purchased and hence the greater is the decline in the quantity of labour demanded to produce it. This is the third condition. The fourth, often referred to as *the importance of being unimportant*, states that the effect of a wage increase on the price of the product will be greater, the larger the proportion of its production costs which are accounted for by wages (Bronfenbrenner, 1971, pp. 144–50; but see Peirson, 1988). Note that both these factors involve changes in the level of output, so that neither is reflected in Figures 2.9 and 2.10, where output remains constant.

Neoclassical economists draw two important conclusions from this analysis. First and foremost, they expect the elasticity of labour demand to be negative, and to differ significantly from zero in almost all cases. Even if substitution in production is impossible, substitution by consumers will reduce the demand for labour when wages rise, since output will fall. Second, elasticity of labour demand will be greater in the long run than in the short run, due to the greater substitution opportunities available to producers and consumers as plant is redesigned and purchasing habits change. Only when these opportunities are blocked, by trade union restrictions or government regulation, will higher wage rates not appreciably reduce the long-run employment of labour.

4   Labour as a semi-fixed cost

We now remove the second assumption made at the beginning of the chapter, and allow for the existence of fixed as well as variable labour costs. The first step is to define the input 'labour'. We can write output per day as:

Number of workers × hours worked per worker per day × hourly output per worker.

In its simplest form the neoclassical theory of labour demand assumes the third component, hourly output per worker, to be a technical datum, entirely determined by the firm's production function and thus constant unless capital per worker alters or there is technological change. It is further supposed, in elementary neoclassical theory, that workers and hours are interchangeable, so that the firm has no reason to prefer an increase (or decrease) in the number of workers employed to an equivalent increase (or reduction) in the hours worked by each employee.

Neither assumption is defensible, and the input of 'labour' has three dimensions: workers, hours and effort. Output per hour worked is not a datum but an economic variable, even with technology and the level of capital per head held constant. Labour productivity varies with the amount of effort supplied by the worker, and hence depends upon motivational factors about which nothing has so far been said. Neoclassical theory is not at its strongest in dealing with this question, as will been seen later in the present chapter. A full discussion must be deferred, however, until Chapter 4.

The second assumption can be justified only if neither the worker's hourly output nor the hourly cost of labour varies with the number of hours worked in a given period (for example, a day). Again, this will not in general be the case. If nothing else, sheer fatigue will certainly lead to a reduction in hourly productivity after some point in the day. More important is the variation in labour costs with the number of hours which are worked. One obvious cause of such variations is the worker's contractual right to premium rates (time-and-a-quarter, time-and-a-third etc.) for overtime hours.

There are also significant non-wage costs of employment, including payroll taxes of various kinds, the administrative costs of hiring workers, and (probably the most important) training costs. The impact of payroll taxes can be extremely complex, depending upon the intricacies of the tax regime (see Bell, 1982 for one example). Hiring and training costs constitute an investment made by the firm in each newly-hired worker; similar investments made by workers are considered in Chapter 3. Since they do not depend on the length of the employment relationship such outlays are necessarily fixed rather than variable in nature, and this makes a major difference to the neoclassical theory of labour demand (Oi, 1962).

Suppose for simplicity that the firm intends the employment

relationship to last for only one period. Assume further that the labour market is perfectly competitive. Then, in the absence of fixed employment costs, the wage is equal to the marginal cost of labour: $W(=ALC)=MLC$. Now introduce hiring and training costs, denoted by H and K respectively. Both the average and the marginal cost of hiring an extra worker will exceed the wage, since $ALC=MLC=W+H+K$.

If the firm expects to employ the worker for t periods, the analysis becomes more complicated. Wages must be paid in each period, but the fixed costs $(H+K)$ are paid only once. The wage component of labour cost over the entire period is the sum of the wage payments, suitably discounted. Where W_0 is the wage rate in period 0, W_1 is that paid in period 1, and so on, and the discount rate r is constant, the present value of the expected labour costs (C) can be written as:

$$C=W_0+W_1/(1+r)+\ldots+W_t/(1+r)^t+H+K \qquad (2.1)$$
$$\sum_{i=0}^{i=t} W_i(1+r)^{-i}+H+K$$

The present value of the employer's returns from employment (V) can be written, quite similarly, as:

$$V=MRPL_0+MRPL_1/(1+r)+\ldots+MRPL_t/(1+r)^t \qquad (2.2)$$
$$\sum_{i=0}^{i=t} MRPL_i\,(1+r)^{-t}$$

where $MRPL_i$ is the marginal revenue product of labour in period i.

The firm is in equilibrium where, for the marginal worker, $C=V$. Unless non-wage costs are zero, this means that the discounted sum of the net returns must exceed the discounted sum of wage payments. What this implies for the relationship between wages and marginal revenue productivity in each period can be seen if we make the simplifying assumption that both W and $MRPL$ are constant over the full length of the employment contract. In this case equilibrium entails that, in every period, $MRPL=W+R$, where R is the sum required by the firm in each period to amortise its investment and to yield the appropriate rate of return (r) on that investment. That is:

$$H + K = R_0 + R_1/(1+r) + \ldots + R_t/(1+r)^t \qquad (2.3)$$

$$\sum_{i=0}^{i=t} R_i (1+r)^{-t}$$

Note carefully the significance of the formula $MRPL = W + R$. It means that the $MRPL$ is, in equilibrium, less than the wage whenever there are fixed employment costs, even if the firm has no labour market power. Hiring and training costs drive a wedge between marginal revenue productivity and the wage, even in perfect competition.

This is especially important because it confers an advantage upon 'insiders' – that is, workers already employed by the firm – over 'outsiders'. Ignoring overtime, the marginal cost of an extra hour of labour performed by an insider (W) is less than the average cost ($W + R$). It is also less than the marginal cost of an hour of labour obtained from a newly-hired worker, which is also $W + R$ since the fixed costs of employment must be incurred before such an outsider can commence work. Thus insiders will be offered overtime in preference to the hiring of outsiders, up to the point where the combined effects of the overtime premium and increasing fatigue make outsiders the more attractive option. There is no reason why extensive use of overtime should be inconsistent with heavy unemployment.

Neoclassical economists use these results to explain some otherwise puzzling phenomena. One is *Okun's law*, named after the US economist Arthur Okun to describe the fact that output fluctuates more in the course of the trade cycle than employment does. In other words, the average productivity of labour ($APPL$) moves procyclically: it rises when employment and output are increasing, and falls when they decline. If MPPL follows a similar course – and there is no obvious reason why it does not – Okun's law appears to be inconsistent with the law of diminishing returns, according to which MPPL falls as employment rises.

Fixed employment costs offer neoclassical theorists a means of escaping from this unpalatable conclusion, since they imply that the firm may be in long-run equilibrium only at the peak of the trade cycle. As product demand falls, the firm cuts back its output level, but it adjusts its employment of labour only after an interval has elapsed. There is here a striking analysis with the proposition that price must fall below average variable cost, not average total cost, before the firm will shut down. Similarly, it is only when MRPL becomes less than W (not less than $W+R$) that the firm will lay off workers. In the interim there will be a growing level of *labour hoarding*, which is reflected in declining average productivity. The converse occurs in the upswing of the cycle, with output growing faster than employment as *dishoarding* takes place.

Labour hoarding may be *paid for*, with the employer accepting a lower level of effort from each hour of employment; or *unpaid*, with the introduction of short-time working (Taylor, 1974). Only paid hoarding will give rise to the cyclical fluctuations in output per hour worked which are required by Okun's law. The argument is illustrated in Figure 2.11. As output declines from OX_1 to OX_2, the number of hours worked falls only from ON_1 to ON_3, and not to the long-run cost-minimising level ON_2; there is labour hoarding of N_3N_2 hours. The firm moves from A to C, rather than to B. Its apparent production function passes through A and C, displaying increasing returns. The true production function is that which would

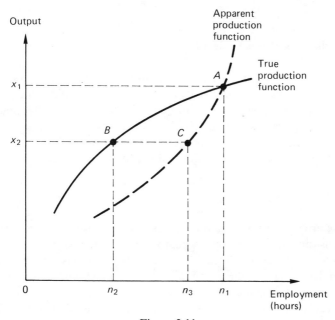

Figure 2.11

have been observed if the firm had fully adjusted the employment of hours to the decline in output. It runs through A and B, with diminishing returns.

Further variations on the theme of labour as a quasi-fixed input can be made by defining R/W as the *degree of fixity*, which will differ from occupation to occupation depending on the level of training costs. The degree of fixity is greatest for the most highly skilled occupations (assuming, once again, that it is the firm and not the worker which has incurred the costs of training). Occupations with a high degree of fixity are expected to display relative stability of employment over the cycle, and this is confirmed (as will be seen in Chapter 10) by the evidence on unemployment rates by skill category. The related implications for cyclical changes in occupational wage differentials are outlined in Chapter 7, Section 2. Finally it should be mentioned that, given H and K, both R and R/W depend on the expected length of the employment relationship. Labour turnover is costly to the employer of quasi-fixed labour, and some of the formal and informal devices which are used to control it will be considered in Chapter 4.

5   Criticisms of neoclassical theory

In this section three important objections to the orthodox analysis of labour demand are discussed. The first concerns the difficulties which arise in applying marginalist equilibrium theory to oligopolistic (and oligopsonistic) markets. Second, there are the implications of non-cost-minimising behaviour on the part of the firm. Finally, the empirical validity of neoclassical theory must be assessed.

(i) Oligopoly

There are two defining characteristics of oligopolistic product markets. Firms are few enough in number for the decisions of any one significantly to affect all the others, and they recognise this mutual dependence. Thus defined, oligopoly is the most common market form, at least in manufacturing industry.

The problem arises because the demand curve of oligopolist A depends significantly on the price-output decisions of rival oligopolists B, C and D, and vice versa. Moreover, each realises that this is the case and is forced to make some estimate of the likely reactions of the other firms to any alteration in price. But, this means that there is something very odd about their demand functions. Generally speaking, a demand curve shows the effect of changes in the price of a commodity on the quantity bought, holding constant consumer tastes, their incomes and the prices of all other goods. These are the *ceteris paribus* conditions, or parameters, of the demand curve. But, in oligopoly, prices are interdependent. The third *ceteris paribus* condition is therefore inevitably violated, since any movement along an oligopolist's demand function results in a shift in the entire curve due to the reactions of rival producers.

One way of dealing with the problem is to assume that oligopolists collude, operating a cartel, a price-fixing agreement, or some other less formal arrangement which eliminates price competition. This allows them to set the price which would be charged by a single monopolist, and to share out the monopoly profits between them. The whole industry's labour demand curve would then be identical to that of a monopolist; the individual oligopolists would simply have a share of the market, and a corresponding share of employment. This model has a long and honourable history (Chamberlin, 1933; Fellner, 1960), but it is not very convincing. Cartels are far too brittle, the temptation to cheat on a price agreement is much too strong, and the dangers of new entry are too acute, for collusion to be acceptable as a general, long-term solution.

An alternative approach emerged at the end of the 1930s, a decade marked by great public and professional concern over price rigidity. Sweezy (1939) and Hall and Hitch (1939) suggested that oligopolists believe themselves to face a *kinked demand curve*: that is, they expect their competitor to follow any reduction in price, but not to react to a price increase. The anticipated elasticity of demand is thus much greater for a rise in price than for a reduction, and it is this which deters the oligopolist from competitive price cuts.

Corresponding to the kink in the average revenue curve is a vertical discontinuity in the marginal revenue function, as shown in Figure 2.12. Since $MRPL = MPPL \times MR$ (see Section 1 above), a similar discontinuity occurs in the firm's labour demand function, making the elasticity of demand for labour with respect to the wage zero over a significant range of wage rates. Sweezy, in fact, regarded this as the most important practical conclusion to emerge from the analysis (Sweezy, 1939, p. 570; Bloom, 1940–1).

However, the kinked demand curve does not explain how the

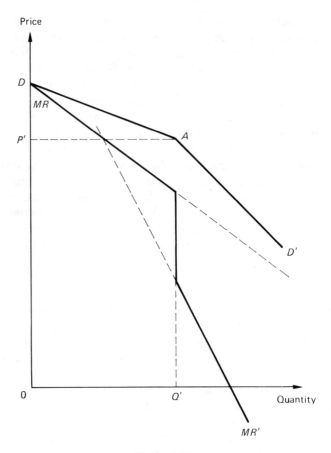

Figure 2.12

price is set in the first place. Nor, rather obviously, does it provide a satisfactory account of price stability in the face of shifting product demand. It has very few supporters today, even Paul Sweezy having renounced it in favour of the collusive, monopoly-price, solution (Baran and Sweezy, 1968, Chapter 3). No refinement of marginalist equilibrium theory is really able to deal with oligopolistic interdependence, since there are no determinate average or marginal revenue functions, and hence no possibility that the firm might equate marginal revenue with marginal cost (Andrews, 1964). An identical problem exists where labour markets are oligopsonistic, that is, where there are so few buyers that each recognises their mutual dependence, so that average and marginal labour cost curves are indeterminate.

To return to the product market, it may be concluded that a quite different theory of price determination is required for oligopoly, and with it an alternative analysis of the demand for labour. These questions are re-examined, in the context of post-Keynesian theory, in Section 6 below.

(ii) X-inefficiency

Conventional economic objections to monopoly, and to other market imperfections which fall short of it, centre upon the inefficiency which results because prices are set too high and output levels too low. Many economists, of non-orthodox as well as neoclassical persuasion, would now agree with Leibenstein (1987) that failure to minimise costs at any level of output is a much more serious source of monopolistic inefficiency. It is competitive pressure which keeps managers on their toes. Take that away, and they can pursue goals of their own – maximising their own utility functions, in which leisure and the pleasures of a quiet life might feature prominently – rather than attempt to maximise profits (Williamson, 1964). The result is *X-inefficiency*, to use Leibenstein's term, or *organisational slack*, in the language of behavioural theorists of the firm (Cyert and March, 1963).

Two cases of X-inefficiency are shown in Figure 2.13. Cost-minimisation would occur at A, where OL_1 units of labour and OK_1 units of capital are employed and the capital–labour ratio is given by the slope of the ray OA. If the firm actually operates at B production is still *technically efficient*, since B is on the isoquant Q_0Q_0; but it is *economically inefficient*, because the relevant isocost line is FBG rather than DAE. The capital–labour ratio, shown by the slope of OB, is lower than at A. At C production is technically inefficient too, since the firm is now operating off the isoquant. Compared with B, it uses L_2L_3 units of superfluous labour and K_2K_1 units of unnecessary capital. By comparison with A, its capital–labour ratio is also too low. Its costs, shown by the isocost line HCJ, are higher than at either A or B.

X-inefficiency leaves the neoclassical theory of labour demand in a parlous state. At B the slope of the isoquant Q_0Q_0 is less than at A, so that the equilibrium condition $MPPL/MPPK = W/P_k$ is violated

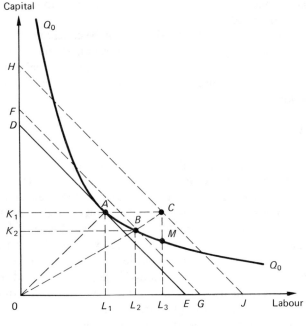

Figure 2.13

(see Section 3 above). The situation at C is even worse, for here the marginal physical product of both inputs is zero. Output need not fall in the course of a move from C to A (involving the use of less labour) or from C to M (using less capital), or from C to B (using less of both inputs). Yet, despite their zero marginal productivity, the owners of both inputs receive a positive price for their services. In short, the X-inefficient firm is off its labour demand curve, and the rigorous neoclassical analysis of Sections 1–4 is no longer valid.

The evidence on the behaviour of labour productivity suggests that X-inefficiency is both widespread and substantial. There are, for example, large international differentials in productivity which cannot be explained by differences in technology or capital–labour ratios. In the 1970s labour productivity in the United States, France and West Germany exceeded that in Britain by at least 50 per cent, and on some calculations by as much as 200 per cent in the case of the US. In individual instances, the most notorious being the motor industry, the gap was even larger. The experience of the 3-day week in 1974 provided further graphic proof that costs were not being minimised. For a period of six weeks the number of hours worked was reduced by 40 per cent, while output fell by only 10 per cent. Average productivity per hour rose by 50 per cent,[8] with capital inputs and the level of technology both unchanged (Hodgson, 1982).

Evidence abounds, too, of the *shock effect* through which unexpected wage increases stimulate productivity so substantially, and so rapidly, that something more must be involved than movement up a neoclassical labour demand curve, even a long-run curve allowing for capital–labour substitution (Reynolds and Gregory, 1965). The 'economy of high wages', it has been argued for more than a century, arises because employers are forced by the pressure of wage increases to come closer to the cost-minimising level of input usage. In a dynamic long-run context, wage rises may also encourage a faster rate of technical change than would otherwise be the case (Rowe, 1969). If labour productivity is in fact a direct function of the wage rate in this way, there are very serious implications for orthodox analysis. Further discussion of this problem will be found in Chapter 4 below.

(iii) Marginal analysis and empirical research

Before it is possible to assess the empirical status of a piece of economic analysis, two questions must be answered. What, precisely, is the hypothesis which is to be tested? And what types of evidence may legitimately be introduced? In the case of neoclassical labour demand theory, both have proved extremely contentious.

The celebrated Lester–Machlup controversy highlights many of the problems which arise. Largely ignoring analytical issues, Richard Lester (1946) attacked orthodox theory on empirical grounds. In a postal survey of a sample of US manufacturing companies, he had asked about the factors behind their employment decisions. By far the most important determinant appeared to be product demand, with the level of wage rates and the speed of wage changes given far less prominence. Those firms with plants in both the South and the North denied that the South's relatively lower wages had induced them to use more labour-intensive techniques in

---

[8] If normal output is 100, normal weekly hours are 40, and normal output per hour is $100/40 = 2.5$, during the 3-day week output fell to 90 while hours declined to 24, giving output per hour of $90/24 = 3.75$, an increase of exactly 50 per cent.

the South. When questioned as to their reactions to an increase in
the relative Southern wage level, most firms gave as much stress to
improving methods and efficiency as to introducing labour-saving
machinery, and slightly more emphasis on improving methods and
efficiency than on changing price or product quality. Almost none
thought in terms of a reduction in output.

For Lester these replies were inconsistent with neoclassical theory.
(Had he been writing 20 years later, he might have cited the concept
of X-inefficiency.) He supported his interpretation with statistical
evidence that a sharp decline between 1937 and 1941 in the North–
South differential in the footwear and clothing industries had failed
to prevent employment in the South from rising more rapidly than in
the North. Within the South employment had risen fastest in just
those firms where wages rose most. Lester concluded that 'for many
manufacturing concerns it is not feasible, or would prove too costly,
to shift the proportion of productive factors in response to changes
in wages, in the manner suggested by marginal analysis'. Employment tended to vary 'simply and directly' with the level of product
demand (Lester, 1946, p. 82). Post-Keynesian theorists have seized
on this final assertion, as will be seen in Section 6 below.

Fritz Machlup's vigorous defence of orthodox theory included
both a critique of the Hall and Hitch article on oligopoly price
determination (see Section 4 above) and an attack on Lester.
Machlup (1946) objected both to the use of questionnaires in general
and to Lester's formulation of his questions. He also criticised
Lester's interpretation of the replies, since the importance placed on
product market demand was entirely consistent with marginalist
theory and entirely predictable: demand tends to fluctuate more
sharply, and more often, than the wage level. A substantial proportion of Lester's respondents had mentioned price and quality
adjustments, and the introduction of labour-saving machinery, in
reply to the question on the effects of a wage increase. The former
reaction, Machlup argued, would also have indirect repercussions
on employment via their effect on the level of output. He concluded
that the wage–employment relationship, and the principle of substitution, remained substantially unimpaired.

There are important lacunae in Machlup's reply, for example his
neglect of the X-inefficiency problem and of the statistical evidence
on the North–South differential. In the long term, however, the
methodological issues raised by his article have proved by far the

most significant. For Machlup, neoclassical theory makes no claims concerning the decision-making process within the firm. Those responsible for pricing the product and hiring labour need not be supposed to calculate marginal revenue and marginal cost, or MRPL and MLC, in order to do what they think best for the profitability of the firm. In any case, 'the raw material for such calculations could not come from any records or documents, but merely from respondents' guesses of a purely hypothetical nature' (Machlup, 1946, p. 548). Questionnaires – and interviews with managers, which Hall and Hitch conducted – cannot, in principle, produce anything relevant to an assessment of marginalist theory. The only legitimate evidence concerns the outcomes of the firm's implicit maximisation behaviour.

In a famous methodological paper, itself partly prompted by the Lester – Machlup debate, Milton Friedman (1953a) drew the more extreme conclusion that only the *predictions*, and not the *assumptions*, of orthodox analysis are the appropriate subjects of empirical research; Lester had been on the wrong track from the start. The great majority of neoclassical economists invoke Friedman's authority to justify their reliance on 'hard' statistical data to the exclusion of more subjective 'anecdotal' sources of economic evidence. Thus empirical testing of the orthodox theory of labour demand involves econometric estimation of elasticities of employment with respect to the wage rate. These estimates differ, often substantially, but they are almost invariably negative, implying a downward-sloping labour demand curve and so, it is claimed, the vindication of neoclassical analysis (Clark and Freeman, 1980; Nissim, 1984a; Symons and Layard, 1984; McCallum, 1985; Symons, 1985; Hamermesh, 1986, pp. 451–5).

There are two sets of problems with this. The first is methodological. Friedman's argument has logical difficulties, since it requires acceptance of demonstrably false assumptions so long as they are consistent with correct predictions. This has led even some neoclassical economists to repudiate it (Samuelson, 1963). It is also vacuous in practice, because it offers no criterion for separating economic statements into two mutually exclusive categories, 'assumptions' and 'predictions'. Hence it is always possible to reformulate neoclassical theory in such a way that some of its assumptions become predictions; and it is far from clear that every conceivable prediction of orthodox analysis has been subjected to empirical scrutiny.

Moreover, there is nothing in Friedman's argument which rules out the case study methods favoured by institutional economists, which often yield evidence contrary to neoclassical predictions (see, for example, Piore, 1968).

There are also more practical objections. Most of the econometric studies cited above rely on estimates of aggregate production functions for the entire economy or a very large part of it (Nissim, 1984a is an exception). There are serious conceptual problems with such functions, as will be seen in Chapter 8 below. And a whole host of microeconomic problems have yet to be addressed by orthodox theorists, still less solved. Thurow (1976, Appendix A) presents an impressive check-list. What is the time period over which workers are paid their MRPL? Each instant, some longer interval, or their whole working life? Are individuals or groups paid their MRPL? If the latter, why, and what determines the scope and size of the group? Until these questions – and many others – are answered, the empirical status of orthodox labour demand theory will continue to be in doubt (see also Blaug, 1980).

6   Non-neoclassical theories of labour demand

Of the alternative schools of economic thought which were discussed in the previous chapter, only green economics does not address itself directly to the question of labour demand. The institutionalists and radical-Marxians are highly critical of orthodox theory, without offering a systematic alternative. Only the post-Keynesians can claim to have a coherent and reasonably comprehensive theory of their own.

The institutionalist critique invokes many of the objections to neoclassical analysis which were noted in Section 5. One central theme is the degree of discretion enjoyed by senior managers over pricing, output and employment decisions. Thus, institutionalists claim, product prices are administered by the firm; wage rates are negotiated with trade unions or set by the personnel department in accordance with an explicit company policy; and X-inefficiency (organisational slack) is pervasive. In the 'planning system', if not in the 'market system' (Galbraith, 1973), economic power is fundamentally important.

Institutionalists repudiate what Latsis (1976) terms the *situational determinism* of orthodox theory, in which all the significant 'decisions' which management must take are effectively dictated by external market forces. For the institutionalists, this greatly exaggerates the impersonal power of the market and underestimates the influence of discretionary individual and (especially) collective behaviour. Once situational determinism is rejected, neoclassical economics takes a back seat and political, sociological and organisational analysis occupies centre stage (McConnell and Brue, 1986, pp. 405–9).

The 1940s and 1950s saw an abundance of institutionalist labour economics in this vein (see, for example, Kerr, 1977, Reynolds, 1951 and Ross, 1953). The same spirit is evident in a more recent critical appraisal of orthodox labour hoarding theory (Bowers, Deaton and Turk, 1982). Even in the most severe depressions, they suggest, enough workers leave their jobs voluntarily for the firm to be able to adjust employment quickly in accordance with declining levels of output. Instead it pursues a policy of 'active labour hoarding', hiring new workers to replace those who leave. Bowers, Deaton and Turk argue that this results from technological inflexibility, but that this itself requires a deliberate decision by the firm, in the interests of workers' co-operation and constrained by union bargaining power and the development of custom and practice. These factors are all essentially non-neoclassical (see also Chapter 4 below).

Like the institutionalists, radical-Marxian theorists accuse orthodox economists of missing all the really important points about the employment relation. Above all they take for granted the definition and structuring of work tasks, completely failing to account for the existence of a hierarchy of jobs. Where this issue is addressed by neoclassical writers, the radical-Marxians complain, job hierarchy is assumed to be an inevitable consequence of modern technology, rather than a conscious attempt by capitalists to undermine workers' solidarity at the point of production. 'Divide and rule' is often profitable even when it is technically inefficient (see Chapters 4 and 6). Inequalities of productivity, status, income and power are among the most important results of profit-maximising behaviour under conditions of class antagonism (Roemer, 1979; Bowles, 1985).

These insights do not add up to a self-contained theory of the demand for labour. Post-Keynesian economics, however, does have such a theory (Applebaum, 1979). It is based on the model of the oligopolistic corporation outlined in Section 4(i). The post-Keyne-

sian 'representative firm' has fixed technical coefficients of production, as in Figure 2.10, and except at cyclical peaks operates below
full capacity. Thus average variable and marginal costs are constant
with respect to changes in the level of output. Both the average and
the marginal physical product of labour remain the same whatever
the level of employment. The product price is set by the mark-up
procedure explained in Chapter 9, Section 3, and (up to capacity) the
firm produces as much as its customers will buy. Employment varies,
as Lester put it, 'simply and directly' with the level of product
demand.

In post-Keynesian theory employment and real wages are determined separately, not simultaneously as with neoclassical analysis.
Employment is governed by the level of product demand, which
depends very largely on aggregate demand conditions in the economy as a whole. Real wages reflect the degree of monopoly power,
and of trade union *countervailing power* (Galbraith, 1952), both in
the whole economy and in the individual firm. Together these forces
establish the money wage within the firm and the overall price level.
There is no reason, a priori, to expect either a positive or a negative
correlation between real wages and employment, because there is no
direct causal relationship which links them. A host of macroeconomic variables, of uncertain size and direction, intervene.

7 Conclusion

How might it be possible to choose between these conflicting
approaches to the study of labour demand? If, ignoring the many
objections to Friedman's principle, we attempt to test only the
predictions of each theory, what would we find?

Only neoclassical theory predicts an unambiguously downward-
sloping labour demand curve. If the econometric evidence cited in
Section 5(iii) is to be believed, there actually is a negative relationship between real wages and employment. The predictions of the
remaining contenders are less clear-cut. Institutionalists place
greater emphasis on company wage policies than do theorists of any
other school. From this it can be deduced that there will be
substantial variation in wage rates between companies, in the same
locality, for apparently similar types of labour. This as will be seen in
Chapter 7, Section 5, is indeed the case. One radical-Marxian

prediction concerns the existence of job hierarchies which have no obvious basis in the technology of work, and such, again, can be readily identified (Stone, 1974). The post-Keynesians, for their part, predict product prices which are rigid with respect to demand but flexible in the face of changing wage levels, and the evidence on inflation which is discussed in Chapter 11 is quite consistent with this.

Clearly there is no hope of choosing between theories on the basis of *verified* predictions, since any theory worthy of the name will be consistent with some aspects of reality. Philosophers of science sometimes argue that *falsification* provides an effective discriminator; scientists should look for evidence which is not consistent with the theory under review. The more often its predictions are not falsified, the more likely it is to be true (Popper, 1959). Economists do sometimes behave in this way, though not as often as they might (Blaug, 1980). Thus neoclassical writers claim to have falsified post-Keynesian analysis by demonstrating that aggregate effective demand has no effect upon employment independent of changes in relative input prices (Symons, 1985). And post-Keynesians interpret the experience of the mid-1930s, when the recovery of employment preceded any significant decline in real wages, as a falsification of orthodox theory (Bonnell, 1981).

As these examples suggest, the falsification principle is itself difficult to implement. If applied systematically, it would undermine any theoretical framework whatever. Popper himself was no theoretical nihilist. According to his 'principle of tenacity', a theory should not be abandoned until it has repeatedly been shown to be false, and a coherent alternative theory is ready to take its place. But this poses a number of questions (how many falsifications are required? how coherent must the alternative be?). Popper's critics have shown that a theory can effectively be insulated from criticism if *auxiliary assumptions* – similar to the *ceteris paribus* conditions of orthodox economic analysis – are invoked on an *ad hoc* basis to explain apparent instances of falsification. According to Lakatos (1978), a scientific research programme is progressive rather than degenerating to the extent that it manages to avoid such *ad hoc* defences, and is able to uncover new and interesting phenomena which have been overlooked by rival theories. This however begs the question as to what counts as 'new' and 'interesting'; as we saw in section 4–5, it is precisely this which divides the various schools of thought on the demand for labour. Although for a time Lakatos's work aroused considerable interest among economists (Blaug, 1975), it too offers no simple criterion for choosing between the competing theories.

3

The Supply of
Labour

1 Introduction

There are several dimensions to the supply of labour, the most
important being quantity, quality, intensity and location. From the
viewpoint of the individual, two decisions determine the quantity of
labour supplied: whether or not to work, and for how long. In
aggregate the supply of labour to the entire economy is the product
of the participation rate, which measures the proportion of the
population which is in work or seeking a job, and the average hours
per person which are worked in each period. The quality of labour
supply depends upon the degree of skill which has been acquired
through education and through formal or informal (on-the-job)
training. The intensity of labour supply is determined by the degree
of effort that is performed. Finally, locational decisions relate to the
firm, industry and region to which labour is supplied.

The next three sections outline the neoclassical theory of labour
supply, while the following section considers the contributions of
rival schools of thought and their criticisms of orthodox analysis.
Sections 2 and 3 deal with the quantitative aspects of labour supply,
and Section 4 with qualitative questions (though locational issues
also occasionally arise). A full consideration of effort and the
intensity of work is deferred to Chapter 4, and locational issues are
discussed more fully in Chapter 7, Sections 4–5.

2   The short-run neoclassical theory of labour supply

In this section the quality of labour is assumed constant. This
confines the analysis to the short run, since the acquisition of skills is
a long-term process. The neoclassical analysis of labour supply then
becomes a fairly straightforward application of the theory of
consumer choice. In its most elementary form it rests upon five
simplifying assumptions. First, all income is derived from work;
there is no unearned income, either positive (interest, dividends,
social security benefits) or negative (for example, liability to a poll
tax). Second, the analysis is confined to isolated individuals whose
decisions are not affected by the labour supply behaviour of their
families. Third, these individuals are free to choose how much
labour to supply, subject only to the limitations imposed by time and
the prevailing market wage rate; there are no further constraints
imposed by employers, and in particular no requirement that a
minimum or maximum number of hours be worked in each period.
Fourth, work and leisure are the only possible uses of time.

These first four assumptions can be relaxed by orthodox theorists
without too much difficulty. This is not the case with the fifth
assumption, which is that people regard work as 'neutral', in the
sense that it is not in itself a source of utility or disutility but merely
involves sacrificing time available for leisure, which does yield
utility. As will be seen in Section 5, the 'non-pecuniary' aspects of
work pose serious problems for the neoclassical theory of labour
supply.

If these problems are ignored, we need deal with only two goods:
income and leisure. As in consumer theory more generally, the
individual is supposed to maximise utility subject to a budget
constraint given by the available income and the relative prices of
the two goods. In Figure 3.1 I_0I_0, I_1I_1 and I_2I_2 are three of a family of
indifference curves reflecting the individual's preferences for income
and leisure. They satisfy the axioms of orthodox consumer theory by
being downward-sloping and convex to the origin; they neither
intersect nor touch either of the axes. The budget constraint is
shown by the line CAB, where OC gives the amount of leisure
available if the individual does not work at all (that is, 24 hours per
day), and OB is the income which could be earned by working 24
hours a day and consuming no leisure. Thus OB represents 24 times
the hourly wage rate, which equals the slope of CAB; it is assumed

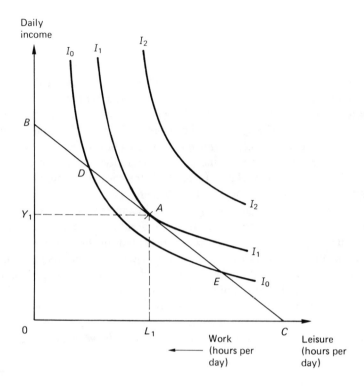

Figure 3.1

for simplicity that this is constant, so that there are no overtime premia. The wage rate, in fact, is the price of leisure: it is the income that the individual must forgo in order to enjoy an extra hour of leisure.

The individual is in equilibrium, with utility at a maximum, at A on I_1I_1 with a daily income of OY_1. Here OL_1 hours of leisure are enjoyed each day, and L_1C hours of work are supplied. (Note that hours of leisure increase along the horizontal axis from left to right, starting from the origin, while hours of work increase from right to left, starting from C.) None of the combinations of income and leisure on I_2I_2 can be attained, while points on I_0I_0 such as D and E are regarded by the individual as inferior to A. In equilibrium the slope of I_1I_1 is equal to the slope of the budget line CAB. More formally the marginal rate of substitution of income for leisure is equal to the ratio of their prices.[1]

A change in the wage rate alters the price of leisure in terms of income. The effects of a wage increase are illustrated in Figure 3.2, where the budget line pivots from CAB to CFH to reflect the new, higher relative price of leisure. The individual moves to a new equilibrium position at F on I_2I_2. As with consumer theory more generally, the *price effect* of the wage increase is the sum of an *income effect* and a *substitution effect*. The income effect is shown by the move from A to G, increasing the individual's income but holding constant the relative price of leisure; the substitution effect is given by the move along I_2I_2 from G to F.

If leisure is not an inferior good, the income effect will always be positive: a wage increase leads the individual to consume more leisure (L_1L_2 more, in the case illustrated in Figure 3.2). The substitution effect, however, is always negative; leisure has become more expensive, so that less is consumed (L_2L_3 less, in Figure 3.2). The price effect is ambiguous, since it depends upon the size of the income effect relative to that of the substitution effect. In Figure 3.2 $L_1L_2 > L_2L_3$, so that the income effect outweighs the substitution effect. Hours of leisure increase, and hours of work decrease, by

---

[1] The individual maximises the utility function:

$$U = U(Y,L)$$

which states that utility comes from income (Y) and hours of leisure (L). This is subject to a time constraint and an expenditure constraint, which together give the budget constraint. If total time available is written as $\bar{T}$ (for example, 24 hours in a day), and H denotes hours of work, then the time constraint is:

$$\bar{T} = H + L$$

This shows that all time is spent either at work or in leisure. With the hourly wage rate equal to w, the expenditure constraint may be written as:

$$Y = wH = w(\bar{T}-L)$$

on the assumption that there is no unearned income.

Totally differentiating the utility function we have

$$dU = \frac{\partial U}{\partial Y}\cdot dY + \frac{\partial U}{\partial L}\cdot dL.$$

Along any indifference curve it is true by definition that $dU = 0$, so that

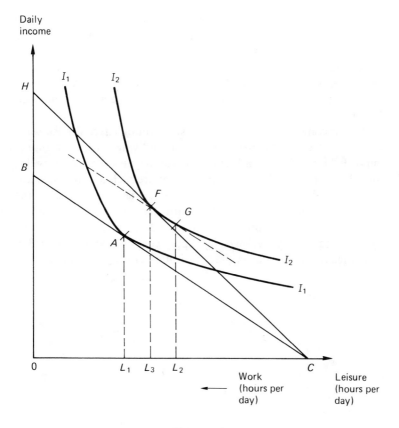

Figure 3.2

$$\frac{\partial U}{\partial Y}\cdot\partial Y = -\frac{\partial U}{\partial L}\cdot dL$$

and the slope of the indifference curve is

$$-\frac{dY}{dL} = \frac{\partial U}{\partial L}\Big/\frac{\partial U}{\partial Y}$$

This is the marginal rate of substitution of income for leisure, or the ratio of the marginal utilities of the two goods. In equilibrium it is equal to the slope of the budget line, which is

$$\frac{dY}{dL} = w$$

This is the price of leisure in terms of income.

L_1L_3. Thus the individual's labour supply curve is backward-sloping over the relevant range, as shown in Figure 3.3. Here A' corresponds to A in Figure 3.2, and F' to F; note that the origin in Figure 3.3, which indicates zero hours of work, is labelled C rather than O. At the lower wage $CW_1(=OB/24)$, L_1 hours of work are supplied. When the wage rate rises to $CW_2(=OH/24)$, the amount supplied falls to CL_3.

If the income effect outweighs the substitution effect also for wage rates above CW_2 and below CW_1, the individual's labour supply curve will look like SS' in Figure 3.3. But there is no reason why this must be so. If the individual's preferences are such that the substitution effect always outweighed the income effect, for example, the labour effect curve would slope upwards from left to right. Various intermediate cases are possible, including the celebrated – but largely hypothetical – *backward-bending* supply curve shown in Figure 3.4. For wage rates below OW_1 the substitution effect predominates and

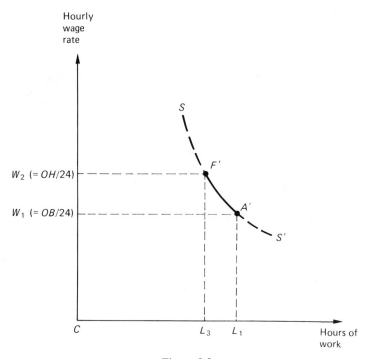

Figure 3.3

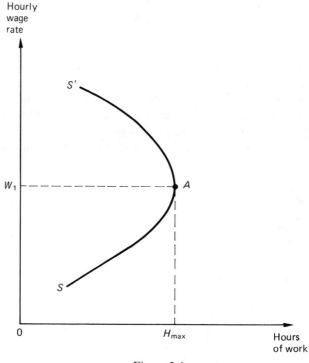

Figure 3.4

hours of work increase with the wage rate, while above OW_1 the income effect is the stronger and the quantity of labour supplied declines. The labour supply curve bends back at A, and there is a maximum number of hours supplied (OH_{max} at OW_1).

The labour supply curve to the whole economy is the aggregation of individual curves, and unless individual preferences are all very similar it is unlikely to look like that in Figure 3.4. The practical significance of this question lies in its implications for taxation policy. It is the post-tax wage rate, not the pre-tax wage, which represents the true price of leisure in terms of income forgone. Thus a reduction in the income tax rate increases the relative price of leisure, with the income and substitution effects which have been described. For an individual with a labour supply curve like that of Figure 3.3, or who is above A in Figure 3.4, tax cuts reduce the amount of work which will be supplied; in popular language, tax reductions provide a disincentive for work, and increased tax rates would be required in order to make people work harder. The empirical evidence on this point is considered in the following section.

One sure way of increasing the supply of work is to offer an overtime premium. This has a very large substitution effect, since it increases the price of leisure at the margin by the amount of the premium (one-quarter, for example, or one-third). The income effect, however, is rather small, since the premium applies only to the overtime hours. In Figure 3.5 this is illustrated by a kink in the

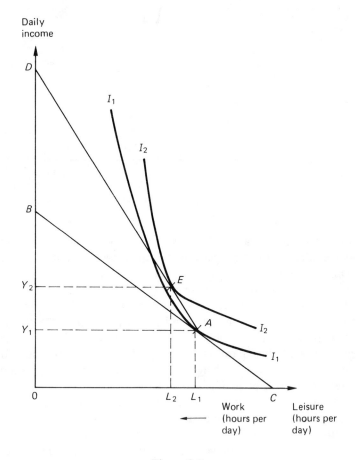

Figure 3.5

budget line at A, with the section AD representing the higher overtime rate. The new equilibrium position is at E, where the individual works L_2L_1 hours of overtime for an extra income of Y_2Y_1. Only if the individual's indifference curves were extremely steep above A, indicating an exceptionally strong preference for leisure at the margin, would the offer of an overtime premium fail to produce an increase in the supply of working hours.

3 Some extensions

(i) Non-wage income

Up to now, it has been presupposed that the individual is a labour market participant. Equilibrium at C in Figure 3.1 is impossible, since the indifference curves do not touch the horizontal axis and some work is therefore always preferable to none, however low the wage rate. Man (and woman) cannot live by leisure alone. Non-participation can be understood only if the first assumption made at the beginning of Section 2 is relaxed to allow for non-wage income.

In Figure 3.6 the individual has a non-wage income of AC. The corresponding budget line is CAB, where the slope of the section AB represents the wage rate and the maximum wage income available to the individual is BD. It is now quite conceivable that a rational individual might choose not to work, and be in equilibrium at A with no wage income at all. Here I_0I_0 touches neither axis (but the extension beyond A is purely notional, since there are only $OC = 24$ hours in a day).

Non-wage incomes can be negative as well as positive. As colonial administrators were well aware, one method of inducing non-participants to enter the labour force is to impose a poll tax. In Figure 3.7 the individual must pay a lump-sum tax of AE per day, and thus faces a budget line of EGF. This is below AB but parallel to it, since the wage rate is unchanged. Equilibrium is at G, where CL_1 hours are worked for a total wage income of JH. This pays part of the tax, the remainder coming from the non-wage income of the individual. In effect the poll tax has a large negative income effect, leading to a sharp reduction in the consumption of leisure.

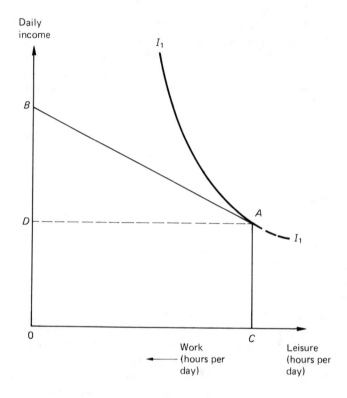

Figure 3.6

(ii) Family influences on individual decisions

One source of income not derived from the individual's own work is
the wage income of other family members. This has become increasingly important in the last two or three generations, when the labour
force participation rates of married women have risen to such an
extent that a married woman without even a part-time job is very
much the exception rather than the rule.

Orthodox models of labour supply allow for the effect of family
influences on individual behaviour in three ways (Brown, 1983,
chapter 8; Killingsworth, 1983, pp. 29–37). In the *male chauvinist*
model, the husband's decisions affect those of his wife but not vice
versa. The wife's labour supply depends upon his earnings, which
she treats as unearned income, but her earnings have no effect on his
labour supply. In addition to what we must now term the 'own-

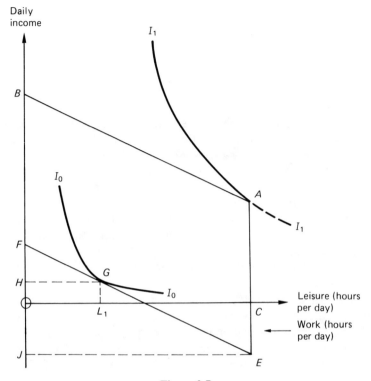

Figure 3.7

income effect' and 'own-substitution effect', as outlined in Section 2, there is a single *cross-income effect*: increases in the husband's wage rate will lead, all other things being equal, to a reduction in the number of hours worked by his wife.

The *family-utility-family-budget-constraint* model postulates a single utility function involving the family's pooled income and the leisure of both partners. There is also a single budget constraint relating family wage income to the work hours supplied and the wage rates paid to both partners.[2] Here there are two cross-income

[2] The family utility function is

$$U = U(Y, L_H, L_W)$$

which is maximised subject to the budget constraint

$$Y = w_H (\bar{T} - L_H) + w_W (\bar{T} - L_W)$$

where the suffixes H and W refer to the husband and wife respectively.

effects, since the wife's decisions now affect those of her husband. And there are two *cross-substitution effects*, which occur because an increase in the wife's wage rate raises the cost of her leisure relatively to that of her husband, and vice versa. The signs of these cross-substitution effects depend upon whether the leisure times of the two partners are complements or substitutes, and cannot be specified in advance.

This second model assumes, in effect, that both parties regard all the commodities consumed by the family as public goods. In the third, *individual-utility-family-budget-constraint* model, the family maximises two separate utility functions subject to a common budget constraint.[3] There are now no cross-substitution effects, but instead there are no fewer than four cross-income effects, two direct and two indirect. The direct cross-income effects operate as before; the indirect effects arise because the own-substitution effects alter the hours worked, and hence the wage earnings, of each partner, and this produces an additional cross-income effect on the labour supply of the spouse.

It is not clear which of these specifications is to be preferred, though the male chauvinist case is of doubtful relevance to the 1990s. One lesson is that empirical research should investigate the labour supply behaviour of men and women separately, preferably also distinguishing between married and unmarried people. There have been several studies concentrating upon married women (Greenhalgh, 1980a; Layard, Barton and Zabalza, 1980). More generally, the evidence suggests that the price elasticity of labour supply is positive for women, and possibly quite large, but small and negative for men. Own-income elasticities are positive, confirming that leisure is a normal, non-inferior good, and own-substitution elasticities are negative with respect to leisure (positive with respect to work).

However, these findings are subject to severe qualifications for both conceptual and practical reasons. Thus C. V. Brown concluded that 'There are *no* studies of labour supply that are not open to serious objection on at least one important ground. Therefore the most intellectually-defensible position is that after a decade and a

[3] The budget constraint is the same as that in note 2, but there are two separate utility functions:

$$U_H = U_H (Y, L_H) \quad \text{and} \quad U_W = U_W (Y, L_W)$$

half of effort we can say very little about labour supply elasticities' (Brown, 1983, p.167). Similar reservations have been expressed in relation to North American research (Killingsworth, 1983, p. 432).

Further unanswered questions remain. Why have participation rates for men declined during the present century while those for women have increased dramatically? Why has the average work-week fallen so little in recent decades, for both men and women, despite a substantial increase in the real wage rate and the attendant and supposedly strong own-income effect? (Killingsworth, 1983, pp. 433–40). Orthodox analysis has not proved very successful in explaining these 'stylised facts' of long-term trends in labour supply.

(iii) Institutional constraints on working hours

Neoclassical theory assumes that individuals are free to vary the numbers of hours worked in accordance with their preferences, subject only to the budget constraint described in Section 2. In practice, of course, this is not so. In the great majority of cases, employers insist upon the working of a specified number of hours per week, and weeks per year, and persistent absenteeism is treated as a serious disciplinary offence. Some flexibility is provided by the availability of second jobs, through part-time employment, and through overtime working, but in the latter two instances the worker's freedom of choice may well be illusory. Overtime is often compulsory and many part-timers would prefer a full-time job if one were on offer.

Thus workers are subject to an institutional constraint, in addition to the market-imposed budget constraint, upon their labour supply decisions. And this points to a further puzzle. The long-run growth in real wages has been a slow, steady process. One might have expected the corresponding effects on labour supply – with the income effect outweighing the substitution effect, at least for men – to have been equally gradual and continuous. In fact, reductions in the standard working week have come in a few major steps, invariably as the outcome of collective bargaining rather than through uncoordinated individual decisions. Large declines in hours in 1919–20, 1946–50 and 1959–66 were all followed by long periods of stability (Bienefeld, 1972; Roche, 1987).

Orthodox economists have been strangely reluctant to offer explanations. One interpretation is that this loss of freedom is the price of a tacit guarantee of secure employment, and that workers pay it willingly (Carter and Maddock, 1984; Killingsworth, 1983, pp. 45–66). But, for the vast majority, it is impossible to opt out of this implicit contract, if such it be. The enforcement of a standard work-week corresponds more closely to the radical-Marxian view of production as an area of social life where power rather than exchange relations predominate, and where class inequalities are of fundamental importance. These issues are considered in much more detail in Section 5, and in Chapter 4, below.

If orthodox analysis cannot account for institutional constraints upon the supply of labour, it does have something to say about their effects. The budget line shrinks to a single point, given by the wage rate and the number of hours which must be worked. Only those workers whose preferences would have led them to choose this combination of income and leisure will be in equilibrium. Everyone else will be either *overemployed* or *underemployed* at the standard work-week (Perlman, 1969, pp. 34–48).

Underemployed workers may choose to moonlight, even at a wage rate lower than that in their primary job. In Figure 3.8 the hourly wage in the primary job is given by the slope of the pseudo-budget line $DABE$. The standard work-week is DL_1 hours, and only point A is actually available to the worker, who would prefer to be at B on I_2I_2, working DL_2 hours. The slope of the segment ACF gives the (lower) wage rate on offer in a second job. (We assume that there are no institutional constraints on working hours in this job, and that its non-pecuniary advantages and disadvantages do not differ significantly from those in the primary job.) The individual's second-best position is C on I_1I_1, where L_3L_1 moonlighting hours are supplied.

(iv) Alternative uses of time

Underlying two-dimensional diagrams such as Figure 3.8 is the assumption that there are only two uses of time: every hour not spent working for wages is treated as an hour of leisure. This is true in a tautological sense, if leisure is defined as encompassing all activities other than paid work. But there are good reasons for distinguishing several different ways in which time can be spent, including consumption, non-market work, and idleness. *Consumption time* is that required for the enjoyment of commodities and

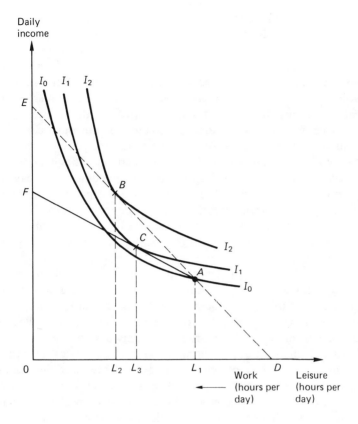

Figure 3.8

services purchased in the market. It ranges from the few seconds needed to gulp down a sandwich to the many long hours absorbed by a colour television. *Non-market work* refers to unpaid time spent in such activities as housework which (for most people) are not pleasurable in themselves but produce substitutes for goods and services which would otherwise be purchased from the market. *Idleness* involves neither consumption nor production, but rather meditation, reflection and rest (Linder, 1970).

Hard and fast distinctions between these types of activity (and inactivity) are difficult to draw. Even yoga requires some minimal clothing and is usually practised indoors, so that a small element of

consumption is entailed; more, if commercial classes are attended.
Home decoration is enjoyment or purgatory, depending upon one's
taste, while cookery can be a delight or a chore; non-market work
and consumption are not always easy to separate. In the most
sophisticated neoclassical theory of the allocation of time (Becker,
1965), there is an indefinitely large number of activities, each
requiring inputs of commodities, purchased on the market, and
time. Decisions to buy consumer goods are simultaneously commit-
ments to the time needed to enjoy them, and the price of 'leisure'
activities includes the cost of the necessary commodities in addition
to the time which they require. Furthermore, goods and time can be
substituted for each other. The labour force participation of married
women, for example, has clearly been encouraged by the mechanisa-
tion of housework, which has increased the goods-intensity of
cleaning and cooking and freed time for use in market work
(Mincer, 1962).

This has one very important implication. Rational, utility-maximising individuals must allocate their time in such a way as to
equalise its marginal productivity, in terms of utility, in all uses.
Otherwise it would be possible to increase one's utility by reallocat-
ing time from relatively unproductive activities to those with a
higher yield in utility at the margin. Rising real wage rates mean that
the marginal product of time devoted to market work increases
inexorably, putting constant pressure on all other uses of time. Most
forms of consumption and non-market work can be mechanised, but
idleness cannot. This helps to explain the decline in pure idleness and
in those cultural pursuits in which it is difficult to increase the input
of commodities per unit of time. It also gives rise to certain
paradoxes. Time is more and more scarce in an age of growing
affluence; people feel increasingly harried as they become more
'leisured'. And it is rational to act irrationally when the time
required for rational decision-making is so expensive (Linder, 1970;
Rubin, 1973). This is a basic inconsistency in the neoclassical theory
of the allocation of time, to which we shall return in Section 5 below.

4   Neoclassical theory in the long run

For our present purposes the long run can be defined as the period in
which the quality of labour, as well as the quantity, is variable. It is

the period in which productive skills can be acquired, and levels of ability changed. In the neoclassical theory of *human capital*, skills are obtained through the investment of time and other resources in anticipation of both monetary and non-monetary returns. Time spent in education, for example, can be regarded as a form of non-market work in which the individual invests time, which would otherwise have been available for market work (or other activities), and commodities such as books, stationery and paid tuition. The returns to education take the form of higher earnings in the future, and perhaps also higher productivity in non-market work (bicycle maintenance classes) or consumption (music lessons).

Rational individuals now maximise utility over their entire life-time, instead of in the single period to which the analysis of Sections 2–3 applies. A very simple model of human investment is illustrated in Figure 3.9 (adapted from Thurow, 1970, p.76). There are only two periods, present and future, which for simplicity are assumed to be equal in length. If no human investments are made, as at P, present and future consumption are equal ($OB = OC$). Investments may be made by deferring consumption to acquire skills which increase productivity in the future. This is shown by the *transformation curve*, or *production possibility frontier*, $PP'E$, which also represents the inter-temporal budget constraint facing the individual. Its gradient at any point gives the marginal productivity of human investment, which is assumed to decline as increasing quantities of human capital are accumulated; this is why $PP'E$ is concave in shape. Finally, I_1I_1 and I_2I_2 are indifference curves reflecting the individual's preferences as between present and future consumption.

Equilibrium occurs at P', where present consumption of $AB(=PF)$ is sacrificed to obtain an increase of CD ($=P'F$) in the future. At P' the marginal rate of substitution between present and future consumption, shown by the slope of I_2I_2, is equal to the marginal rate of return on the investment, given by the slope of the transformation curve (effectively, the budget constraint) $PP'E$. The *average* rate of return is

$$\frac{CD - AB}{AB} = \frac{CD}{AB} - 1 \quad \text{equal to} \quad \frac{P'F - PF}{PF} - 1$$

and is greater than the marginal rate due to the existence of diminishing returns.

62

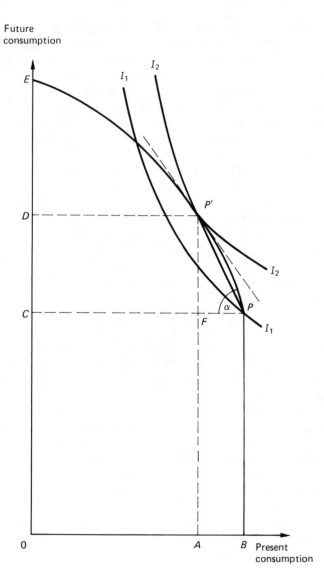

Figure 3.9

Estimates of the rate of return on education vary, but nearly all lie within a fairly narrow range. In the United States, investment in a high school education at the end of the 1960s brought a return of between 14 and 20 per cent, while the rate of return on a college education was very similar. In Britain the decision to remain at school until A level (age 18) yielded between 11.7 per cent and 16.6 per cent, while acquiring a University degree had a return of 9.6 per cent to 22.5 per cent (Siebert, 1985, pp. 29–30). In Australia rates of return in the 1970s ranged from 2.3 per cent to 21.2 per cent depending on the level of schooling concerned and on the sex and national origin of the individual, most being between 10 per cent and 20 per cent (Miller, 1984, Table 2.1, p. 24).

Evidently education is for most people a profitable investment, and to that extent the neoclassical analysis is supported by the evidence, though there is very little sign of diminishing returns. The argument can be extended to cover industrial training, migration decisions and job search behaviour. Many productively-relevant skills are acquired away from the classroom, in formal or informal training. Employer-financed training was discussed, in the context of labour as a quasi-fixed input, in Chapter 2. Becker (1964) claimed that employers will be prepared to finance only *specific* training, which does not raise the worker's productivity in other firms, as only then can it pay a wage rate less than the worker's marginal revenue productivity and obtain a return on its investment. *General* training, generating skills which can be used in other firms, must be financed by the worker, since any attempt to pay a wage rate below marginal revenue productivity will induce the worker to move to a better-paid job and deprive the firm which has provided the training of any return to it.

Apprentices and other trainees have always earned less than fellow-workers who are not undergoing training, which suggests that employee-financed training is indeed important. For most workers, too, earnings rise steadily with age well beyond the period of formal education, indicating returns to skills picked up long after schooling has ended (Mincer, 1974; Miller, 1984). But there are other interpretations of this phenomenon, as will be seen in Section 6. Issue may be taken with Becker on the grounds that his argument assumes a perfect labour market, in which mobility is costless and differences in wage rates for workers with identical skills are eliminated instantaneously. If employers expect workers to be slow to move, they may be willing to invest even in general training; and workers who anticipate long tenure in their jobs may accept temporarily lower wage rates in the hope of higher earnings in the future. Specific training gives rise to *bilateral monopoly*, since the firm's monopsony power is matched by a corresponding monopoly of skilled workers over the supply of their skill. The wage rate depends upon the relative bargaining strengths of the parties, with a lower limit set by the marginal revenue product of untrained labour in other firms and an upper limit given by the marginal revenue product of the specifically trained worker.

The issues raised by industrial training are given further consideration in Chapter 4. Quite early in its development, human capital theory was also applied to the analysis of migration (Sjaastad, 1962) and job search behaviour (Stigler, 1962). In both cases the principle is similar: the individual decides whether to move by comparing the discounted sum of the costs and benefits which are involved (Molho, 1986). As regards migration, the evidence is, perhaps not surprisingly, consistent with the predictions of the human investment model. Geographical mobility is stimulated by differences in the level and stability of earnings between one region and another, reflecting the monetary benefits of moving, and discouraged by the distance between regions, which affects the pecuniary and non-pecuniary costs of migration (Langley, 1974; Greenwood, 1975).

One particularly interesting use of the theory is in explaining rural–urban migration in underdeveloped countries. Villagers who move to the city do so despite massive rates of unemployment in urban areas throughout the Third World, and in search of something more tangible than bright lights. Wages are so much higher in the cities than in the countryside, and informal earnings opportunities in self-employment and petty trading are so widespread, that migration makes good economic sense, even though the probability of quickly finding a steady job in the high-wage modern sector is quite small (Harris and Todaro, 1970; Todaro, 1976). The human investment model makes it possible to predict the demographic and social characteristics of those who move, and those who stay behind (Lucas, 1985). It even explains why, in the early 1980s, rural blacks in South Africa were willing to risk imprisonment by seeking work illegally in urban areas. A Ciskei villager who spent nine months in gaol for breaches of the pass laws and the remaining three months unlawfully employed in Pietermaritzburg would improve his annual income by some 230 per cent (Laurence, 1981).

Finally, three important implications of orthodox analysis must be noted. First, the long-term increase in the population's human capital endowments may be a major source of economic growth. Neoclassical researchers who try to attribute growth in output over long periods to increased employment of working hours and of capital invariably find that there is an unexplained *residual element*. They ascribe this partly to economies of scale and technical progress, but the expansion of education and training is often argued to be its largest component (Denison, 1974).

Second, both wage differentials between occupations and the distribution of earnings between individuals will be heavily influenced by the dispersion of human capital between workers. And it should be possible to explain a large proportion of the inequality in earnings by studying differences in human capital endowments. Thus any increase in educational opportunities, for example through government subsidies to post-compulsory education, is expected to result in a reduction of the rate of return to the investments in question and a narrowing of the wage advantage enjoyed by those with the relevant qualifications.

Third, there is a strong *prima facie* case for state intervention in the market for human capital. Education, training, migration and job search are all semi-public goods, with benefits to society as a whole in addition to those which accrue privately to the individuals. Moreover, the finance for human investments is almost certainly obtained in an imperfect market, since in the absence of serfdom or slavery no gilt-edged security can be offered for loans. Human capital theorists therefore argue for a government manpower policy to encourage mobility and job search, and for subsidies to education and industrial training.

5 Criticisms and alternatives

Some of the problems with the orthodox theory of labour supply have already been identified. In particular, its exclusive concentration on individual and family behaviour is unwarranted. Decisions on hours of work are in practice taken collectively, as we saw in Section 3(iii). There are also good reasons to believe that individuals

are motivated by relative wages, and act on the basis of comparisons
with the earnings of others; the absolute level of wage income, which
together with leisure determines their utilities in the models used in
Section 2, is only part of the story. Thus for Keynes (1936, p. 264),
British workers' resistance to money wage cuts between the wars
reflected not some irrational 'money illusion' but rather a perfectly
sensible desire to maintain their position relative to that of other
workers. The principle of *comparative wage justice* is, however, very
difficult to incorporate in neoclassical models of labour supply. This
point will be amplified in Chapter 5, in the context of trade union
wage policy. But the majority of the criticisms directed against
orthodox analysis by institutionalist, post-Keynesian, radical-Marxian and green economists are concerned with two rather different
questions: the meaning of work, and the theory of human capital.

(i) The meaning of work

We noted in Section 2 that neoclassical theory treats work as not-
leisure, or more generally as neutral in the sense that it merely
detracts from the time available for other activities without being a
source of utility or disutility in its own right. This is not quite the
orthodox economist's last word on this issue, however. The theory
of *compensating wage differentials* allows for variations in the degree
of danger, discomfort, tedium and strain in different occupations,
which are offset by differences in earnings. Although it has a very
long pedigree (Smith, 1776, pp. 112–23), there are two powerful
objections to this approach. The first is purely empirical. As early
institutionalists noted, and modern researchers have confirmed,
there is very little evidence that heavy, dangerous, boring, stressful
work actually does command a wage premium, *ceteris paribus*, over
more pleasant jobs (Wootton, 1955; Groshen, 1988, p. 30).

The second problem is more fundamental: according to many
critics of neoclassical theory, its entire conception of work is at fault.
At issue here is the nature and meaning of work as a human activity.
In orthodox analysis work is an input; it imposes a cost upon its
suppliers, who are compensated by higher or lower wage rates
depending upon the extent of the sacrifice which is required. For
green economists like Schumacher, work is primarily a medium of
self-expression, self-development and social service; or, rather, this is
what it should be:

there are three things healthy people most need to do: to act as spiritual beings, that is to say, in accordance with their moral impulses – *man as a divine being*; secondly, to act as neighbours, that is to say, to render service to their fellow man – *man social*; thirdly, to act as persons, as autonomous centres of power, that is to say, to be creatively engaged, using and developing the gifts that have been laid into them – *man himself*. These are man's three fundamental needs, and in their fulfilment lies his happiness. In their un-fulfilment [*sic*], their frustration, lies his unhappiness.

'Good work' encourages creativity, altruism and sociability; 'bad work' does not. And it is bad work which is characteristic of the jobs offered by large organisations which use mass-production technologies. In Schumacher's conception of work, 'what the work does to the worker' is a 'decisive criterion of efficiency'; and yet it is totally ignored by neoclassical economics (Schumacher, 1974a, pp. 1–2; 1974b, p. 13).

Significantly, Schumacher cites Karl Marx on this question, and his discussion draws heavily upon the radical-Marxian theory of *alienation*. Marx too regarded work as a means of self-realisation. He defined the communist society of the future as one in which people would view work as an end in itself, develop a wide range of productive skills and interests, co-operate voluntarily with others at work, and be free to do (or not to do) all these things (McLellan, 1969). The alienated labour which was performed in capitalism failed, Marx argued, on all counts. The worker treated it as a vicious but unavoidable evil, 'shunning it like the plague' whenever possible. An intense and ever-increasing division of labour stultified the creative powers of the labourer, 'reducing the workman, from his very childhood, into part of a detail machine' in which he becomes a 'mere living appendage' of the inanimate instruments of production. Social cooperation at work was perverted by the 'barrack-discipline' of the factory, under a regime in which the employer 'confiscates every atom of freedom, both in bodily and intellectual activity' (Marx, 1867, pp. 367–4; cf. Marx, 1844, Meszaros, 1972, and Reich and Devine, 1981, pp. 30–1).

Thus, for green and radical-Marxian economists, work is very much more than the diversion of time from other, more pleasurable activities. It is, or should be, an end in itself. It follows that there are two distinct types of output: goods and services for sale on the market; and workers with capabilities, attitudes and beliefs which have been altered by their participation in the process of production. Changed workers are a joint product, along with output as conventionally defined (Gintis, 1976). There are significant differences of emphasis between the green and radical-Marxian schools, with the greens stressing the importance of organisational scale and technical complexity while the radical-Marxians emphasise the social relations of ownership and managerial control. Both agree, however, that the freedom enjoyed by the wage labourer is to a significant extent illusory, and that neoclassical analysis evades the main issues with its theory of compensating wage differentials. Market relations are part of the problem, and cannot provide a solution to it. They concur, too, in broadly accepting the feminist critique of a society in which women's domestic labour – 'non-market work' – is trivialised and undervalued, and its role in reproducing capitalist relations of production is not understood (Himmelweit and Mohun, 1977; Beechey, 1987; Chapter 6, section 3, below).

It might be objected that these criticisms are purely normative, reflecting adversely upon the nature of modern society rather than on the coherence and relevance of the orthodox analysis of that society. Thus, while they entail rejection of neoclassical welfare economics (Gintis, 1972), they leave the positive theory of labour supply intact. There is an element of truth in this. If workers really are alienated, they actually do treat work in the instrumental way assumed by neoclassical theory, that is, as an evil (a source of disutility) to be minimised subject to the constraint imposed upon them by their need for wage income. Many people do voluntarily work overtime, and moonlight, as neoclassical theory suggests. And there is no superior green or radical-Marxian analysis – indeed, no alternative analysis at all – to explain their (alienated) behaviour.

The problem with this defence of neoclassical theory is that it ignores a very basic market failure. The evidence is overwhelming from their own statements, from attitude surveys, from reports by participant observers, and from studies of strikes on the issue, that working people do feel the deprivations of alienated labour which the greens and radical-Marxians have identified. But they are powerless to do anything about them. There is simply no market in self-actualisation or industrial democracy; there is no way in which the individual can 'buy' job control or satisfying work by giving up income at the margin, as leisure time can be bought (within quite narrow limits) by sacrificing wage-income. Even job enrichment plans, and schemes for worker participation, are introduced at the prerogative of management subject only, in some cases, to consultation with trade unions. Work relations are authoritarian, and no theory of free and voluntary market exchange can hope to deal adequately with them. This problem is related to the institutionalist complaint that neoclassical labour economists assume the existence of markets and cannot account for their non-existence (Marsden, 1986). We shall return to these questions in Chapter 4.

(ii) Problems with human capital theory

The core of human capital theory is the relationship between schooling, the acquisition of productively-relevant skills, and the consequent increase in wages. While the evidence cited in Section 4 on the rate of return to schooling is firmly established, the neoclassical interpretation is far from universally accepted. One difficulty concerns the proportion of the variance in individual earnings which can be explained by differences in formal education. In one important study (Mincer, 1974) this was found to be no more than 7 per cent, implying that schooling is of quite minor importance in accounting for inequality in the labour market. An alternative way of looking at the same problem is in terms of the dispersion in rates of return to education. An average return of 10 per cent means that a quarter of all individuals get more than 20 per cent and, at the bottom end, the return to another quarter is actually less than zero (Siebert, 1985, pp. 39–40).

Mincer managed to increase the explained variance to 30 per cent by adding years of experience, which he regarded as a measure of individuals' investments in on-the-job training. This, however, is extremely contentious. For one thing, skills acquired at work may cost little or nothing in forgone output. Moreover, as we saw in Section 4, any such investments are as likely to be financed by the employer as by the employee. Finally, the supposed connection between experience and productivity is purely speculative; Mincer offers absolutely no evidence for it. Using job performance ratings by the immediate supervisors of professional and managerial staff in two large companies, Medoff and Abraham (1980) found there to be no correlation between years of experience and productivity, although there was a close relationship between experience and earnings. Rewards for seniority, it appears, need not reflect improved quality of work or an increased quantity of effort. What, exactly, they do represent will be considered in Chapter 4.

To return to formal education: there is a real problem with neoclassical analysis in the case of non-vocational courses, where no directly relevant skills are acquired. The *screening hypothesis* suggests an alternative explanation. Employers may use educational qualifications as a screen or filter when recruiting labour. That is, they believe that educational attainments indicate the individual's suitability for employment and (especially) for training, even if these qualifications have no direct bearing on the work which is to be performed. Diplomas and degrees are 'certificates of ability, perseverance and docility' (Wiles, 1974, p. 45), irrespective of the content of the course. If this is the case the externalities of non-vocational education are very small, since a good one-day test of docility, perseverance and ability, costing (at 1974 prices) about £20 instead of £300 would do as well (ibid., p. 45). Individuals are acting rationally in obtaining credentials, since the *private* returns are substantial, and firms are rational in using them to reduce their hiring costs. But the *social* benefits are not significantly greater than the private advantages, and the case for subsidising education is very weak.

The great difficulty in deciding between the human capital and screening theories is that both predict significantly higher earnings for the better-educated. It is thus not at all easy to choose between them on empirical grounds (on this see Willis, 1986, pp. 591–5). Although not all advocates of the screening hypothesis would describe themselves as institutionalists, the underlying argument does fit rather neatly into an institutional view of the labour market. Thurow (1976), for example, uses it to reject the entire neoclassical approach to wage determination. He proposes an alternative model of *job competition*, in which most important productive skills are obtained informally, through training while on the job. In the job competition model everything hinges upon access to training opportunities, which are allocated according to educational credentials. Changes in equality of access to education may affect the distribution of individuals among jobs without greatly altering the returns to schooling or the distribution of earnings. We shall return to these questions in Chapters 7 and 8.

Radical-Marxian objections to human capital theory are quite different. Although they agree that schooling does indeed increase workers' productivity, radical-Marxian writers argue that neoclassical analysis takes an unduly narrow view of the way in which this is achieved:

> The worker attributes which are valued by employers and which therefore constitute 'human capital', are not limited to technical skills and abstract productive capacities. In particular, such ascriptive attributes as race, sex, age, ethnicity, and formal credentials, often held to be irrelevant in the logic of capitalist production, are used to fragment the work force and reduce the potential formation of coalitions within the firm. . . . Moreover, as Richard C. Edwards has shown, such work-relevant personality traits as resignation to or approval of the structure of control and distribution of rewards in the enterprise, dependability and orientation to authority within this structure, and propensity to respond individualistically to incentive mechanisms are directly relevant to extracting work from workers.

Thus

> the educational system does much more than produce human capital. It segments the work force, forestalls the development of working class consciousness, and legitimates economic inequality by providing an open, objective, and ostensibly meritocratic mechanism for assigning individuals to unequal occupational positions (Bowles and Gintis, 1975, pp. 76–8; cf. Edwards, 1975).

Hence it comes as no surprise to radical-Marxian theorists that there are significant differences in rates of return to education, both for individuals and between the sexes and racial groups (see also Chapter 6). They also reject the neoclassical growth accounting model outlined in Section 4, which ignores too many of the wider social effects of schooling to be at all convincing. Moreover, for radical-Marxian theorists human capital explanations of income distribution ignore demand conditions, which depend on structural characteristics of the capitalist economy and are more important than individual supply behaviour in determining the pattern of economic inequality. Finally, orthodox analysis takes individual tastes and preferences as given, neglecting the fact that education inevitably alters preferences; on this point, radical-Marxian critics are at one with the institutionalists (Bowles and Gintis, 1975, pp. 80–2).

6 Conclusion

The full extent of the differences between the various schools of thought is perhaps more apparent in connection with the theory of labour supply than in any other area of labour economics. The neoclassical principle of individual (or family) utility maximisation does offer a precise and rigorous way of thinking about some significant problems, for example the effects of tax changes on hours of work, and individual decisions to undergo vocational education or training. The limitations of the orthodox approach are also evident, most notably its narrowly instrumental understanding of the nature of work and education and its unsubstantiated assertion that there is a close connection between job experience and the acquisition of skill. These are issues of fundamental importance, which have a profound effect on economists' perceptions of the way in which work is organised (see Chapter 4 below) and earnings differences are to be explained (Chapters 5–8). Although not fully developed, the institutionalist, green and radical-Marxian alternatives to neoclassical analysis form a basis for critical discussion of all these questions.

4

Internal Labour Markets and the Organisation of Work

1 The internal labour market

In this chapter we bring together a number of issues which were touched upon, but not adequately dealt with, in Chapters 2 and 3. One concerns the level of effort supplied by the worker, which was identified as an important determinant of labour productivity but was itself left unexplained. Closely related to this is the organisation of work in capitalist society, which, being both hierarchical and authoritarian, is very difficult to reconcile with the neoclassical view of the employment relation as a free, non-coercive market exchange. There is also evidence that relationships between employers and workers are typically long-term in nature, which distinguishes them very sharply from the mass of buyer–seller transactions. Finally, the rigidity of both money and real wages with respect to changes in labour demand is a real puzzle in its own right, and has major implications for unemployment, inflation and macroeconomic efficiency.

All these problems are connected with the *internal labour market*, a concept which originated with the institutionalists of the 1940s and early 1950s (Kerr, 1977) but which is now common currency among labour economists of all persuasions (Creedy and Whitfield, 1988). The defining characteristics of internal labour markets are threefold (Doeringer and Piore, 1985, Chapters 1–4). First, there must be a substantial degree of permanency to the attachment between employer and worker, which is reflected in the length of the typical job. Second, there must be substantial opportunities for advancement within the firm through internal training and promotion, with a corresponding restriction of hiring from the outside market into higher-level jobs. Hence there are only a limited number of 'ports of entry' into the internal labour market. Third, the allocation of tasks and rewards, as well as the imposition of sanctions, must be subject to a well-defined framework of rules prescribing the rights and obligations of employer and workforce. These will normally include an internal wage structure, so that the pattern of wage relativities is laid down by administrative procedures in isolation (to a greater or lesser extent) from the influence of the external labour market. Probably the best known, and by far the most extreme, case of internal labour markets is the life-time employment system which is commonly practised by large Japanese companies (but which is much rarer in the small business sector). In its pure form the Japanese system is inconsistent with any inter-firm mobility of labour whatever, and wages depend entirely on length of service and not at all on the differential skill or productivity of the individual worker (Dore, 1973).

There is nothing quite like this anywhere else in the world, but recent research does suggest the existence of less rigidly structured internal labour markets in all advanced capitalist countries. In 1981 the median duration of current jobs in Britain was 5.5 years, compared with 3.3 years in Australia, 4.2 years in the United States and no less than 13.0 years in Japan (Mulvey *et al.*, 1985, p. 116). Norris estimated the *completed* length of jobs held by Australians in 1976 at 18.0 years, only slightly less than in the United States or Great Britain. For administrative, executive and managerial jobs the estimated duration was 21.9 years, and for no occupational group was it less than 10 years. 'The main implication', he concluded, 'is that internal labour markets must be typical across a wide range of industries and, further, that these markets must be relatively "closed" rather than "open". Job durations of the order of 18 years for males are entirely consistent with the existence of job ladders, seniority rights, and of employer policies that encourage workers to remain with them for long periods.' (Norris, 1984, p. 198; cf. Hall, 1982 and Hashimoto and Raisian, 1985).

Such phenomena are frequently interpreted as *prima facie* evidence of labour market inefficiency. The existence of internal labour markets means that workers' mobility between employers is severely restricted, perhaps to the extent that we can identify a 'new industrial feudalism' (Ross, 1958). Job incumbents are immune from outside competition except in the early stages of their careers and in a narrow range of entry occupations, and in consequence wage rates are insulated from normal competitive pressures. When the demand for labour falls, wage rates are slow to respond, and – neoclassical economists argue – heavy unemployment is an inevitable consequence. What Kerr (1977) termed the 'balkanisation' of the labour market thus seems to muffle market signals and to delay or distort the necessary adjustment mechanisms. As we shall see in the next three sections, in their very different ways neoclassical, institutionalist and radical-Marxian schools all question the validity of these conclusions.

2 Neoclassical economics and the internal labour market

There are several strands in the neoclassical argument. One follows directly from the concept of quasi-fixity (see Chapter 2, Section 4, above). Employers incur fixed costs in hiring and training labour. This makes labour turnover costly, since it reduces the period over which the returns to the firm's investment can accrue, and makes 'insiders' preferable to 'outsiders', even when they are willing to work for a lower hourly wage rate. The firm rewards loyalty with seniority bonuses and internal promotion to better-paid jobs, and has strong incentives to do so. The internal labour market must therefore be viewed as an efficient cost-minimising device (Okun, 1981).

This argument can be extended by defining 'loyalty' more broadly to include satisfactory (or exemplary) effort levels, and by setting out a theory of hierarchy in production. Orthodox economics is primarily a theory of exchange, in which individuals with differing tastes and asset holdings relate to each other on an equal footing through market transactions. In the neoclassical story a labour market emerges when those with relatively small stocks of physical capital obtain the consumer goods which they desire by supplying the use of their time to those better endowed with capital; that is, they work for a wage. But they do so as employees, carrying out the instructions of

their employers, rather than as independent contractors who orga-
nise their own work. Why, then, does production typically take place
inside hierarchical organisations known as firms? Why, in an
economy supposedly regulated by the market, does so much econo-
mically-relevant activity go on outside the market-place? We shall
see in Section 4 that Marxian political economy does not find this at
all problematical, since it regards the structural subordination of the
proletariat as a defining characteristic of the capitalist mode of
production. It is much less easy to reconcile with the individual
freedom and equality required by the neoclassical analysis of
economic exchange.

Since the seminal work of Coase (1937), orthodox economics has
answered these questions in the following way. The enormous
technical advantages of 'team production' make it inevitable that
production is a collective rather than an individual activity, so that a
theory of organisation is required to supplement the established
model of market exchange. Due to the complexity of modern
technology, it is impossible for contracts of employment fully to
specify the tasks demanded from the worker without incurring
unacceptably high costs. To avoid these costs, contracts are left
open-ended, giving the employer the right to issue detailed instructions in the process of production and requiring the worker's
obedience to all reasonable directions (Simon, 1951). But this
involves no serious breach of the canons of economic liberalism, for
workers' submission to their employers' authority is given voluntarily in return for the material rewards of higher output. Monitoring
and disciplinary arrangements are also freely accepted, as it is in
everyone's interest to deter shirking. It is therefore misleading,
neoclassical economists argue, to regard the employment relationship as an authoritarian one. It is simply an efficient means of
facilitating mutually beneficial exchanges (Alchian and Demsetz,
1972).

Further refinements follow from the observation (shared with the
X-efficiency theorists) that intensive supervision is subject to diminishing returns. For Williamson (1975, chapter 4), conditions of
'information impactedness' prevail inside the firm: management is
never fully aware what is going on. Williamson's is a Hobbesian
world (Bowles, 1985), in which individuals seek to maximise their
utilities 'opportunistically', where opportunism is defined as 'self-
seeking with guile'. Unless dissuaded by an appropriate incentive

structure, workers will not only restrict their effort levels but will also conceal them and distort the flow of information about their job performance. Their ability to do so is enhanced by the degree of 'idiosyncrasy' in their skills, which arises from the fact that the knowledge required for particular sequences of tasks is often obtained informally on the job through repeated practice instead of through formal education and training programmes. Such knowledge thus can never, in principle, be fully available to managers and supervisors who are not themselves directly engaged in production. This introduces an element of bilateral monopoly into labour market transactions, since skills are acquired which have few sellers and even fewer buyers; it offers scope for opportunism on both sides. Under these circumstances, Williamson concludes, employers will often find it profitable to offer incentives for workers to cooperate voluntarily, including seniority payments, security of employment, and prospects of promotion. Job hierarchies are created to motivate the workforce.

Motivational considerations are also invoked by some neoclassical writers to explain wage rigidity. When the demand for labour falls, employers may avoid wage reductions for fear of damaging employee morale, which would reduce effort, increase opportunism and accelerate labour turnover. According to what has come to be termed the *efficiency wage* hypothesis, productivity varies directly with the wage rate. Employers are concerned to minimise the labour cost per unit of output, and this may require the payment of wage rates in excess of the market-clearing level (Yellen, 1984; Stiglitz, 1987). It is only a short step from this to the conclusion that unemployment – or more accurately, the fear of unemployment – acts as a disciplinary device, and that the threat of dismissal is used to maintain satisfactory work performance (Shapiro and Stiglitz, 1984). One impeccably neoclassical writer even refers – in a celebrated Marxian phrase – to the establishment of a 'reserve army of the unemployed' (Rosen, 1985, p. 1146). The effect is to require the repeal of the law of supply and demand (Stiglitz, 1987, pp. 4–7), since permanent excess supply is now consistent with an unchanged wage rate even in a perfectly competitive labour market.

This is one variant of *implicit contract theory*, according to which the firm agrees to maintain wage rates in exchange for co-operation in production. In the best-known model (Baily, 1982), it is supposed that workers are more risk-averse than their employers. The firm provides what is in effect insurance against deteriorating labour market conditions, promising not to reduce wages and obtaining in return higher productivity, and paying lower wage rates over the cycle, than would otherwise be the case. Why such contracts are not explicit, and how they are enforced, remains contentious (Rosen, 1985).

3 Institutionalist perspectives

It is difficult to decide exactly where the neoclassical analysis of the internal labour market ends and institutionalism begins. When Doeringer's and Piore's influential book *Internal Labor Markets and Manpower Analysis* first appeared in 1971, it was widely regarded as being profoundly critical of orthodox labour economics. Today its treatment of employer-specific training and the costs of labour turnover have been so thoroughly absorbed into mainstream theory that institutionalists now cite it as a neoclassical text (Marsden, 1986, pp. 144–5). Even the traditional institutionalist complaint that 'the average worker has a narrowly confined view of the market, and, in addition, is not an alert participant in it', has been taken over by orthodox economists who distinguish between 'job shoppers' and 'careerists' (Kerr, 1950, p. 281; cf. Darby, Haltiwanger and Plant, 1985).

What remains distinctive about institutional analysis is, firstly, its emphasis upon collective as against purely individualistic behaviour; second, its treatment of custom and habit; and, finally, its insistence that markets are themselves institutions whose existence cannot simply be assumed but must be explained. Surveying attempts to incorporate their treatment of internal labour markets into neoclassical theory, Doeringer and Piore insisted, fifteen years on, that 'we do not believe that internal labour markets can be understood in terms of a theory which starts with individuals as the basic unit of analysis'. Much more fundamental is 'the interplay of formal and informal groups, exerting various kinds of social pressures', which involve 'group behaviours – solidarity and collective goals, concern with the distribution of benefits relative to other workers in the group instead of distribution relative to individual productivity, kinship and friendship obligations, political factions, and concern with fairness and legitimacy – which are irrelevant to individuals, except as they are members of groups'. To understand group behaviour, they concluded, 'one needs to move away from the research techniques and models of neoclassical economics towards other social science disciplines, particularly sociology and economic anthropology' (Doeringer and Piore, 1985, pp. xxii–xxiv; original stress deleted).

In an ambitious attempt to do just that, Akerlof (1982) argued that labour contracts should be interpreted as the exchange of gifts. Workers do not consistently minimise the amount of effort they put into the job, nor do employers reduce wages to the bare minimum. Excess effort is exchanged for excess income, not in any calculating way but as a gift. Akerlof's workers act collectively, showing an emotional commitment both to each other and to the employer, which is reciprocated. They show loyalty to the firm, and also to other workers. It is this which prevents the dismissal of slower workers who are unable to make effort gifts; this would be viewed as unfair, and adversely affect the supply of effort.

Akerlof's social anthropological approach is entirely consistent with the possibility, indicated in Chapter 3, Section 5 above, that workers may be less concerned with the absolute wage rate than with the relation which it bears to pay rates of other individuals or groups. Where internal labour markets exist, intra-firm comparisons will be especially pertinent, but relativities with the outside world will also be taken into account. The internal wage structure is most unlikely to be disturbed by the emergence of excess labour supply in any one occupational group, and the firm may also be reluctant to respond even to a more general weakening of the demand for labour. Jobs are more than a source of income; they also assign one a place in the social order. They are 'positional goods' (Hirsch, 1977), since the benefits derived from them depend not only upon one's own level of consumption but also on the benefits consumed by others. Notions of fairness and justice cannot be ignored in labour economics (see Akerlof and Yellen, 1988), but they seriously weaken the force of the neoclassical distinction between efficiency and distributive equity (Sen, 1979; Turk, 1983). To this extent institutionalism must be seen as something more than a primitive and imprecise version of orthodox economic analysis.

Some would go much further than this and argue, with Doeringer and Piore, that institutionalism offers the more general analysis:

While the neoclassical firm would still have a place in such a theory as a special type of labour market institution, it would exist only as one of many forms of organization. Similarly, internal labour markets as described in this book would be only one variant of a more general phenomenon. That phenomenon would encompass not only internal labour market structures found in other countries but also work groups embodied in families, kinship groupings, and many types of informal associations of workers. (Doeringer and Piore, 1985, pp. xxxii).

In a similar vein, Marsden (1986, Chapter 7) suggests that the multi-employer occupational labour markets upon which neoclassical theory focuses are not viable without institutional support, and that the pressures towards internalisation are often irresistible. Occupational markets require the transferability of skills between employers, and this in turn necessitates standardisation of job descriptions and the content of training. Workers will bear the costs of general training only if guaranteed a return on their investment, for example by the enforcement of apprenticeship regulations. Employers who finance general training face the poaching of skilled workers by their competitors and in self-defence resort to internalisation – specific training, which creates employer-specific or idiosyncratic skills. Only occupational licensing, or some device to share the costs of training fairly among employers, can ensure the survival of multi-employer labour markets.

The implications of institutionalism can best be seen if we return to Thurow's (1976) distinction between the *wage competition* and *job competition* models (see Chapter 3, Section 5, above). In the wage competition model, which corresponds to the (neoclassical) occupational labour market, an increase in the demand for a particular type of labour (due perhaps to a shift in product demand or to a technical change) results in an immediate increase in its relative wage. In the short term this induces labour mobility, as some of those who possess the relevant skill but are not at present employing it leave their current jobs and move to secure the new higher rewards. Others invest in acquiring the skill, increasing the long-run elasticity of its supply. Thus relative wage flexibility and mobility of labour between employers are the two basic requirements for labour market adjustment in the wage competition model.

Neither need occur in the job competition model, where the internal labour market is given pride of place. Here excess demand for a particular skill is unlikely to induce an increase in relative earnings, which would upset the internal wage structure and damage morale. The firm's initial response is more likely to involve obtaining an increase in the effort level and hence in the productivity of its existing labour force, with a corresponding decline in labour hoarding. If this proves inadequate the vacancies will be filled by internal promotion, with any necessary training being provided by the firm itself either formally or through instruction on the job by those already performing it (for which their co-operation is again needed). The existing internal wage structure will offer sufficient incentives for lower-level workers to accept promotion, but the firm may have to relax its criteria and accept less well-qualified trainees. Vacancies will now exist lower down the job ladder. They will be filled in the same way, with outside hiring confined to entry occupations, where standards may (once again) need to be reduced. Adaptation occurs without wage changes and with little, if any, inter-firm labour mobility. The relevant skills are acquired within the firm itself, and the only impact on the external labour market of the entire adjustment mechanism is a shortening of the 'queue' of unemployed workers.

4 The radical-Marxian approach

The objection to all this, from the radical-Marxian viewpoint, is that it pays insufficient attention to class conflict at the point of production. Oddly enough the same accusation can be levelled at Karl Marx. Although he denoted lengthy sections of the first volume of *Capital* to a dissection of the contemporary factory, Marx believed that the organisation of work in 'modern industry' – that is, machine production – was dictated by the capitalist employer. The capitalist's power in the factory was conclusively established by industrial technology and was reinforced by the inexorable pressure exerted on those in work by the reserve army of the unemployed. Marx would have had no complaint against the Shapiro–Stiglitz conception of unemployment as a worker disciplinary device. For him the workplace had ceased to be a significant site of class conflict, as it had been in the pre-machine or 'manufacturing' phase of industrialisation; the class struggle had moved outside the factory, into the political arena.

Later generations of Marxists were largely content to follow Marx in this; Braverman (1974) was a late, and very influential, example. Things began to change in the late 1960s when developments in the world economy forced a reconsideration of Marxist theory (Howard and King, 1991, chapter 16). Economic stagnation after 1973 seemed to be bound up with a decline in the rate of growth of labour productivity, and this in turn was due, to a very considerable extent, to a decline in effort levels and the intensity of work. Worker motivation had declined, it was argued, along with the effectiveness of employer control at the place of work. This 'Marx effect' explained a large proportion of the decline in US productivity growth between 1948–66 and 1973–9 (Weisskopf, Bowles and Gordon, 1983).

The three authors of this study were all Marxists, albeit of an unorthodox kind. They and many others, mainly in the United States, had come to realise that Marxian political economy offered an extremely valuable (and almost entirely neglected) conceptual key to the analysis of work organisation. This is Marx's distinction between labour and labour power. The commodity *labour power* is what is traded on the 'labour market'; it is the worker's capacity to work, and is measured in units of time. In itself this is of no use to its purchaser, the capitalist employer, who profits only from the human activity of *labour*, the performance of work. The extraction of labour from labour power lies at the heart of the production process. All other things being equal, the greater the intensity of labour the more surplus value (and hence the more profit) will accrue to the capitalist, per hour of labour power which is purchased. As we have seen, Marx deemed the capitalist to have unchallengeable control over the intensity of labour. In a very influential article Gintis (1976) rejected Marx's pessimism on this question, placing worker resistance at the forefront of the labour process and concluding that employers require power over the work-force in order to secure the performance of labour at an adequate level of intensity. Capitalist production is therefore always joint production, in which two types of inputs – raw materials and workers with a particular form of consciousness – give rise to two types of outputs – the product, and new workers with transformed consciousness (see Chapter 3, Section

5, above). Workers' consciousness is a major determinant of the profitability of production. This serves to distinguish exchange in the market for labour power from all other exchanges, in which only the attributes of things are relevant, and not the characteristics of people.

Radical-Marxian economists conclude from this that career structures, pay scales, promotion criteria and job hierarchies are all arranged to facilitate the manipulation of workers' consciousness. Far from evolving into a single homogeneous mass, as Marx had predicted, the working class has become increasingly fragmented as capitalists bolster their power by creating artificial divisions between workers. Wage differentials by race and sex are part of this strategy of 'divide and conquer' (see Chapter 6 below). A reserve army of the unemployed is created to give credibility to the threat of dismissal, and wages are to a considerable extent insulated from external market pressures. But although they are profitable, the hierarchical forms of work organisation developed under capitalism are not economically efficient. The failure of 'worker sovereignty' – the counterpart in production to the 'consumer sovereignty' which is supposed to characterise consumption activities – is easily explained: the production process is dominated by the (non-market, extra-economic) power of the capitalists, who are able to override workers' preferences for better conditions and more satisfying work.

Two applications of the radical-Marxist framework have modelled the division of labour within the firm and the intensity at which work is performed. Reich and Devine (1981) contrast the 'Smith effect' and 'radical effect' of increasing the division of labour. The Smith effect (which also dominated Marx's writings on the subject) concerns the purely technical advantages of a very fine subdivision of tasks, while the radical effect focuses on its ability to divide workers from each other by reducing their opportunities for interaction and communication, thus obstructing the growth of solidarity and the potential for collective action. Reich and Devine show that the capitalist division of labour will be taken further than the Smith effect requires, and that worker co-operatives, where there is neither conflict between capital and labour nor the radical effect, will be more efficient than capitalist enterprises. Bowles (1985) constructs a model of profit maximisation in which a 'labour extraction function' is added to the conventional production function and product demand curve facing the firm. This relates the amount of labour performed per hour to the inputs of supervision and surveillance used to elicit work from the labour force. He demonstrates that the need to manage class conflict renders the capitalist firm inefficient, and shows that wage discrimination is profitable because of its effects in preventing unity among different groups of workers. Bowles concludes that technology is more an expression of class interest than a neutral engineering datum. Pay differentials and the allocation of tasks are structured to aid in the division of the labour force, and involuntary unemployment is central to the survival and growth of the capitalist system.

5   Conclusion

These issues have an important bearing on the analysis of wage differentials, economic inequality, unemployment and wage infla-tion. Unfortunately all three of the approaches outlined in this chapter are flawed (neither post-Keynesian nor green economists have anything distinctive to say on these questions). The efficiency wage hypothesis is the strongest element of the orthodox argument, though institutionalists might claim to have invented it first (see Rowe, 1969 for an early example). The neoclassical suppression of authoritarianism and conflict in employment relations is, however, unconvincing, and the empirical status of implicit contract theory is very doubtful (Kniesner and Goldsmith, 1987, pp. 1273–5). There is clearly something in the quasi-fixity or turnover-cost minimisation model, but it is difficult to believe that this is the whole story.

Many of the institutionalist arguments are intuitively appealing. As yet, however, they have not produced a coherent non-neoclassi-cal analysis of the problems with which this chapter began. The closest approximation is probably Akerlof's model of partial gift exchange, but even this fails to confront alternative explanations of the phenomenon of surplus effort. It may be that boredom and strain are reduced by working at a steady pace, even when the employer does not insist upon it (Baldamus, 1961), and a desire to safeguard one's job by not 'sailing too close to the wind' may also play a part.

The radical-Marxian analysis is in some ways the most promising, being able to explain hierarchy, authoritarianism and (as will be seen more clearly in Chapter 6) also the racial and sexual segmentation of the labour force. However, it is unlikely that the full complexity of task divisions or job structures can be encapsulated in a single measure like Reich's and Devine's 'division of labour', or that Bowles's 'work intensity' variable captures everything that is important about the performance of labour. Both must thus be regarded as first approximation to a more thorough and more elaborate model, which would also allow for the idiosyncratic skills, defective information and imperfectly competitive markets from which Bowles (1985, p. 20n7) explicitly abstracts.

There is also the neoclassical objection that capitalist work organisation is after all efficient, and that the advantages of worker cooperatives, alleged in the neo-Marxist literature, are illusory:

> It may be asked why, if observed organisational forms are not efficient, they are not competed out of existence. Our argument shows clearly why capitalists do not seek alternatives in competition with one another. But why, for instance, do not workers hire capital and institute their own organisation? I take this to be an open question. It may be that workers simply do not have the collateral to borrow large amounts of capital, or that if several workers did decide to 'go it on their own' they would hire labour as well and in effect cease being workers. (Gintis, 1976, p. 52n10; cf. Reich and Devine, 1981, p. 32).

A final unresolved problem with radical-Marxian analysis operates at the methodological level. Both Reich and Devine and Bowles assume maximisation by (non-colluding) capitalists, who act as individuals and not in any conscious way as part of a class. In this sense their analysis is neoclassical, and the mathematical structure of their models (which use the standard techniques of constrained optimisation) is identical with that of orthodox microeconomics. They are in this respect more conventional than institutionalist writers like Doeringer and Piore, and Akerlof. But it is probable that capitalists, like workers, are motivated by class solidarity, and it may be that it is this rather than considerations of individual profitability which inhibits them from introducing non-hierarchical work structures (or non-racist, non-sexist recruitment and promotion systems). Such collective behaviour would cast doubt upon the significance of any purely 'economic' theory of work organisation. Perhaps for this reason, it has proved unpalatable to neoclassical and neo-Marxist theorists alike.

5

Trade Unions

1 Neoclassical models of union behavior

Three issues are central to the economic analysis of trade unions. The first is the formation of union goals and policy. Second is the bargaining process which determines the degree to which these goals can be achieved. Third, there are the effects of union activity on the level and structure of wages, on the distribution of income, and on output and productivity. These questions cannot always clearly be isolated, but for convenience they will be treated separately, and in sequence, in this chapter.

In the earliest neoclassical model of union wage policy (Dunlop, 1944), the total wage bill took the place of profits (for the firm) and utility (for the individual consumer or worker) as the magnitude which the union was supposed to maximise. This, however, was essentially arbitrary. In more modern versions of this *labour monopoly* model the union itself has a utility function, derived in some way from the preferences of its members; we shall have more to say about this in Section 3. Typically the wage rate and the level of employment are the two 'goods' which provide utility to the union's members. The union is assumed to be run either directly by the members or by professional officers who must reflect the members' preferences in order to keep their jobs. It seeks to maximise its corporate utility subject to the budget constraint imposed by the firm's labour demand (MRPL) function, which represents the various combinations of the wage rate and the level of employment at which the firm maximises its profits.

The analysis is illustrated in Figure 5.1, where I_0I_0, I_1I_1 and I_2I_2 are three union indifference curves, and D_1D_1, D_2D_2 and D_3D_3 are three corresponding MRPL or labour demand functions. Note that the firm is assumed to be a perfect competitor in its labour market, even before the appearance of the union (see Chapter 2, Section 2). For simplicity the labour demand curves have been drawn as parallel straight lines, though there is no reason why demand conditions should be so neat (Oswald, 1985, pp. 168–9). The three equilibrium positions A, B and C are points on the union's *wage preference path*, which traces its response to shifts in labour demand. It is broadly analogous to the income consumption curve used in orthodox consumer theory. In Figure 5.2 labour demand is unaltered, but there has been a shift in union preferences, due perhaps to an increase in members' tastes for leisure, or to higher rates of unemployment benefit. The effect is to pivot the union's indifference curve from I_0I_0 to I_1I_1. At the new equilibrium position B the union

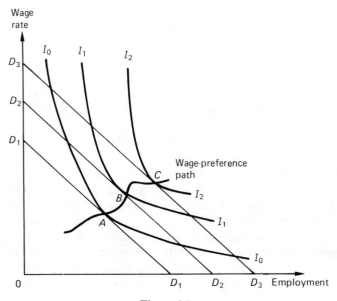

Figure 5.1

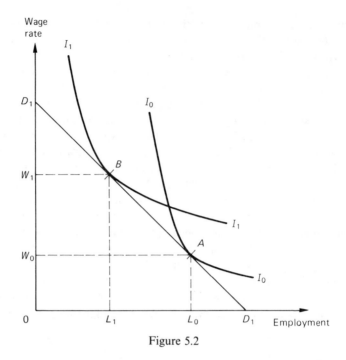

Figure 5.2

seeks a higher wage rate, and is prepared to accept less employment, than at A.

It is presumed, in this simple model, that the union is content to secure the wage rate of its choice, leaving it to the firm to determine the level of employment. If, however, the average revenue product function had been included in Figures 5.1 and 5.2 it would have been apparent that the firm is making excess profits, since $ARPL$ is above $MRPL$, which is equal to the wage rate. This suggests that the union could do even better for its members by specifying a level of employment as well as a wage rate. The limit to this is set by the $ARPL$ curve, since if the firm is forced to pay a wage greater than $ARPL$ it will make less than normal profits, and leave the industry. If, in Figure 5.3, the union had successfully negotiated a wage rate of $0W_0$ and allowed employment to be set at $0L_0$, the firm would have made excess profit of W_0ACD (since $0W_0 = ALC = MLC$, and $ARPL = L_0C$). Union members' utility would be increased by moving to B, on I_1I_1 rather than I_0I_0, where the wage equals $ARPL$ and excess profits have been eliminated.

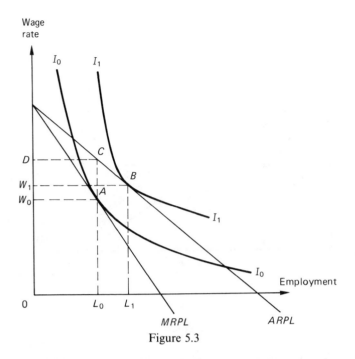

Figure 5.3

An extension of this argument leads to an alternative neoclassical model of union behaviour, based on the requirement that any agreement between employer and union be efficient (Pareto-optimal), so that it is impossible to make one party better off without making the other worse off (MacDonald and Solow, 1981). An essential tool of this *efficient bargaining* analysis is the firm's *isoprofit curve*, which needs a little explanation. In Figure 5.4 operation at A gives the firm excess profits of W_0ACD. It could obtain the same profit if the wage rate were lower, at $0W_1$, by employing either less labour, or more, than $0L_0$. Points E and F represent combinations of the wage rate and employment which yield the same level of profits as A, since $W_1EHK = W_1FGJ = W_0ACD$. Hence E, A and F lie on the same isoprofit curve and the firm will be indifferent between them.

There is one isoprofit curve for each level of profits; the further to the south-east the curve lies, the higher the firm's profits are. In Figure 5.5, for example, there are two isoprofit curves. It is easy to show that A is not efficient, since it is possible (i) to increase the firm's profits without making the union worse off, by moving from A

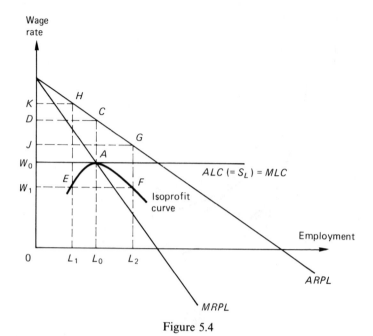

Figure 5.4

to *C*; or (ii) to increase the union's utility without reducing profits, by moving from A to B; or (iii) to make both parties better off, by moving from *A* to some point within the shaded area *ACEB*, all of which (apart from *A*) lies above the *MRPL* curve. A similar argument reveals that *D* is not efficient either. In general, efficient bargains are those on the *contract curve* which links points of tangency, such as *B* and *C*, between isoprofit curves and union indifference curves. The contract curve, as can be seen from Figure 5.5, lies above the firm's labour demand curve.

The only circumstances under which this is not so are illustrated in Figure 5.6, where the union's indifference curves are horizontal over the relevant range. Now *A* is on the contract curve, and there exists no combination of wage rate and employment which is superior (in the Pareto sense) to OW_0, OL_0. Here the marginal utility of employment is zero. There are two cases in which this might be a reasonable assumption (Oswald, 1985). The first is where the union's membership is closed at OL_1, union members have preference in employment, and the utility of non-members does not affect that of the members.

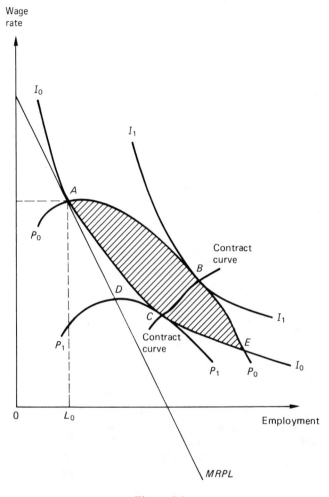

Figure 5.5

In the second case redundancies are made on a last-in-first-out basis, and employment is high enough, relative to the size of the union's membership, for only relatively junior employees to fear dismissal as a consequence of an increased wage rate. The *median voter*, whose support is necessary if the union leadership is to retain power, will be unconcerned with employment, since his (or her) own job is safe (Booth, 1984).

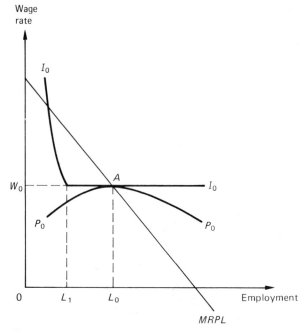

Figure 5.6

2 Some objections

The argument is necessarily incomplete, since nothing has been said about the point on the contract curve at which agreement will eventually be reached. This question is deferred to Section 3. Here we are concerned only with trade union wage policy. An early and very influential institutionalist critique of the labour monopoly model came from Ross (1953), whose objections apply equally to efficient bargaining theory. Ross stressed, firstly, that unions are organisations whose leaders have goals of their own, distinct from and often in conflict with those of the members. Union officers are especially interested in the survival of the organisation and in maintaining their own control over it. However, the very fact that they have control tends to insulate them to some extent from the rank-and-file, making it quite implausible that a union's utility function can be reduced to the individual preferences of its members.

Ross's second criticism concerned the extent of the information which union leaders were assumed to possess. To be neoclassical utility maximisers, trade union officers need reliable information on the position and slope of the firm's labour demand curve, which acts as their budget constraint. Ross suggested that this is most unlikely to be the case (and his argument is equally relevant to the efficient bargaining model, since isoprofit curves will be no easier to identify than the MRPL function). Frequent changes in product demand, technology and the prices of other inputs make it difficult for union leaders to distinguish movements along a given labour demand curve from shifts in the entire function. The problem is compounded in oligopoly, where product demand curves are indeterminate (see Chapter 2, Section 5(i) above). Moreover employers have a powerful motive for providing misleading information about the elasticity of labour demand: bluff and deception are an integral part of the bargaining process.

Finally Ross noted several ways in which the actual conduct of unions in the United States had been inconsistent with neoclassical theory. They tended to form coalitions to bargain with employers, increasing the elasticity of the demand for their members' services in apparent defiance of the Marshallian 'importance of being unimportant' (see Chapter 2, Section 3). Instead of squeezing the maximum possible wage increase from each individual employer they tried to enforce the 'common rule' of equal pay for equal work, a principle of great antiquity also in Britain (Webb and Webb, 1897). They appeared more concerned with relative than with absolute wages, using 'coercive comparisons' in an effort to ensure that their members fared no worse than those of rival organisations. All this implied, for Ross, that trade unions could not be treated as maximisers at all, since they aspired to satisfactory, not optimal, solutions. Union wage policy was more a matter of politics than economics.

Ross made no attempt to develop a formal model of union activity from a political perspective, and it was left to orthodox economists to explore the possibilities. The median voter analysis discussed previously is one application of the theory of public choice, which argues that the essence of political and institutional decision-making can be captured by the neoclassical theory of individual self-seeking (Mueller, 1979). Another, rather more subtle variant is the three-way bargaining model of Ashenfelter and Johnson (1969), which will be outlined in the following section.

Ross's way of thinking about unions, however, corresponds more closely to Herbert Simon's neo-institutionalist theory of the firm, in which *satisficing* replaces maximising, and *bounded* rather than *global rationality* prevails (Simon, 1982). Ironically it was a neoclassical writer (Reder, 1952) who developed this theme, suggesting that unions rarely exploit their full bargaining power in times of prosperity, preferring to keep a margin of reserve power for the bad times which they suspect to lie ahead. This drives a wedge, it should be noted, between union power and the effects of its use.

Dunlop found Ross's arguments so convincing that he effectively abandoned his neoclassical model of union wage policy in favour of a concept of 'wage contours' which are Ross's 'orbits of coercive comparisons' in all but name. Most orthodox economists, however, continue to treat the union as a utility maximiser, whether in the labour monopoly or the efficient bargaining framework. In both cases the union's indifference curves can be derived in one of two ways (Oswald, 1985). In the *expected utility* formulation the union's utility is the sum of that of its (identical) members. Each member's utility is itself the sum of the utility derived from employment, multiplied by the probability that he or she will be employed; plus the utility obtained (through leisure and social security benefits) while unemployed, multiplied by the probability of unemployment.[1] The *utilitarian* version of neoclassical theory expresses the union's utility as the sum of the utilities of its employed and unemployed members.[2]

There are several institutionalist objections to this. The two variants are equivalent only when the size of the union's membership is given. Hence a theory of trade union membership must form an integral part of any orthodox analysis of union wage policy. One

---

[1] The union's expected utility is

$$U = \frac{N}{M} \cdot U(W) + \frac{(M\text{-}N)}{M} \cdot U(B),$$

where W is wage income; B the level of social benefits available to the unemployed; N the level of employment; M the union's membership; and $U(W)$ and $U(B)$ are the utility functions of individual members.

[2] Defined in a utilitarian manner, the union's utility is

$$U = N \cdot U(W) + (M\text{-}N) \cdot U(B).$$

early (and only partly facetious) model envisaged a continually declining membership:

> If I were running a union and were managing it faithfully in the interest of the majority of its numbers, I should consistently demand wage rates which offered to existing firms no real net earnings but only the chance of getting back part of their sunk investment at the cost of the replacement outlays necessary to provide employment for most of my constituents during their own lifetimes as workers. In other words, I should plan gradually to exterminate the industry by excessive labor costs, taking care only to prevent employment from contracting more rapidly than my original constituents disappeared by death and voluntary retirement. (Simons, 1944, p. 8).

The indifference curves of such a union would pivot continually upwards to the left, as in Figure 5.2. A less extreme, nepotistic version would slow the decline in membership by allowing the admission of close relatives of existing union members. Alternatively, the union may seek to maintain a stable membership, or to expand. At the other extreme to Simons's case, the syndicalist dream was to unite all the workers of the world into One Big Union.

Which of these models of union membership is to be preferred? The answer will depend upon the distribution of power within the union, for it cannot be presumed that members and leaders will have the same views on the issue, nor for that matter that the attitudes of all the existing members will be identical, as the expected utility model supposes. In multi-union industries it may also be necessary to take account of differences in the preferences of the various unions, for example between those representing craftsmen and non-craft workers. The outcome will also be affected by union members' implicit theory of society and of the place of working people in it, in short, by what radical-Marxian economists term ideological factors (Harris, 1971). All this is a far cry from the neoclassical approach to union wage policy, which involves little more than individual tastes for income and leisure.

There is one final objection to orthodox analysis, which again unites its institutionalist and radical-Marxian critics (and, following their lead, post-Keynesian economists). This is the narrow individualism of the neoclassical approach, which makes it very difficult to explain why unions find people who are willing to join. Outside the closed shop, where membership is compulsory, there is a serious *free rider* problem for trade unions. This is common to all voluntary associations which provide public goods, since a rational, utility-maximising individual who can obtain the benefits of membership without contributing to the costs has no motive to join (Olson, 1965). Wage increases and the advantages obtained by unions do tend to be public goods, since both employers and unions are – for different reasons – reluctant to allow the pay and conditions of non-unionists to fall below those enjoyed by union members.

Orthodox theorists must then explain why anyone should go to the trouble and expense of becoming a union member in such circumstances. Part of the answer lies, as Olson suggests, in the selective benefits (private goods) offered by the union, which are only available to members: individual representation in grievance cases, discounted insurance, and other perquisites. More important, however, is the fact that free riding offends people's sense of justice and fair play, in a way which cannot be reduced to any statement about individual utilities. In joining a union, as in taking their litter home or visiting the local bottle bank, individuals are asserting their membership of a wider community. They are giving the lie to Margaret Thatcher's claim that 'there is no such thing as society, only individuals and families', and in so doing they are exposing a fundamental weakness in neoclassical economics.

3 The bargaining process

Setting aside the controversy over trade union goals, the next issue which arises is the union's ability to achieve them. One well-known neoclassical response is the claim by Milton Friedman (1951) that trade union power is an illusion, except for a relatively small number of craft unions. For Friedman there are two preconditions for unions to exercise power: monopoly control over the supply of labour, and inelastic labour demand. His argument is illustrated in Figure 5.7, which relates to a competitive industry (not an individual firm). Before the formation of the union, equilibrium is established at A with a wage rate of OW_0 and employment of OL_0. This is unsatisfactory to the union, which would prefer to move from I_0I_0 to a higher indifference curve. By enforcing a pre-entry closed shop the

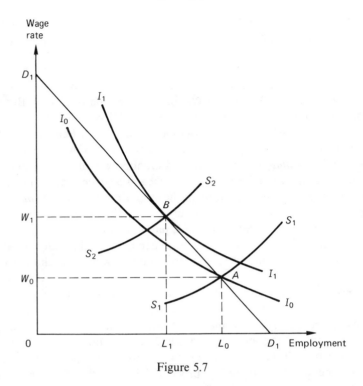

Figure 5.7

union restricts the number of workers available to the industry, shifting the labour supply curve from S_1S_1 to S_2S_2. A new equilibrium emerges at B, with a higher wage rate (OW_1) and a lower level of employment (OL_1). The union is now on indifference curve I_1I_1.

In Figure 5.7 the labour demand curve is quite inelastic between A and B, perhaps because the elasticity of technical substitution between craftsmen and machines is low, or due to the 'importance of being unimportant' (their wages account for only a small proportion of the total costs of production). If demand had been more elastic the maximum possible gain in the union's utility would have been smaller. Similar arguments apply to situations where the union is able to force firms onto their $ARPL$ curves, except that it is now the elasticity of $ARPL$ with respect to the wage, and not $MRPL$, which is relevant.

Friedman's analysis of union power does not allow for bargaining. Unions push up wages for their members by manipulating the supply of labour, and leave normal competitive market forces to do the rest. He is quite correct in arguing that only a few privileged unions can do so. As early as the 1890s, the majority even of craft unions in Britain had abandoned any pretence at restricting entry (as opposed to enforcing a post-entry closed shop, or compulsory membership rule: Webb and Webb, 1897, volume II, p. 474). But it does not follow that other unions are completely powerless.

The early institutionalist economists Sidney and Beatrice Webb distinguished three 'methods of trade unionism', of which only the *method of mutual insurance* required monopoly control over labour supply. In addition there was the *method of legal enactment*, involving reliance on state regulation of the labour market, and the *method of collective bargaining* backed up by the threat of strike action (Webb and Webb, 1897, volume I, part I, chapters I, II, IV). Craft and non-craft unions alike may be able to achieve, through bargaining, what they could never hope to obtain by restricting the supply of labour.

Over a century ago the neoclassical economist F. Y. Edgeworth voiced the suspicion of his colleagues that bargaining was not susceptible to orthodox analysis: 'contract without competition is indeterminate' (Edgeworth, 1881, p. 20). This, however, is slightly too negative. It is possible at least to set lower and upper limits to the outcome of the bargaining process. The gap between them is influenced, as Friedman suggests, by the elasticity of MRPL (and ARPL). The lower limit is clearly set by the pre-union level of wages and employment, for example by OW_0, OL_0 in Figure 5.7. At the upper end, the union will in the long run be unable to force the firm above its ARPL curve (that is, to move to an indifference curve higher than I_1I_1 in Figure 5.3), since the firm would leave the industry if it were unable to obtain normal profits. Hence the contract curve in Figure 5.5 ends on contact with the ARPL curve (which is not shown in that diagram).

Between these limits there is scope for the exercise of *bargaining power*, which is defined as follows. The bargaining power of one party is the perceived cost to the other party of rejecting its terms, relative to the perceived cost of accepting them (Chamberlain and Kuhn, 1965, Chapter 7). It is assumed that unions and employers undertake a calculating appraisal of the costs and benefits of reaching a settlement, as against digging in for a strike.

Assume that the firm (or an association of employers) has made

an offer less favourable than the union would have liked. The costs
to the union of rejecting the offer are equal to the cost of the strike
which its rejection might entail – the wages lost by the membership,
less any increased utility from the additional leisure time, both
depending on the strike duration – multiplied by the probability that
a strike will in fact occur. If the union accepts the offer it forgoes the
gain in utility from the better deal which the employer might be
prepared to offer in order to avoid a strike, multiplied by the
probability that a higher offer will be forthcoming. This is the cost of
agreeing. The ratio of the two sums is the employer's bargaining
power.

Now assume that the union makes a counter-proposal. The cost
to the employer of rejecting it is equal to the profits lost in any
ensuing strike (which again depend on the expected length of the
strike), multiplied by the probability of its occurrence. And the cost
to the employer of accepting the union's demands equals the profits
forgone by paying a higher wage rate than would otherwise have
been offered, or employing more labour, or both. The ratio of these
two magnitudes is the union's bargaining power.

Of these quantities, only the fourth – the cost to the employer of
accepting the union's claim – can be calculated with any degree of
certainty, and then only on the premise that the union is bargaining
in good faith and will not increase its demands at the first sign of
weakness. The other three magnitudes must be estimated from the
inevitably incomplete and often conflicting information available to
the parties. The union must decide how likely it is that the firm will
in fact come up with a better offer. Both employer and union must
form a view of the likelihood that a strike will occur, and of its
anticipated duration. Each has an obvious incentive to mislead the
other party, though the benefits from doing so must be set against
the advantages (themselves very uncertain) of establishing relations
of mutual trust. Both parties must also consider the effect of their
bargaining stance in the present period on the other party's perceptions of their bargaining power in subsequent negotiations.

A determinate solution can be arrived at by imposing special
restrictions on the calculations of the union and the employer. Thus
Hieser (1970) concluded that a bargain would be struck, by rational
profit and utility-maximising parties, at that point on the labour
demand curve where elasticity equals $-5/3$. The objection to models
like Hieser's is that only small adjustments to their simplifying

assumptions make the outcome vastly more complicated (see for example Johnston, 1972). For this reason many institutionalists, following Ross (1953), reject the neoclassical cost-benefit framework in favour of a satisficing model in which the majority of collectively-bargained wage rates are determined by comparisons. Most negotiations simply follow the patterns set in a small number of *key bargains*. However, this approach leaves the terms of the key bargains themselves undetermined. There is evidently much to be said for Edgeworth's pessimistic view of the prospects for a theory of bargaining which was cited earlier.

One final problem is the economic interpretation of strikes. The suspicion is that strikes are irrational, because they cause losses to both parties. In a world of perfect information about the present, and perfect certainty concerning the future, it is indeed difficult to see how 'economic' strikes could ever be justified (strikes aimed at securing political change are another matter). If both parties can calculate the outcome of a strike it will pay them to settle on the relevant terms immediately, avoiding the loss of profits and wages which a dispute would involve. Where there is ignorance and uncertainty, however, this is no longer necessarily true. Strikes can then be seen as accidents, that is, as one expected possible outcome of rational behaviour which nevertheless cannot individually be foreseen or prevented (Siebert and Addison, 1981). They may also result from differences in the parties' views of future economic prospects. This might explain the well-documented increase in the number of strikes at the peak of the trade cycle, when market conditions are changing rapidly and the signs of an impending downturn are apparent to employers before they become evident to the union (Mayhew, 1979). Or strikes may act as an educational mechanism by means of which trade union leaders teach their sceptical rank-and-file that less can be obtained from the employer than they had previously believed (Ashenfelter and Johnson, 1969; cf. Johnes, 1985).

4 The economic effects of unions

There are two sharply contrasting approaches to studying the economic effects of trade unionism. One is derived from the *labour monopoly* analysis which was outlined in Section 1. The other is the

collective voice/institutional response model set out by Freeman and
Medoff (1984) in their book *What Do Unions Do?* The former is a
straightforward application of neoclassical theory, while the latter
draws heavily (but not exclusively) on institutional labour economics.

Most of the central propositions of the labour monopoly model
are illustrated in Figure 5.8, which is adapted from Rees (1963). One
grade of homogeneous labour is employed in a single industry with a
perfectly competitive labour market. For simplicity the supply of
labour to the industry is assumed to be perfectly inelastic, as shown
by *SS*. The industry will shortly be divided between a union sector
and a non-union sector, whose labour demand (*MRPL*) curves are
the parallel straight lines D_uD_u and D_nD_n. These can be summed
horizontally to give the total labour demand curve D_tD_t. In the
absence of a union, supply and demand are equalised at *A*, establishing the single wage rate $O\bar{W}$, which equals *MRPL*.

A union now organises part of the industry, obtaining the higher
wage rate OW_u. Employers in the union sector adjust to the higher

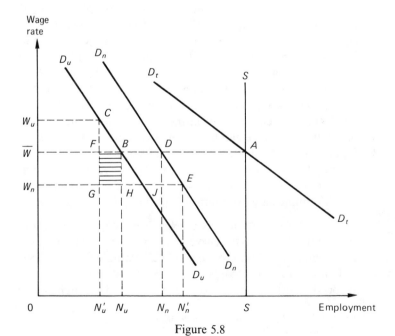

Figure 5.8

wage by moving up their labour demand curve from B to C, reducing employment from ON_u to ON_u'. Workers displaced from the union sector seek work in the non-union sector, increasing the labour supply in that sector from ON_n to ON_n'. Non-union employers move down their labour demand curve from D to E, reducing the non-union wage rate to OW_n. The economic effects of unionisation are thus:

(i) The establishment of a *wage gap* between union members and non-members equal to W_uW_n or, in proportional terms, W_uW_n/OW_n;

(ii) A corresponding increase in the degree of inequality among the labour force, since before the union came into existence every worker earned the same amount ($O\bar{W}$);

(iii) A decline in allocative efficiency, since there is now a difference between the MRPL in the union sector (which is $OW_u = N_u'C$) and that in the non-union sector ($OW_n = N_n'E$). This departure from Pareto-optimality corresponds to a reduction in total output. In the union sector, where employment has fallen, output contracts by an amount equal to the area $N_u'CBN_u$. This is so because the area under the *MRPL* curve is, by definition, equal to the total revenue product, which is simply total output in money terms. Employment rises in the non-union sector, giving rise to an increase in output there of N_nDEN_n'. But this is less than the decline in the union sector. Since D_uD_u and D_nD_n are parallel, the lost output can be calculated precisely. It equals the decrease in employment in the union sector, multiplied by one-half of the wage gap beteen the two sectors. It is shown in Figure 5.8 by the shaded rectangle $GFBH$.[3]

The possible effects of unions on relative factor shares, and on the rate of wage inflation, will be discussed in Chapters 9 and 11. Two immediate extensions of the analysis are possible:

(iv) If the union directly affects the firm's employment decisions, forcing it off the *MRPL* curve, there may be an increase in X-inefficiency in addition to the loss in allocative efficiency shown in Figure 5.8; and

(v) If social security payments to the unemployed are high enough

---

[3] Since $N_u'GHN_u = N_nJEN_n'$, and (by similar triangles) $FCB = JDE$, the difference between $N_u'CBN_u$ and N_nDEN_n' is the area $GFBH$.

to offer an attractive alternative to employment at low wages, the wage rate in the non-union sector may not fall to OW_n. This will reduce the union wage gap, but also lead to unemployment. In the extreme case, where the non-union wage remains constant at $O\bar{W}$, the wage gap is $W_u\bar{W}/O\bar{W}(< W_u W_n/OW_n)$ and unemployment is $N_n N_n'$, equal to the number of workers displaced from the union sector. The loss of output is now given by the (much greater) area $N_u' CBN_u$.

This is not the only possible neoclassical approach to the problem. The full implications of the efficient bargaining model, for example, have yet to be explored. And the merits of the labour monopoly framework depend heavily on the validity of its assumptions that labour markets would be competitive, and firms fully efficient, in the absence of unions. These assumptions will be questioned shortly. There are also many difficulties facing empirical researchers, especially in attempting to estimate the *wage gain* from union membership ($W_u\bar{W}$ or, in proportionate terms, $W_u\bar{W}/O\bar{W}$, from data on the wage gap (Lewis, 1986). In the first place the labour force is not homogeneous, and the skills and other personal characteristics of union members are not in general the same as those of non-members. These differences are in part the effect of unionism, since high-wage unionised employers are able to recruit and retain better-quality workers than their non-unionised competitors. This poses severe problems for econometric work (Parsley, 1980; Treble, 1984).

There are also *spillovers* from the impact of unions on the wages of their members to the wage rates of non-members. One such (negative) spillover is illustrated in Figure 5.8. But there may be positive spillovers, too, if non-union employers pass on negotiated wage rises to maintain morale or to forestall unionisation among their own workers. This *threat effect* of union activity is not easy to allow for in assessing the size of the union wage gain. A final source of difficulty comes from the different levels of aggregation at which research is carried out, and from the different data bases which have been employed. Not surprisingly, estimates of the union–non-union wage differential show considerable variations.

In their survey of the US literature on this question, Freeman and Medoff cite Johnson's calculations for the period 1920–1980, which show a union wage gain ranging from 2 per cent in the late 1940s to 46 per cent in the early 1930s. By the late 1970s the figure was 30 per cent (Freeman and Medoff, 1984, p. 53; see, however, Pencavel and Hartsog (1984) for contrasting estimates). Freeman and Medoff also report very substantial differences between different types of union members, with blacks and the poorly-educated, for example, doing much better as a result of their union membership than other categories of worker (ibid., p. 49).

British research on this question began much later, and no systematic studies are available before the 1960s. Once again there are large differences in the various estimates. Using individual data Stewart (1983a) found an average union–non-union wage gap of 7.7 per cent in 1975, with large discrepancies between different unions and industries. Table 5.1 shows Blanchflower's (1986) estimates of the wage gap in 1980, distinguishing several occupational groups in addition to manufacturing and non-manufacturing industry, and public and private employment. The table reveals little evidence of any union wage effect for many groups of members. Significant effects greater than 10 per cent are very exceptional.

Table 5.1 *Wage gaps in Britain 1980 (%)*

	Manual		Non-manual	
	Semi-skilled	Skilled	Clerical workers	Middle managers
Great Britain	10.2	− 0.4*	0.7*	4.0
Manufacturing	2.0*	− 0.7*	3.0*	2.6*
Non-manufacturing	14.0	− 0.9*	− 0.5*	3.5
Private sector	7.8	− 1.0*	1.3*	2.3*
Public sector	25.5	6.7*	12.4	3.5*

* Coefficient not significantly different from zero at the 5 per cent level.
Source: Blanchflower (1986), table 1, p. 200.

It follows from this that, even if the assumptions of the labour monopoly model are accepted, the loss in allocative efficiency due to trade unionism is very small. Freeman and Medoff (1984, pp. 57–8) calculate it to have been no more than 0.2–0.4 per cent of US gross national product in 1980. In the UK, where a much larger proportion of the labour force is unionised but the relative wage effect seems to be smaller, the loss of output can hardly have been any greater.

Freeman's and Medoff's alternative approach to the economic impact of unions can best be described as semi-institutionalist, since they make some concessions to the labour monopoly model while arguing that its quantitative importance is limited. For Freeman and Medoff trade unions have offsetting and beneficial effects which orthodox analysis ignores. In particular:

(i)   Unions increase economic equality among workers by enforc-ing a standard rate ('equal pay for equal work') both within and across firms. This reduces or eliminates wage differentials based on discrimination or monopoly power, which were stressed by earlier institutionalists (for example Reynolds, 1951) but neg-lected by neoclassical economists; and

(ii)   Unions reduce X-inefficiency by lowering the quit rate, improv-ing worker morale, and keeping management on its toes. Unions allow workers a collective voice, making their prefer-ences known to the employer more clearly than is possible on a purely individual basis, and encouraging the growth of senior-ity-based fringe benefits which serve to reduce labour turnover.

The evidence, Freeman and Medoff conclude, is that productivity is higher in unionised then in non-union plants, although profits are lower:

> The paradox of American unionism is that it is at one and the same time a plus on the overall social balance sheet (in most though not all circumstances) and a minus on the corporate balance sheet (again, in most though not all circumstances). We believe that this paradox underlies the national ambivalence toward unions. What is good for society at large is not necessarily good for GM (or any other specific company).
> (Freeman and Medoff, 1984, p. 248).

Trade unionism is a public good and, shorn of its residual monopoly power, they argue, should be encouraged by government policy.

Freeman and Medoff acknowledge some of the limitations of the model:

> Unionism may have much more pervasive effects on the economy

than indicated by our estimates. It is possible that workers in the least unionized sectors of the economy benefit from unionism. It is also possible they lose from unionism. Economic theorists have specified conditions under which one result will occur and conditions under which the other will occur. In an economy with little foreign trade, workers in the nonunion sector would be expected to gain if the union sector were more heavily capital-intensive. Then the contraction of the union sector could free capital for the nonunion sector more than it freed labor, raising the amount of capital used per worker in that sector, and most likely raising wages. Contrarily, if the union sector were labor-intensive, the contraction of employment would send more workers than capital to the nonunion sector, reducing the wages of nonunion workers. In an economy with considerable foreign trade, gains or losses depend on whether the union sector produces goods that are traded or goods that are not and the extent to which capital is mobile across countries, as well (Freeman and Medoff, 1984, p. 160).

As this quotation suggests, Freeman and Medoff are by no means implacable opponents of neoclassical labour economics. Nevertheless their analysis does lend support to institutionalist critics of orthodox analysis by stressing the importance of managerial discretion, company policies and imperfect labour markets. *What Do Unions Do?* was hailed as a vindication of the institutionalist approach (Lipsky, 1985), and described by a more orthodox reviewer as 'a landmark in social science research' (Mitchell, 1985, p. 253). But it has also been criticised on several counts. The evidence on productivity levels in unionised and non-union plants is hotly debated (Hirsch, 1985; Addison and Barnett, 1982). Any such productivity gap may in any case (as Freeman and Medoff realise) be nothing more than the corollary of the union wage gap ($W_n W_u$ in Figure 5.8). And many of the productivity advantages claimed for union activity seem to be the product of internal labour markets, which (as we saw in Chapter 4) can be explained without invoking trade unionism.

5   Conclusion

The present chapter has dealt entirely with neoclassical and institu-tionalist writings, and this has been quite unavoidable. There is no green economic analysis of trade unionism. Post-Keynesian econo-mists have yet to offer a distinctive and systematic treatment of any of the problems discussed above, but draw on the orthodox and institutionalist literature as and when they need to. The radical-Marxian school, for its part, has been concerned more with the broader political economy of unions than with these essentially microeconomic questions. Many Marxian economists, following the lead of Marx himself, doubt that unions can exercise any significant power in a capitalist economy except through political institutions (Hyman, 1971). When Rosa Luxemburg described collective bar-gaining as 'the labour of Sisyphus' she was not far from Milton Friedman's 'illusion theory' of the trade union economic impact.

Neither neoclassical nor institutionalist theory scores very highly in their treatment of unions. On the question of union wage policy, neoclassical theory is subject to all the criticisms discussed in Section 2, while institutionalism has little of any substance to contribute on the determinants of those 'key bargains' which are the object of 'coercive comparisons' in the other sectors. A solution to the venerable problem of wage-fixing under bilateral monopoly is as remote as ever, and the economic effects of unions remain pro-foundly controversial. The only safe conclusion is that unions *do* matter, but that the degree (and often even the direction) of their economic influence is still unclear.

6

Labour Market Discrimination

1 The evidence

The large and enduring differential in pay between blacks and whites in the United States is documented in Table 6.1. Note that this relates to income from all sources, including property, self-employ-

Table 6.1 *Ratio of nonwhite to white median income. United States, 1950–86*

	Men	Women
1950	0.54	0.49
1955	0.53	0.54
1960	0.53	0.70
1965	0.54	0.73
1970	0.60	0.92
1975	0.63	0.92
1980	0.63	0.96
1985	0.66	0.88
1986	0.64	0.88

Sources: 1950–75: Reich (1981), Table 2.3, p. 32; 1980–6: US Bureau of the Census (1988).

ment and social security payments, not only from employment: the trends in black–white earnings differences are, however, broadly comparable. Down to 1965 the incomes of black men were only a little more than half those of whites, increasing thereafter to around two-thirds. The incomes of black women rose spectacularly between 1955 and 1970 in relation to those of white women, and increased again in the late 1970s before falling back somewhat in the 1980s. Relatively to whites, black women now do very much better than black men.

There are no time-series of black earnings in Britain, although there have been appreciable numbers of non-white workers since the mid-1950s. Table 6.2 gives details of racial wage differences in one industrial city in 1982–3. Taking all workers surveyed, West Indians earned about 85 per cent, and Asians 89 per cent, of the pay of white workers. Racial differentials for unqualified workers were very similar, while in the engineering industry non-whites fared slightly less well: West Indians earned 79 per cent and Asian workers 87 per cent of the white average.

The extent of the gap in pay between men and women is revealed in Tables 6.3 and 6.4. In 1978 British women earned, on average, only slightly more than half as much as men, and there is very little evidence from the data presented in Table 6.3 of any substantial improvement this century. Female semi-skilled manual workers, indeed, were paid much less in 1978, relatively to men, than was the case in 1913–14. A slightly different picture is obtained from Table 6.4, which points to a significant, and permanent, increase in the relative earnings of women between 1970 and 1975. This also shows up in Table 6.3, where a comparison of the columns for 1970 and

Table 6.2 *Male earnings by race in Birmingham, 1982–3 (£)*

	White	West Indian	Asian	All
Average	111.7	94.4	99.3	104.5
Unqualified workers	106.8	90.2	96.8	—
Workers in engineering and related industries	112.0	88.8	96.9	—

Source: McCormick (1986), Table 1, pp. 101; figures are full-time weekly earnings before overtime for heads of household.

Table 6.3 *Women's pay as a percentage of men's, 1913–14 to 1978*

		1913 –14	1922 –4	1935 –6	1955 –6	1960	1970	1978
1A.	Higher professional	—	—	—	(75)	(75)	84	81
1B.	Lower professional	57	67	69	72	72	65	72
2B.	Managers and administrators	(40)	33	38	54	54	55	63
3.	Clerks	42	46	46	57	61	63	74
4.	Foremen	46	57	57	61	59	61	69
5.	Skilled manual	42	48	44	51	50	47	52
6.	Semi-skilled manual	72	78	75	57	58	50	62
7.	Unskilled manual	44	57	57	52	53	53	67
All (current weights)		53	57	56	50	54	48	56
All (1911 weights)		53	58	56	52	54	51	59

Source: Routh (1980), Table 2.28, p. 123.

Table 6.4 *Ratio of women's to men's earnings United Kingdom, 1950–87*

1950	0.60
1955	0.59
1960	0.60
1965	0.59
1970	0.58
1975	0.66
1980	0.67
1987	0.66

Sources: 1950–1980: Zabalza and Tzannatos (1985), Table A1, p. 695; 1987: HMSO (1989, Table 5.4, p. 87).

1978 indicates an increase for all occupational groups except the higher professionals (who initially earned by far the largest proportion of male pay). Wage differentials by sex are an international phenomenon. At the start of the 1970s women's earnings were approximately 60 per cent of the male average in the United States, Canada and Australia, and between 65 per cent and 70 per cent in France, Finland, Norway, Israel and several Eastern European countries. There has been some recent narrowing of the differential in several of these countries (Sloane, 1985, pp. 84–5).

Conceptually, if not always so easily in practice, wage differentials by race and sex can be broken down into pre-employment and employment components. The former include differences in *innate ability*, physical and intellectual; variations in the level and quality of *schooling* between the demographic groups; and differences in *attitudes and motivation* toward education and work. Factors which operate after entry into employment are *occupational segregation*, which is the tendency for blacks and women to be concentrated in low-paid occupations and to progress less rapidly in the course of their working lives; and *wage differences within occupations*. These elements interact in complicated ways. Black workers and women have less schooling, on average, than whites and men. To some extent this is due to differences in their aspirations and ambitions, which are in turn partly attributable to the realistic expectation that their human investments will be relatively poorly rewarded. Some of the difference in occupational attainment can then be ascribed to the gap in educational qualifications, which may also be invoked to explain part (in all likelihood a rather small part) of differences in pay within occupations.

Discrimination can be defined as 'unequal treatment in terms and conditions of employment for groups of equally productive workers' (Sloane, 1985, pp. 78–9). It is evident from the complications described in the previous paragraph that measuring discrimination is no simple matter, since it may operate at several stages in the worker's life-cycle. Moreover discrimination may itself influence human investment decisions, which cannot, therefore, be regarded simply as the outcome of exogenously-determined tastes and preferences. If there are differences between races or sexes in the quantity or quality of schooling, workers with identical innate abilities will no longer be 'equally productive' at the end of their formal education. And these productivity differences will be increased by differential access to skill-enhancing work experience, and to training and promotion opportunities inside the internal labour market. For all these reasons, empirical estimates of discrimination have to be approached with some caution.

Most researchers measure discrimination from an essentially neoclassical, human capital, perspective. They estimate earnings functions of the type described in Chapter 3, Section 4, and encountered again in Chapter 5, Section 4, which relate individual earnings to the personal characteristics of the worker. The next step is to calculate, for each sex or racial group, the rate of return to various types of human investment. For the United States it is very well-documented that black workers obtain, on average, a lower return than whites to both schooling and experience. The evidence for Britain is similar, if less abundant. One study found that in 1975 the rate of return to education for blacks was only half that for whites: no less than 93 per cent of the black-white earnings differential was due to the lower rate of return to blacks' individual, productivity-enhancing characteristics (Blackaby, 1986). McNabb and Psacharopoulos (1981a) found that the marginal return to a year of schooling for whites was 8.5 per cent, but for blacks only 6.1 per cent: the return to formal educational qualifications was also lower for blacks. This is confirmed by McCormick (1988, p. 106, Table 104), who reports racial earning differentials of between 2.1 and 15.8 per cent for workers with equal qualifications. Blacks also obtain lower rates of return to additional years of work experience (7.5 per cent, as against 9.1 per cent for whites), indicating a flatter earnings-experience profile and the existence of discrimination in on-the-job training and internal promotion opportunities (McNabb and Psacharopoulos, 1981a). Limited access to higher-level occupations, rather than slow progress within a particular occupation, seems to be the key factor in restricting black advancement (Stewart, 1983b).

In the case of sex discrimination there is an additional consideration. It is often argued that women's attitudes to work differ significantly from those of men, since child-rearing leads women both to interrupt their work experience and to make smaller human investments after the completion of formal education. In fact, however, 'female attachment to the labour force is less peripheral than is generally supposed. Interruptions to work experience are the norm for married women, but they are usually few in number and their total duration is small in comparison with the total length of working life.' But they do have a substantial private cost (quite apart from the social cost in terms of skill depreciation). If married women were able to pursue the same work pattern as married men, their occupational status would be higher and they would earn, *ceteris paribus*, 40 per cent more than they do (Stewart and Greenhalgh, 1984, p. 514).

One way of controlling for such attitudinal factors is to assume that single women have a career orientation comparable to that of single men (married men with family responsibilities may be supposed to be even more highly-motivated). In 1975 'the overall variation in earnings between men and women with similar characteristics can be expressed as a multiple of three roughly equal ratios: married men to single men: single men to single women: single women to married women: each ratio being close to 1.1' (Greenhalgh, 1980b, p. 771). The 10 per cent advantage of single men over single women with the same human capital endowments can be interpreted as a (rather conservative) estimate of sex discrimination. It is consistent with the 8 per cent differential reported by Siebert and Sloane (1981).

Miller (1987) focused on married women, who in 1980 earned on average only 60 per cent as much as men (unadjusted for differences in human capital). Of this differential, approximately two thirds was 'justified' by differences in education and experience, and the remaining one-third was the result of discrimination. (Note that this is almost certainly an understatement of the full effect of discrimination, given its impact on human investment decisions.) Interestingly, and in clear contrast with the evidence on racial wage differentials, occupational segregation appears to be relatively unimportant compared to sexual wage differentials within occupations (Miller, 1987, pp. 893–4). This conclusion may be due to the very broad occupational categories which Miller employs. It is not supported by Greenhalgh and Stewart (1985), who report significant inequality in the occupational status of men and women, which is however less acute for single women. Married women tend to be concentrated in low-status, part time jobs, and paid accordingly.

2 Neoclassical models of discrimination

There are three distinct neoclassical models of discrimination, two assuming perfect competition in the labour market and one based on monopsony. The first originated with Becker (1957), and represents one of the earliest attempts to apply the orthodox theory of individual maximising behaviour to an apparently 'non-economic' problem. Drawing on the economic and political history of the South after the American Civil War, Becker suggested that whites and blacks could be regarded as two separate societies, rather like the independent nations which are the focus of neoclassical trade theory. They own homogeneous labour and capital of identical quality, and have access to the same technical knowledge, but white society has very much more capital, per unit of labour, than its black counterpart. If there is no trade between the two societies, the higher white capital-labour ratio will make the marginal revenue productivity of white labour higher, and that of white capital lower, than is the case for blacks. White wages are higher than the black wage rate, and the rate of return on white capital (r_W) is lower than that prevailing in black society (r_B). Thus

$$MRPL_W = W_W > MRPL_B = W_B, \text{ and}$$
$$MRPK_W = r_W < MRPK_B = r_B \tag{6.1}$$

where the suffixes W and B refer to whites and blacks respectively.

The model is illustrated in Figure 6.1, where Q_0Q_0 is the common isoquant for the two societies. Their initial endowments are given by OK_W, OL_W and OK_B, OL_B, which place them at W and B on the isoquant, and the two isocost lines tangent to Q_0Q_0 at W and B show the corresponding relative prices of labour and capital. In the normal course of events, market forces would eliminate these differences. Capital would flow from white to black society and labour would move in the opposite direction, as shown by the arrows in the diagram, establishing a single capital–labour ratio somewhere between OK_W/OL_W and OK_B/OL_B. In both sectors the marginal revenue products and the prices of the two inputs would be equalised, so that

$$MRPL_W = W_W = MRPL_B = W_B, \text{ and}$$
$$MRPK_W = r_W = MRPK_B = r_B \tag{6.2}$$

Black workers and white capitalists would have gained from this; white workers and black capitalists would have lost. But their losses would have been mitigated by an increase in total output, brought about by the equalisation of the marginal products. Taking the two

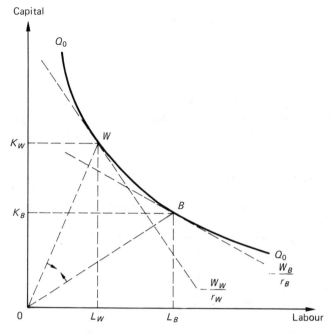

Figure 6.1.

societies as a whole, production is now Pareto-optimal, which was not the case before the introduction of free trade between them.

Becker now posits a white 'distaste' for blacks, which inhibits white capital from employing black labour unless it is cheaper than the services of white workers. The full cost to a white employer of an hour of black labour now has two components: the black wage rate, and a *discrimination coefficient* $(d_B > 0)$ which reflects the additional disutility incurred by associating with black workers. An alternative way of thinking about d_B is to treat it as a factor reducing the perceived worth of the black worker's output, in effect reducing the demand curve for black labour below the *MRPL* function. This means that, in equilibrium, the black wage rate will be below the black marginal revenue product. Conversely, if white capitalists obtain utility from the employment of white workers, the discrimination coefficient for whites $(d_W \leqslant 0)$ will be negative, and they will be paid more than their marginal revenue product: if d_W is zero, the employer treats them neutrally and the white wage will equal marginal revenue productivity. The equilibrium outcome[1] is now:

$$MRPL_W = W_W + d_W, \; d_W \leqslant 0, \text{ and}$$
$$MRPL_B = W_B + d_B, \; d_b > 0 \tag{6.3}$$

Becker argued that discrimination was similar in its effect to transport costs in the theory of international trade, preventing the equalisation of capital–labour ratios which would otherwise have occurred. It follows, if this is correct, that:

$$MRPK_W = r_W < MRPK_B = r_B. \tag{6.4}$$

so that white capitalists pay for discrimination by sacrificing profits in order to exercise their prejudices. White workers and black capitalists gain but, because production is less efficient than it might have been, the sum of the gains is necessarily less than the sum of the losses.

The weaknesses in Becker's conclusions were demonstrated by Thurow (1969, chapter 7), whose analysis is illustrated in Figure 6.2. Here the demand curve for black labour is shown as D_B, which is below $MRPL_B$ because of white employers' distaste for hiring blacks. In case (a) black labour is in perfectly inelastic supply. Employment and output are unaffected by discrimination, which

---

[1] The following version of Becker's model is derived from Arrow (1972b). The firm's utility depends on profits (π), and on the number of blacks (B) and whites (W) employed. Profit depends on revenue (a function of employment) and on costs (which depend on employment and on the wage rates paid to blacks and whites, W_B and W_W).

The firm accordingly maximises

$$U = U(\pi, B, W)$$

subject to

$$\pi = F(B + W) - W_B.W - W_W.W$$

where

$$\frac{\delta U}{\delta \pi} = MU_\pi > 0;$$

$$\frac{\delta U}{\delta B} = MU_B < 0;$$

$$\frac{\delta U}{\delta W} = MU_W \geqslant 0.$$

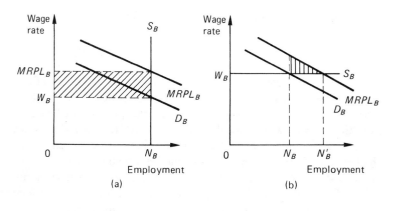

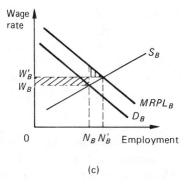

Figure 6.2

The solution to this constrained maximisation problem is $MRPL_B = W_B + d_B$, where $MRPL_B$ = the marginal product of blacks and the discrimination coefficient

$$d_B = -\frac{\delta U}{\delta B} \Big/ \frac{\delta U}{\delta \pi} = -\frac{MU_B}{MU_\pi} > 0.$$

This is the marginal rate of substitution of profits for black labour. Moreover, $MRPL_W = W_W + d_W$, where $MRPL_W$ = the marginal product of whites and the discrimination coefficient

$$d_W = -\frac{\delta U}{\delta W} \Big/ \frac{\delta U}{\delta \pi} = -\frac{MU_W}{MU_\pi} \leqslant 0,$$

which is to be interpreted analogously to d_B.

Hence $W_B + d_B = W_W + d_W$, so that the equilibrium racial wage differential is $(W_W - W_B) = d_B - d_W$. In the simplest case, where $MU_W = 0$, this becomes

$$(W_W - W_B) = -\frac{MU_B}{MU_\pi} = -d_B.$$

merely transfers income from black workers to white capitalists. The size of the transfer is shown by the area of the shaded rectangle. White employers gain, unequivocally, from discrimination. Case (b) shows the opposite situation, with a perfectly elastic labour supply curve. Here the effect of discrimination is to reduce employment and output. The black wage remains equal to marginal revenue productivity, so that there are no gains for white employers. In fact they lose the profits which would have accrued to them had they employed the additional $N_B N_B'$ workers: these are depicted by the shaded triangle in Figure 6.2(b). In the intermediate case (c), there are simultaneously gains and losses. In the absence of discrimination, ON_B' blacks would be employed at a wage (equal to marginal revenue productivity) of OW_B'. In fact employment is only ON_B, and the wage is OW_B. White employers gain to the extent of the shaded rectangle in Figure 6.2(c). But total output and employment have fallen, and the shaded triangle in the figure reveals the profits forgone by employers as a result. Whether, on balance, white capitalists gain or lose financially from discrimination is determined by the relative sizes of the two shaded areas in Figure 6.2(c). Given the discrimination coefficient against blacks, this depends on the elasticity of black labour supply.

An even more serious objection to Becker is apparent once the full implications of competition between employers are taken into account. Since black and white workers are assumed to be identical in their skills and productive ability, a non-prejudiced employer will always hire black workers, and only black workers, when the black wage is less than that which must be paid to whites. In the long run they would force the higher-cost, prejudiced capitalists out of business or, at the very least, bid away all their black employees and leave them to indulge their prejudices by operating an all-white workplace. The total elimination of wage discrimination could be prevented only if the expansion of non-discriminating firms was hindered by diseconomies of scale, for which there is little or no empirical evidence. Becker's model may permit *racial segregation* in employment, but it is not consistent with persistent differences in wage rates between black and white workers.

An alternative neoclassical model which retains the assumption of perfectly competitive labour markets is provided by the theory of *statistical discrimination* (Arrow, 1972a). It has the twin advantages that it can explain the persistence of racial wage differentials and is also applicable to discrimination against women (for which Becker's model was not designed and is not well-suited). Arrow starts from the premise that the employment relationship is typically a long-term one. Employers are therefore concerned with the quality of new recruits, and in particular with their suitability for training and with the probability that they will leave before any investment in their specific job skills has been repaid. If there are believed to be systematic differences between the races, or sexes, in their reliability, aptitude or job stability, this will be sufficient to establish a permanent differential in wages between them. Race or sex acts as a screening device or filter (see Chapter 3, Section 5(ii), above), in a similar way to education. As it is an expensive and uncertain business to test each individual applicant's ability and motivation, employers simply assume them to have the average characteristics of the demographic category into which they fall. If most blacks are thought to be unreliable, and most women are expected to leave work in order to start a family, then all blacks and all women are tarred with the same brush, and will be hired only at lower wage rates than those paid to whites, and to men.[2]

Statistical discrimination requires no distaste for or prejudice against those who suffer from it: employers discriminate because they believe it to be profitable for them to do so. The problem is that it is actually not profitable, given the assumption that there are in fact no relevant differences between the sexes and racial groups. Non-discriminators who employed exclusively women, or blacks, at just a small premium over their prevailing market wage, would find their costs to be appreciably lower than those of their competitors. Discrimination would eventually be eliminated by the same competitive process which applied in the case of Becker's model.

A third and final neoclassical explanation is provided by the model of *discriminating monopoly*. No distaste or prejudice is

---

[2] In the simplest model of statistical discrimination (Arrow, 1972b), it is assumed that workers are either suitable or unsuitable for the job. If p_B is the employer's perceived probability that a black applicant is suitable, and p_W is the corresponding probability for a white applicant, then the profit derived from employing a black is $p_B(MP_B - W_B)$ and the profit derived from hiring a white is $p_W(MP_W - W_W)$. At the margin these must be equal; and by assumption $MP_B = MP_W = MP$. Hence

$$\frac{MP - W_W}{MP - W_B} = \frac{p_B}{p_W} < 1 \text{ if } p_B < p_W,$$

so that $W_W > W_B$.

involved, nor any miscalculation of the long-term productivities of the respective groups, only differences in their labour supply elasticities. If, for example, black labour is in less elastic supply than white labour, the gap between average and marginal labour cost (see Chapter 2, footnote 4, above) will be greater for blacks than for whites. Both groups will be paid less than their (common) marginal revenue product, but the discrepancy is greater for blacks than for whites. Blacks are discriminated against because of profit maximising behaviour on the part of white employers.[3] In Figure 6.3 the marginal labour cost and supply (average labour cost) curves of blacks and whites are MLC_W, S_W and MLC_B, S_B respectively. They are summed horizontally to give MLC_t and S_t. The profit-maximising firm equates MLC_t and $MRPL_t$, with total employment of $ON_t = ON_B + ON_W$, and corresponding wage rates of $OW_W > OW_B$. (If discrimination were impossible a single wage of $O\overline{W}$ would instead be paid.) Profits are increased by discrimination, and white workers gain (since $OW_W > O\overline{W}$).

The theory of discriminating monopsony was first elaborated over half a century ago by Robinson (1933), but it was long neglected in the orthodox literature. In part this reflects the very narrow, 'company town' conception of monopsony which prevails among neoclassical economists (Cain, 1986, pp. 718–9), which leads to the presumption that nearly all labour markets are perfectly competitive. As will be seen in the following chapter, this belief is unfounded. There are, however, two further problems. First, the analysis entails the absence of discrimination when there actually is perfect competition in the labour market, and there is no evidence whatever for this. Second, it seems to be the case that black and

---

[3] To maximise profits the employer equates the (common) marginal revenue productivity of labour ($MRPL$) with the marginal cost of blacks (MC_B) and of whites (MC_W). By definition

$$MC_B = \frac{\mathrm{d}}{\mathrm{d}b}(B . W_B) = W_B + B . \frac{\mathrm{d}W_B}{\mathrm{d}B}$$

and the elasticity of supply of black labour is

$$\varepsilon_B = \frac{\mathrm{d}B}{\mathrm{d}W_B} . \frac{W_B}{B}$$

so that $MC_B = W_B[1 + (1/\varepsilon_B)]$.
Similarly $MC_W = W_W[1 + (1/\varepsilon_W)]$ and,
since $MC_B = MC_W$, it follows that $W_B(1 + \varepsilon_B) = W_W(1 + \varepsilon_W)$
and

$$\frac{W_B}{W_W} = \frac{1 + 1/\varepsilon_W}{1 + 1/\varepsilon_B} < 1 \text{ if } \varepsilon_B < \varepsilon_W.$$

121

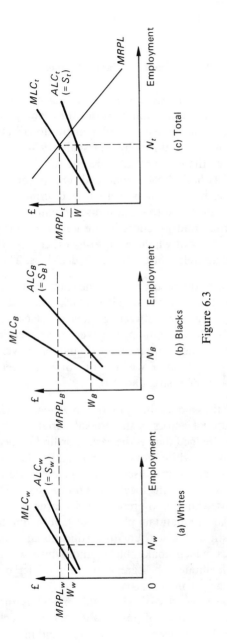

Figure 6.3

female labour supply is more elastic than that of whites and men, not less elastic (Reich, 1981, pp. 213–4).

3   Institutionalist and radical-Marxian models

More perhaps than any other labour market phenomenon, the persistence of discrimination cries out for a non-neoclassical interpretation. Some of the elements of an institutionalist theory of racial discrimination are outlined by Marshall (1974), for whom social groups, rather than individuals, are the focus of the analysis. As Arrow (1972a) had already conceded, group norms may override individual motivations in perpetuating discrimination. Indeed, if they do not it is difficult to see how discriminators are able to enforce prejudicial rules and practices in the long run. Similarly, it is the marginal products of whole groups of workers, not those of individuals, which are relevant to the firm's decisions. The employer

> must calculate the costs to him of the reaction of the whites as well as the gains from hiring a qualified black. This often will become a bargaining problem between groups of blacks and their supporters (the black community, government agencies, etc.), white workers and their organisations, and employers. The *power relations* will determine whether or not blacks get hired   (Marshall, 1974, p. 863; stress added).

Marshall's is thus a bargaining model, in which the relative power of various groups of actors is the crucial variable. These actors are more broadly defined than is the case in orthodox theory, to include white employers, white workers, craft and industrial unions (the latter being generally anti-discriminatory), black workers, the wider black community, and the local and national state. The objective of discriminating whites is to preserve their status *vis-à-vis* blacks, not (as with Becker) to maintain physical distance from them. Discrimination is institutionalised, creating educational and occupational disadvantages which make black and white workers imperfect substitutes, facilitate job segregation and render overt wage discrimination largely unnecessary.

One of the strengths of Marshall's model is that it treats as endogenous a number of important factors which neoclassical analysis regards as exogenous. This is apparent in his explanation of the decline in racial wage differentials in the Southern states. There was nothing automatic about this process, Marshall argues, and the principal motor of change was industrialisation rather than competition. The industrialisation of the South introduced achievement instead of ascriptive norms for hiring and promotion decisions. It led to large scale urbanisation, and a corresponding weakening of the monopsony power of employers in small rural markets. And, crucially, it broke up the conservative Democratic monopoly of political power and allowed blacks to invoke the state in their struggle against racism (Marshall, 1974, p. 865).

Almost in passing, Marshall mentions the value to employers of strategies which divide the workforce along racial lines and thus prevent effective trade unionism, reduce the wages of all workers, and increase the level of effort which can be extracted from them. This policy of 'divide and conquer' forms the basis of radical-Marxian models of discrimination. Roemer (1979) assumes that the reservation wage of both black and white workers – that is, the lowest wage at which they are willing to work – varies inversely with the degree of racial integration in the labour force. As illustrated in Figure 6.4, reservation wages are greatest when there is complete segregation, since an all-white or all-black workforce has greater cohesion and solidarity than one which is racially mixed. For the

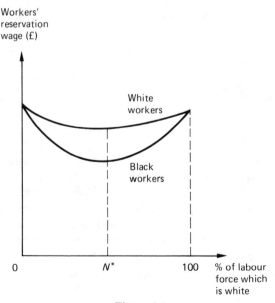

Figure 6.4

employer the optimum percentage of white workers is ON^*, where the ratio of black to white wages is lowest and the wage rates demanded by both groups are at a minimum. The very similar model of Reich (1981) is illustrated in Figure 6.5. Here workers' bargaining power is regarded as a function of the racial wage differential and the employment mix. In Figure 6.5(a), which is drawn for a given ratio of black to white employment, bargaining power declines steadily as white wages increase, relatively to black wages. Figure 6.5(b) assumes a given relative wage and shows how bargaining power is increased as the proportion of whites employed varies, in either direction, away from ON^*, which is the employment mix which maximises effort and minimises labour costs.

These two models are complementary, since Roemer concentrates on the effect of discrimination on wages while Reich focuses upon the supply of effort. In contrast to orthodox analysis they predict that employers always gain from discrimination while both groups of workers lose. (Institutionalist theory is ambiguous on this important question.) Reich cites historical and econometric evidence in support of this conclusion. The use of black strikebreakers to undermine white unions is well documented in the United States, especially but by no means exclusively in the South. Racism enabled Southern Democrats in Congress to block for generations social welfare reforms which would have benefited white workers as well as blacks (Reich, 1981, chapter 6). And the degree of inequality in white incomes increases, across major US cities, with increases in the wage advantage enjoyed by white workers over blacks (ibid., chapters 4 and 7). Thus 'white workers lose from racism, while rich whites, capitalists and a few privileged white workers benefit' (ibid., p. 109); most of the latter are members of a handful of powerful craft unions.

The radical theory of discrimination is a very clear example of what was described in Chapter 1, Section 5, as 'rational choice Marxism'. Its advocates argue that 'divide and conquer' is 'a competitive, profit-maximising strategy' which has no need to assume collusion, group loyalties or 'irrational, profit-reducing strategies' (Roemer, 1979, pp. 696, 703) and does not rely upon 'mass conspiracy' hypotheses (Reich, 1981, p. 108). In this sense it is fully consistent with the methodological individualism of neoclassical economics, and might indeed be deemed a superior orthodox theory of racial discrimination. This is a weakness to the extent that, as Roemer (1979, p. 704) recognises, the radical Marxian model fails

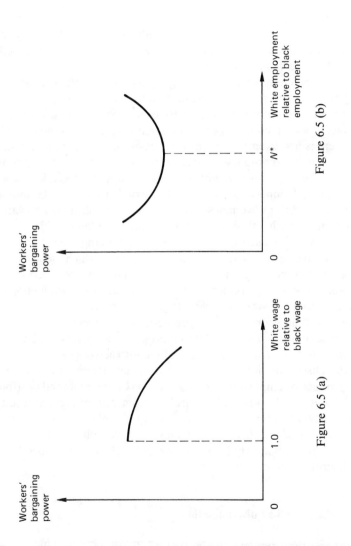

Figure 6.5 (a)

Figure 6.5 (b)

to explain why white workers are susceptible to 'divide and conquer' strategies in the first place. The group loyalties and institutional pressures which are central to Marshall's bargaining model are probably indispensable elements in any such explanation. A second criticism concerns the role played in radical-Marxian theory by the racial integration of the labour force, which is difficult to reconcile with the observed importance of occupational segregation, not least between men and women. This highlights a final, and very serious, objection to the radical-Marxian model. This is its concentration upon racial discrimination, and its corresponding failure to deal explicitly with labour market discrimination against women.

There is a substantial feminist literature on this question, which has much in common with institutionalism and radical-Marxian analysis but, by contrast with the latter, emphasises gender rather than class. Feminists argue that the sexual division of labour in society conditions women's consciousness and attitudes towards work, predisposing them to opt for enjoyable but low-paid jobs with flexible hours or part-time status, and constraining their 'taste' for human investment. The preference structures which neoclassical economists take for granted are thus, for feminists, endogenous to the economic system, broadly defined to include the reproduction of human labour power. 'We need to jettison the view that "production" or "the economy" are gender-neutral terms, and to think about labour markets and labour processes as places [sic] where gender relations are constructed and reconstructed' (Beechey, 1987, p. 16). Discrimination by sex is thus more fundamental than 'a mere by-product of employers' strategies to maximise profitability' (ibid p. 145); it is a deep-rooted cultural phenomenon of great antiquity (cf. Purdy, 1988, pp. 155–60). Thus occupational segregation results from the social construction of men's work as skilled, and women's as unskilled, not merely from the physical exclusion of women from high-status occupations.

4 Policies against discrimination

Although the complete elimination of discrimination will require far-reaching changes in the consciousness of ethnic majorities, and of men, some of its grosser manifestations can be controlled by political means. The clearest evidence of the effectiveness of antidiscrimination policy comes from the United Kingdom, where the Equal Pay Act of 1970 – which became fully effective at the end of 1975 – outlawed the payment of unequal wages for equal work. Table 6.4 on p. 110 shows there to have been a significant and permanent increase in women's relative earnings between 1970 and 1975, after at least two decades of stability. This occurred despite an increase in the relative supply of female labour and the growth of part time employment, which would have been expected to have an adverse effect. It is consistent with the experience of countries such as the United States (Beller, 1979) and Australia (Bonnell, 1987), where comparable legislation was enacted at this time. On one recent estimate, the increase in the relative earnings of women which was needed in 1970 to do away with discrimination was between 28.9 and 36.7 per cent. By 1975 the Equal Pay Act had achieved an increase of 19.4 per cent, or more than one-half of the required amount. The incomes policies of the early 1970s raised women's pay relatively to that of men by another 1.5 per cent. However, the growth of the female labour supply restricted the actual increase in relative earnings to approximately 15 per cent, that is, from 58 per cent of the male average in 1970 to 66 per cent of the male average in 1975 (Zabalza and Tzannatos, 1985, p. 694).

Impressive though this is, there remains substantial discrimination against women. Since 1975 this has taken the form of occupational segregation rather than straightforward wage discrimination, and this seems to have been little affected by the passage of the 1975 Sex Discrimination Act, which required the provision of equal employment opportunities. Discrimination against black workers also remains considerable, as we saw in section 1, in spite of two decades of statutory prohibition. In the United States, too, blacks are still at a great disadvantage when compared to whites. Table 6.1 reveals a real improvement for black men associated with the civil rights victories of 1965–75, and little progress since then. The relative advance of black women has been even more striking, though much of it came in the 1950s, when the political climate was less favourable than it later became.

Further significant reductions in wage differentials by race and sex would require the tightening and rigorous enforcement of the legislation against occupational segregation. 'Affirmative action', committing employers to positive measures which promote the hiring, training and promotion of blacks and women, has had some success in the United States (Gunderson, 1989; Sloane, 1985, pp. 140–2). Its more general acceptability in the United Kingdom presupposes a shift in the balance of political power, away from those who believe themselves to have a stake in the continuance of discrimination; where gender is concerned, this still involves the majority of men. Certainly there is nothing to support the neoclassical prediction that competition alone is sufficient to eliminate discrimination.

7

Wage differentials

1 Introduction

The structure of income from employment can be viewed from several perspectives. Differences resulting from trade union activities, and from discrimination by race and gender, were assessed in the previous two chapters. Here we investigate wage differentials between occupations, industries and regions, and discuss the differences in pay for broadly comparable work within the local labour market, before considering the interpretative framework offered by dual and segmented labour market theory. In each case the competing analytical approaches which were outlined in Chapter 1 will be called upon, where possible, to explain the phenomena which are identified. All these dimensions of economic inequality involve comparisons between classes of worker. The dispersion of pay among individuals forms the subject of the next chapter.

2 Pay differences between occupations

In 1988, among non-manual workers, average weekly earnings for adult men ranged from £511.5 for medical practitioners to £149.3 for salesmen, shop assistants and shelf-fillers. Among manual workers the range was slightly less, with general farm workers at the bottom of the league table with weekly earnings which averaged £145.5, and face-trained coal-miners at the top with £281.6 (HMSO 1988a, Table 8).

There is nothing immutable about these phenomena. As we shall shortly see, there have been very significant changes in occupational wage differentials in Britain in the course of the present century. Other economic systems generate distinctive occupational pay structures of their own. Table 7.1 shows the overall monthly earnings of selected groups of Czech workers in 1965, before the 'Prague Spring', in an economic regime of highly centralised state planning. Bricklayers obtained only a small premium for their skill, but miners and train drivers were very much higher in the earnings league than their Western counterparts, with managers, doctors and teachers very much lower. In Czechoslovakia, as in the West, occupations dominated by women were poorly paid, though with a striking exception in the case of dairywomen. On the whole, pay differentials between occupations were considerably lower than those found in

Table 7.1   *Occupational wage differentials in Czechoslovakia, 1965*

Occupation	Average monthly earnings (crowns)	Index
Senior manager (engineering)	4692	314
Coal-face miner (skilled)	3521	236
Chief doctor of a regional hospital	3381	226
Locomotive driver	2363	158
General practitioner (with wide experience)	2243	150
Bricklayer	1865	125
Labourer (5th wage class)	1757	118
Dairywoman	1632	109
Average of all labour force	1493	100
Primary school-teacher	1288	86
Nurse	1178	79
Shop assistant	1011	68

Source: Adapted from Krejci (1972), Table 29, p. 72.

capitalist economies. Similar patterns prevailed throughout Eastern Europe, and to a considerable extent they still do (Lane, 1982).

In an early anticipation of neoclassical analysis, Adam Smith (1776, pp. 112–23) pointed to five reasons for differences in wages between occupations in the long run. The first was what he termed the 'agreeableness' of the job. *Compensating differentials* would be paid to those in dirty, dangerous, monotonous or stressful occupations. Second came 'the degree of constancy of employment', reflecting the *incidence of unemployment* in different occupations. Smith's third reason was 'the probability of success'. The *dispersion of earnings within occupations* will affect individuals' willingness to enter them, depending on their attitudes to risk, and hence the average earnings between occupations. These two factors indicate that expected lifetime earnings, rather than pay in any one month or year, are relevant to rational occupational choice. Fourth came 'the trust to be reposed in the worker', or the *degree of responsibility* of the work. Goldsmiths in Smith's day, technicians maintaining expensive and delicate machinery in our own, are well paid on this account. Lastly, Smith introduced the theory of *human investment* by referring to 'the cost of learning the trade'.

Abstracting from the first four factors, the fifth suggests a simple human capital theory of occupational wage differentials, in which the long-run supply curves of labour to occupations are perfectly elastic at wage levels which equalise the marginal rates of return on the investments which each requires. In such a long-run equilibrium, demand is irrelevant to the determination of relative wages. In the short run, however, supply curves will be upward-sloping because the acquisition of skills takes time, and wage differentials will be affected by shifts in demand.

This essentially neoclassical argument is, somewhat strangely, also the basis of Marx's explanation of occupational wage differentials. He maintained that real wages tended, in the long run, to equal the value of labour power, by which he meant the quantity of labour needed to produce the goods and services consumed by workers and their families. The longer the training period, and the shorter the worker's productive life, the greater the value of labour power (per year of work) will be. The higher, therefore, is the equilibrium wage rate of the workers concerned:

All labour of a higher or more complicated character than average labour is expenditure of labour-power of a more costly kind, labour-power whose production has cost more time and labour, and which therefore has a higher value, than unskilled or simple labour-power. This power being of a higher value, its consumption is labour of a higher class, labour that creates in equal times proportionately higher values than unskilled labour does (Marx, 1867, p. 197).

Thus all the objections raised against the human capital theory of wage differentials apply with equal force to Marx (Howard and King, 1985, pp. 123–6). Many radical-Marxian economists have in effect abandoned his analysis in favour of a (very different) theory of segmented labour, as we shall see in Section 6.

Extending the neoclassical argument to allow for employer-financed training, the theory of labour hoarding (see Chapter 2, Section 4) predicts counter-cyclical fluctuations in occupational wage differentials. Skilled labour is more likely to be hoarded than unskilled. Thus in a recession the demand for skilled labour will fall less rapidly than that for unskilled workers, and it will increase more slowly in the upswing (Oi, 1962). Similar conclusions can be drawn from a consideration of internal labour markets, where higher-level jobs are filled by promotion from within rather than through recruitment from the external market (see Chapter 4). In boom conditions, employers relax their promotion criteria, allowing less well-qualified workers to progress and increasing the supply of skilled labour relatively to that of the unskilled. In a slump, standards are tightened and fewer workers are deemed to be skilled (Reder, 1955). Oi's argument focuses on cyclical shifts in demand for different levels of skill, while Reder's relies on changes in supply. Both are consistent with neoclassical theory; Nissim (1984b) concludes in favour of Oi on the basis of evidence from the British engineering industry.

What did Adam Smith leave out? Writing at the end of the eighteenth century, he could not reasonably have been expected to say much about the impact of *trade unions* on occupational wage differentials. Given the size of the union/non-union differentials reported in Chapter 5, and the existence of substantial variations in union power across occupations, such effects may be significant. Nor did he emphasise the 'crowding' mechanism described in Chapter 6, whereby sexual (and racial) *discrimination* reduces the average earnings of all workers in predominantly female (or black) occupations. Smith minimised the importance of the *innate ability* required in different occupations, since he believed that most skills could in fact be acquired through training and practical experience. In the few occupations for which this is not the case, the supply of labour will be more or less inelastic. At the extreme, the relative earnings of international footballers and opera singers (for example) are purely demand-determined. Finally, he attributed little significance to a variety of *institutional factors* which are often regarded as relevant, including custom, status, notions of fairness, and the existence of socio-cultural barriers to entry into particular occupations. Such factors may help to explain why occupational wage differentials do not fully reflect the influences identified by Smith, and are often stable over very long periods during which these influences are themselves changing (Wootton, 1955).

Phelps Brown (1977, chapter 3) summarises trends in occupational differentials in the very long run, for manual workers in several countries. In the case of craftsmen and labourers in the British building industry, data are available since about 1300. They show an almost constant ratio of approximately 3 to 2 for the five centuries down to 1914. In other occupations and other economies, there is strong evidence of a widening of differentials in the early stages of industrialisation, probably because early industrial technologies increased the demand for skilled labour more rapidly than that for unskilled workers. There may also have been a tendency for the earnings of professional people to draw ahead of manual workers' wages, though the extent of such a widening of the white-collar differential remains in dispute (Williamson, 1985; Jackson, 1987). Phelps Brown found very little sign of substantial changes in occupational wage differentials between 1850 and 1914 in Britain, Germany or the United States.

As for the twentieth century, there is almost universal agreement that skill differentials of all types narrowed significantly between 1914 and 1920, in virtually all advanced capitalist economies (Phelps Brown, 1977, p. 73, Table 3.2). The only dissenting voices come from the authors of two detailed local studies, of the International Harvester Company's Chicago plant (Ozanne, 1968) and the cotton spinners of Rochdale (Penn, 1983). After 1920 generalisation becomes more difficult. Routh found a discernible increase in both white-collar and skilled manual differentials in Britain between 1920 and 1933, followed by further narrowing in 1934–44 and virtual stability between 1944 and 1950. The renewed contraction of occupational differentials in the early 1950s was followed by a general widening between 1955 and 1960. After this, differentials were largely stable, but there was a decline in the relative position of the higher professions in the 1960s and a deterioration in the relative position of managers in the following decade (Routh, 1980, pp. 178–80). Since 1979 there has been an appreciable widening of occupational differentials of almost all kinds.

Table 7.2 gives an overview of changes in relative earnings between 1913–14 and 1978. For men the evidence of contracting differentials is abundantly clear, and the further up the occupational ladder one goes, the more pronounced it is. The position is less certain where women are concerned. The lower professionals have fared relatively badly – there were too few women in higher professional jobs in 1913–14 for comparisons to be meaningful – and unskilled manual workers have done extremely well. In general,

Table 7.2 *Changes in occupational wage differentials in Britain, 1913–14 to 1978*

	Occupational class	Annual earnings; 1978 as a multiple of 1913–14		Annual earnings as a percentage of the mean for all groups; 1978 as a multiple of 1913–14	
		Men	Women	Men	Women
1.	Professional				
	A. Higher	26	—	0.5	—
	B. Lower	35	44	0.7	0.9
2B.	Managers, etc.	40	63	0.8	1.3
3.	Clerks	37	61	0.8	1.2
4.	Foremen	38	56	0.8	1.2
5.	Skilled manual	41	51	0.8	1.1
6.	Semi-skilled	55	47	1.1	1.0
7.	Unskilled	54	81	1.1	1.6

Source: Adapted from Routh (1980), Tables 2.27 and 2.29, pp. 120–1 and 124.

occupational differentials among women have, if anything, increased. At all levels except that of the semi-skilled, women's pay has increased much faster than that of men, confirming the accuracy of the picture painted in Chapter 6, Section 4.

Thus the evidence lends some support to human capital theory, since part of the long-run decline in differentials must be attributable to the massive expansion in state educational provision, successively at the primary, secondary and tertiary levels. Increased equality of access to education has reduced the rate of return to human investment (or so we must surmise, as there exist no estimates for earlier decades). The problem is that major shifts in occupational wage differentials have tended to be sudden and discontinuous, and this is difficult to reconcile with neoclassical analysis. The reduction in the relative earnings of white-collar and skilled manual workers between 1914 and 1920, for example, can have owed very little to changes in educational endowments, which have been a much more gradual affair. Moreover, narrowing skill differentials seem to be associated with two other developments, neither of them obviously consistent with neoclassical theory. One is rapid inflation, compensated for by flat-rate rather than proportional wage increases. The other, which is closely related to it, is the growth of mass unionism and the relative decline in the power of craft unions. These factors suggest an alternative explanation of changes in occupational wage differentials, in which shifts in relative labour demand and supply curves play only a permissive role, requiring specific institutional forces to bring them into operation. Post-Keynesian as well as institutionalist economists could accommodate such an interpretation.

One final phenomenon must be mentioned, since it casts doubt upon the importance of wage differentials by occupation. Table 7.2 reveals unskilled and semi-skilled manual workers to have greatly improved their position relatively to that of skilled labour. But the distribution of pay among individuals reveals no such tendency. The upper and lower deciles of male manual earnings were in almost exactly the same ratio to the median in 1974 as they had been in 1886: 68.6 and 68.6, and 143.1 and 144.1, respectively (Routh, 1980, p. 214); by 1988 inequality was appreciably higher than in 1974, and the corresponding figures were 63.5 and 157.1 (HMSO, 1988a, Table 1). Evidently the degree of inequality within occupations has risen sharply over the past century. The increasing heterogeneity of occupations in terms of both earnings and tasks performed was noted many years ago (Rowe, 1969, chapter V). Further evidence of this 'balkanisation' of labour markets (see Chapter 4, Section 1) will be discussed in sections 3 and 5 below, and its theoretical significance will become fully apparent in Section 6.

3 Inter-industry differentials

In 1988 average earnings for adult men in manual occupations were £200.6 per week. The best-paid industry was printing and publishing, with average pay of £268.8. The lowest-paid workers were found in agriculture and horticulture, with median earnings of £152.2 (HMSO, 1988a, Table 4).

The neoclassical explanation of inter-industry wage differentials begins by assuming a perfect labour market with homogeneous labour in each occupation. All workers in a given occupation are paid the same, and average earnings will differ between industries only because of variations in the skill-mix, or quality, of the labour force. Only the proportion of workers in the various occupational categories will matter. High-wage industries will be those which are relatively skill-intensive, and vice versa. Changes in an industry's relative pay will reflect variations in occupational wage differentials in the entire economy, or alterations in its particular skill-mix. In the short run there will be an additional factor at work. Occupational labour supply curves will be less than perfectly elastic, so that industry wage levels will incorporate the influence of recent shifts in the demand for labour, and changes in inter-industry differentials will be positively correlated with relative changes in employment. In the long run, however, demand factors will be irrelevant (Reder, 1962).

In the late 1940s and 1950s, institutionalist empirical research in the United States cast doubt upon this neoclassical model (Slichter, 1950; Reynolds and Taft, 1956). These studies have recently been rediscovered, and their results replicated for the 1980s. Thus Krueger and Summers (1987) found that controlling for differences in labour force quality between industries reduces the dispersion in their wage levels, but does not significantly alter the ranking of industries. In the United States the 1984 league table of industry wages was quite similar to that reported by Slichter for 1923, and also closely resembled the wage structure in thirteen other advanced capitalist countries. One further regularity of some importance is the similarity in the ranking across occupations: high-wage industries tend to pay all their workers well. These long-term, systematic discrepancies in pay between industries are a major source of wage differences among individual workers (Dickens and Katz, 1987).

Among the characteristics of high-wage industries are several which indicate *ability to pay*, including profits per worker; the capital–labour ratio and the proportion of labour cost in the total cost of production (together confirming the Marshallian 'importance of being unimportant' discussed in Chapter 2, Section 3); and the degree of product market concentration, reflecting the degree of competitive pressure. Unionisation is also positively correlated with earnings, but the nature of the causal relationship between them (if any) is uncertain. Unions tend to be better represented in capital-intensive oligopolies than in more competitive, labour-intensive industries, giving rise to problems of multicollinearity in econometric estimates of their significance. In the United States, moreover, most high-wage industries were high payers before the arrival of mass unionism; and they tend to be so in other countries where the relative strength of unions may be much less pronounced (Krueger and Summers, 1987).

Broadly comparable findings from a number of other studies are summarised by Groshen (1988). Some comfort for human capital theory is afforded by the finding of Dickens and Katz (1987) that years of education do significantly affect individual earnings. Also important, however, are the proportion of the industry's labour force which is female (lending support to the 'crowding hypothesis' described in Chapter 6, Section 1); trade union strength; and a number of factors associated with ability to pay. These include the capital-labour ratio; profits per worker, despite an a priori expectation that paying high wages would depress profitability; and plant size, which also proved to be significant in a – relatively rare – British study (Hood and Rees, 1974). Again there is a strong correlation among several of these variables, most notably between concentration, plant size, union density, the capital-labour ratio, and the proportion of men in the industry's labour force. Dickens and Katz concluded that three factors stand out: education, profitability, and plant size (or the capital–labour ratio). The first is clearly consistent with orthodox theory, but the second and third are not.

Neoclassical economists account for these patterns of inter-
industry wage differentials with the argument that the characteristics
which institutionalists regard as measures of ability to pay in fact
reflect either unmeasured differences in the quality of labour; or
compensation for non-pecuniary job attributes which serves to
equalise net advantages between industries; or some combination of
both. Consider, for example, the existence of wage differentials by
establishment size. Big plants pay higher wages, on the neoclassical
interpretation, to provide incentives against shirking in conditions
where the monitoring of worker performance is relatively expensive,
and also to reward workers for accepting the greater regimentation
which is inevitable in larger and more bureaucratic workplaces. (A
radical-Marxian economist might agree with this last point, arguing
that alienation increases with the size of the plant.) Similar explanations are held to apply to the other industry characteristics associated with the payment of high wages.

There are many objections to this neoclassical defence (Krueger
and Summers, 1987). Variations in education, age and work experience must capture a very large part of the differences in labour
quality between industries, but controlling for these factors does not
greatly reduce the dispersion in pay, holding occupation and gender
constant. Longitudinal data are also hard to reconcile with orthodox
theory: as workers move from industry to industry, their earnings
change, while their individual endowments and personality traits do
not. What evidence there is on compensation for non-pecuniary job
attributes lends no support to neoclassical analysis, and the same is
true of fringe benefits (Mellow, 1982).

An alternative interpretation, conforming to the spirit if not using
the vocabulary of the original institutional studies of inter-industry
wage differentials, is that workers in high-wage industries are
sharing in the monopoly rents which would otherwise accrue to the
owners of capital alone. There are a number of variants of this *rent-
sharing* hypothesis. Trade unions may play a central role, directly or
(through the 'threat effects' discussed in Chapter 5, Section 4)
indirectly. Or there may be 'expense preference' on the part of
management, who take advantage of the independence which they
obtain from the separation of ownership and effective control: 'the
middle managers who set wages are likely to internalize the welfare
of their subordinates as well as that of the stockholders' (Krueger
and Summers, 1987, p. 40).

The effect of rent-sharing on profits will be reduced if *efficiency wage* considerations are also relevant, and workers' inputs of effort are positively related to their earnings (see Chapter 4). This is a neoclassical argument only if one is willing to believe that the effects of higher wages on effort levels are the same in all occupations. Otherwise institutionalist or post-Keynesian notions of 'fairness' (Akerlof and Yellen, 1988) or 'horizontal equity' (Krueger and Summers, 1987) are needed to explain why inter-industry wage differentials are similar between occupations, while their impact on productivity almost certainly is not.

We shall encounter wage differences between industries in two subsequent sections of this chapter. They help to explain the extent of wage dispersion in local labour markets (Section 5), and supply one cornerstone of the theory of dual and segmented labour markets (Section 6). First, however, we turn to the question of wage differentials by region.

4 Geographical differentials

The most celebrated example of regional wage differentials comes from the United States where, around 1900, average earnings in the South were approximately 50 per cent of their level in the North. By 1945, this had increased to around 75 per cent, and by 1954 to 80 per cent (Scully, 1969, p. 757). Sixteen years later, in 1970, the ratio of Southern to Northern wages was 81.9 per cent. After allowing for regional differences in the cost of living the figure was 93.3 per cent, and standardising for regional differences in the age, educational attainments and race of the labour force increased it further to 100.0 per cent, entirely eliminating the century-old North–South differential (Bellante, 1979, p. 169).

In Britain, before the Industrial Revolution, wage levels were highest in southern counties of England and lowest in the north, the south-west and the Celtic fringe. Industrialisation reversed this pattern, establishing a very substantial wage advantage for the more highly-developed manufacturing areas of the Midlands and northern England (Hunt, 1973). Since 1914 the reversal of the previous North–South divide has re-established a structure of regional wages rather similar to that prevailing in the eighteenth century. This is, however, true only for money wages. Regional variations in living costs make a very great difference to the ranking, as can be seen from Table 7.3, where data for average earnings are corrected for differential endowments of human capital.

Outside remote rural areas, it is the cost of housing which accounts for most of the regional variation in living costs. (Note that Table 7.3 relates to 1973, before the further increase in relative house prices in southern England.) For private tenants – and to a lesser degree those renting from local authorities – these differences in the cost of housing constitute a genuine increase in their lifetime outgoings. For owner-occupiers, however, they are a form of forced saving and cannot be reckoned as an unqualified reduction in the standard of living (Blackaby and Manning, 1987, p. 179). Their interpretation in neoclassical theory is also somewhat unclear. Setting aside the non-pecuniary aspects of the migration decision, orthodox economists would expect real, not money, wage differentials to determine the movement of labour between regions. Workers will move until the marginal rate of return on their human invest-

Table 7.3 *Wage differentials in Britain, 1973*

	Money wages		Real wages	
	Index	Rank	Index	Rank
Greater London	123.4	1	94.1	8
South-East England	120.3	2	92.5	9
West Midlands	112.3	3	102.7	2
North-West England	108.9	4	99.6	5
Scotland (West Coast)	108.8	5	83.3	11
Wales (South-East)	108.1	6	95.3	6
South-West England	105.3	7	87.8	10
Scotland (East Coast)	105.2	8	82.4	12
East Midlands	105.0	9	110.7	1
East Anglia	103.1	10	94.3	7
Yorkshire and Humberside	102.0	11	101.9	3
North-East England	100	12	100	4
Scotland (North)	98.6	13	77.7	14
Scotland (South)	95.7	14	75.5	15
Wales (remainder)	91.6	15	79.9	13

Source: Adapted from Shah and Walker (1983), Table 2, p. 511.

ment falls to that available on other assets, for examples to the interest rate on savings accounts (see Chapter 3, Section 4). In practice this implies something very close to the equalisation of real wages across regions, since for young people the financial costs of migration are very small by comparison with the life-time benefits. But migration of capital must also be considered. The owners of capital will be interested primarily in money wage variations, and regional differences in the cost of living will be relevant to their decisions only if they reflect differences in non-labour costs of production (factory and office rents, for example). Ignoring this qualification, mobility of capital will tend to equalise money wages across regions even if the non-pecuniary costs of migration greatly restrict the geographical mobility of labour (Bradfield, 1976).

An elementary neoclassical model of regional wage differentials was first developed in the United States to account for the North–South differential and to explore the prospects for its eventual disappearance. The analysis is almost identical to that used by Becker in his theory of racial wage discrimination (see Chapter 6, Section 2). Assume that in both regions capital and labour are homogeneous, and that the technical constraints imposed by the production function are also the same. For historical reasons, however, the South has a much lower capital–labour ratio than the North. This means that the marginal physical product of labour is lower, and that of capital is higher, in the South. Hence Southern labour is cheaper than in the North, and capital is more highly rewarded there. In consequence, capital will flow south, and labour will move north, until inter-regional equality is established in capital–labour ratios, marginal products, and rates of return on physical capital, and regional wage differences have been eliminated. *Mutatis mutandis*, the process is illustrated by Figure 6.1 on p. 115 above.

Orthodox economists can claim considerable success in explaining the origins, narrowing and – for real wages – the ultimate extinction of the North–South differential. Migration of both capital and labour took place in accordance with the predictions of the theory, and by the 1960s the ratio of capital to labour was actually a little higher in the southern states. Any remaining wage gap could be traced to differences in human capital endowments, which meant that production functions also differed between the regions. In Figure 7.1 the isoquants represent the same level of output in both

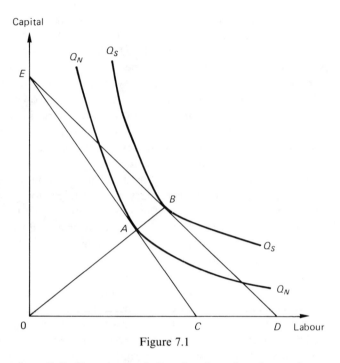

Figure 7.1

cases, but Q_sQ_s lies above Q_nQ_n, showing that larger inputs of capital, or labour, or both, are required in the South than in the North because of the relatively poor quality of southern labour. Assuming an equal capital-labour ratio, represented by the slope of the ray OAB, equilibrium in the North will be at A, with an isocost line EAC. Similarly, the South's isocost line is EBD, and equilibrium is at B. A given outlay buys the same amount of capital (OE) in both regions, but more labour in the South than in the North $(OD > OC)$. Thus, as the rate of return on capital is equal, there is no incentive for further inter-regional capital flows. Average earnings are lower in the South, but this is due to quality differences. Southern workers would gain nothing from moving to the North. The wage differential is therefore an equilibrium one, which will persist in the long run (Scully, 1969).

An analogous story can be told for Britain, and in a very general sense it is a convincing one. Geographical wage differentials over the last two and a half centuries have, broadly, corresponded to regional discrepancies in the level of economic development, which presumably were themselves associated with differences in the amount of capital per worker. In the eighteenth and again in the twentieth century, the South of England was relatively advanced, and paid the highest wages; in the nineteenth, the Midlands and the North had the advantages. Moreover, regional wage differentials are very much less now than they were a century ago, implying that there has indeed been migration of labour and capital in the expected directions. These are not, however, very demanding criteria for the evaluation of neoclassical theory. There is, first of all, a genuine problem for the human capital variant of orthodox analysis. Although there are indeed differences in both the quantity and the quality of schooling between regions, we know that experience and not formal education is most important in accounting for variations in earnings between individuals (see Chapter 3, Section 5(ii)). Skills are learned more readily on the job than in the classroom, and it is the lack of jobs which must be held primarily responsible for the poor development of skills in low-wage regions. Human capital differentials are more the result of regional underdevelopment than an independent cause of geographical wage differences.

Institutionalists raise further objections to neoclassical analysis. They argue that the closing of the North–South differential took much longer than might reasonably have been inferred from orthodox theory. Critics also point to the existence of sizeable and sustained differentials in unemployment between regions, and ask why it is that they have not been dispelled by appropriate changes in the regional wage structure. In the case of the United States they point to the causal significance of a number of non-competitive factors. These include trade unionism; average city size, which indicates the degree of monopsony power available to employers; and labour market discrimination, which has disadvantaged workers in the Southern states where blacks are both a larger proportion of the labour force and suffer more severely from racial prejudice. Finally, they attribute much of the narrowing in the North–South differential to federal minimum-wage legislation and to the impact of inflation in the two World Wars. Some of these objections apply with equal force to Britain, where the egalitarian impact of mass trade unionism, combined with government wage policy, gave rise to a very sharp narrowing of regional wage differentials between 1914 and 1920. At least some of the inequality revealed in Table 7.3 can be attributed to the effects of monopsony in rural areas. And the very low average earnings of workers in Northern Ireland may well be due, in some measure, to discrimination against Catholics in the province.

These institutionalist arguments receive some confirmation in recent empirical research. Shah and Walker (1983) corrected for inter-regional differences in both education and experience; as Table 7.3 reveals, significant differences remained in both real and money wage levels. Blackaby and Manning (1987) found evidence of significant regional differences in the rate of return to human capital. At the county level there is no clear negative relationship between wage levels and unemployment rates (Freeman, 1988, Table 2, p. 298; in the United States, there is a significant positive correlation). Although there is evidence both of a convergence in regional unemployment rates and wage levels, and of a negative association between wage inflation and unemployment by region, geographical wage differentials have not been eliminated by labour market pressures. The South-East appears to operate as a 'leading sector' – a concept analogous to the 'key bargains' discussed in Chapter 5 – with wage increases initiated in this prosperous area spilling over to less-favoured regions. As with occupational and industrial differentials, so with the geographical dimension: institutional forces play a very important role in wage determination (see also Withers, Pitman and Whittingham, 1986).

5 The local labour market

Further light is shed on the determinants of inequality in pay by a consideration of wage differentials, within a given occupation, in a particular locality. The local labour market can be defined, from the viewpoint of the employer, as the potential catchment area for recruiting labour. From the worker's perspective, it defines the geographical limits to job search. According to one version of neoclassical theory it is also the area in which the 'law of equal price' is expected to prevail, in the sense that wages will tend to equality for all workers in comparable jobs.

There is a wealth of evidence, dating once again from the institutionalist researchers of the 1940s and early 1950s, that this is not so, even when, as in some studies, the data refer to wage dispersion within a single industry. Reynolds (1951, p. 190), in a study of 26 firms in a number of industries in one US city, found the starting rate for common labour to vary by 70 per cent from the highest-paying firm to the lowest; the interquartile range was 19 per cent. Similar results have been reported for a number of occupations in Chicago (Rees and Schultz, 1970), the Wirral (Robinson, 1970), and Birmingham, Glasgow and other towns (MacKay *et al.*, 1971). The degree of wage dispersion appears to be more or less constant over time, and to vary only slightly from country to country in spite of sharp distinctions in the nature of wage-fixing institutions. Brown *et al.* (1980) compared earnings differences in six occupations in three cities, as measured by the coefficient of variation (that is, the standard deviation divided by the mean). In Coventry, in 1974, the coefficient of variation ranged from 10.53 per cent to 13.78 per cent. For Adelaide, in the same year, the range was 7.73 per cent to 19.66 per cent, and in Chicago (in 1963) the lowest coefficient was 5.70 per cent and the highest was 15.10 per cent.

Early institutionalists concluded that mobility within the local labour market was quite inadequate to enforce the law of equal price, leaving considerable scope for the operation of *company wage policies*, using employer-specific job evaluation and work study procedures, in substantial isolation from external competitive pressures. Where wage uniformity did prevail, they argued, it was 'as a consequence of policy and not the operation of market forces' (Kerr, 1950, p. 283). There is much to be said for this interpretation. Neoclassical economists, however, propose quite different explanations (Groshen, 1988, pp. 27–33). Wage differentials may simply compensate for differences in the *non-pecuniary advantages and disadvantages* of the jobs offered by employers, for example in non-wage benefits, working conditions or travel-to-work costs (the latter being emphasised by MacKay *et al.*, 1971). To the extent that this proposition is not tautological, and hence non-falsifiable, it seems in general to be false (see Section 3 above). Fringe benefits tend to be positively correlated with earnings, and there is very little evidence that monotonous, unpleasant or dangerous jobs consistently pay more, *ceteris paribus*, than more pleasant work. Substantial wage dispersion exists even in small labour markets where commuting costs are not significant (Nolan and Brown, 1983, p. 280).

A second possibility suggested by orthodox economists is that differences in the wages offered by employers within a locality are *random variations*, which would be competed away if only workers' job search was more intensive. Given imperfect information about the distribution of job offers, the human capital theory of job search predicts that workers will, entirely rationally, accept work on terms less favourable than they might have obtained from continued search. There is no inconsistency between neoclassical analysis and continuing wage dispersion (Stigler, 1962; cf. Chapter 2, Section 4, above). The objections to this explanation are twofold. First, and most important, it is inconsistent with the evidence that wage differentials within local labour markets are stable over time, and (as will shortly be seen) associated systematically with certain characteristics of the firm. Hence they cannot be regarded as random. Second, the argument is asymmetrical, focusing on the labour market behaviour of workers and ignoring the wage policies of employers, who are treated as being entirely passive (Nolan and Brown, 1983).

This last criticism is avoided in the remaining three interpretations, each of which postulates differences in conscious employer policy as the root cause of dispersion in pay. One proposes a process of *sorting by worker quality*. High-paying firms, it is suggested, select the most capable workers for their innate ability, educational qualifications or work experience, leaving those employers who choose a low-wage strategy with a less able labour force. If job stability is regarded as a dimension of labour quality, there is some empirical support for this argument, since quit rates are inversely related to average earnings within the local labour market (MacKay *et al.*, 1971). A related suggestion concerns *efficiency wages*, with relatively high rates of pay being used to motivate workers and encourage above-average levels of effort (Nolan and Brown, 1983; cf. Chapter 4 above). Finally, there is the possibility of *rent-sharing*, which is confirmed by a number of pieces of evidence. The local wage hierarchy tends to be stable, both over time and – crucially for this hypothesis – between occupations; high-wage firms tend to pay all their workers well, and vice versa. Broadly speaking, firms occupy the same position in the local wage league table from year to year, and do so for all grades of labour. Moreover, their league position reflects those indicators of ability to pay, based on the degree of product market power, which were found in Section 3 to be important influences on inter-industry wage differentials (Brown *et al.*, 1984; but see Hodson, 1983).

Taken together, these last three factors do offer a convincing explanation of wage dispersion within the local labour market.

Although they are now advanced by neoclassical economists, they fit more comfortably into the institutionalist framework of analysis, which has always emphasised the discretionary power of the firm and the significance of its conscious wages policy. Indeed, like post-Keynesians, institutionalists attribute more importance to relative wages than is customary among orthodox theorists, and in consequence pay more attention to the stability of companies' internal wage structures. If neoclassical writers are increasingly aware of the motivating effects of 'fair' and 'reasonable' pay relativities, it is proof that they are becoming subject to institutionalist influences (Stiglitz, 1987, pp. 7–10).

Wage differentials of the magnitude considered in this section are not trivial. They indicate that earnings are significantly influenced by factors other than the occupation, industry and region of employment. In determining the level of pay, much depends on the policy of the individual employer. Some jobs are better than others, even though they involve the same type of work in the same locality. A more systematic distinction between 'good' and 'bad' jobs will be drawn in the following section.

6 Dual and segmented labour markets

The concept of segmented labour markets was explicit in the discussion of inter-industry wage differentials in Section 3, and in the analysis of wage dispersion in the local labour market in the previous section. It is closely related to the notion of 'balkanisation' found in the early institutionalist literature which was alluded to in Chapter 4. Kerr (1977) used the term to describe the fragmentation of the labour market into a large number of separate units which correspond to the internal labour markets of individual firms and are, to a considerable degree, isolated from one another. As he was well aware, many workers find employment outside any structured internal labour market, whether in the union-dominated, multi-employer craft labour markets which characterise the construction industry in the United States, or in structureless casual labour markets like those for seasonal agricultural workers (Fisher, 1951). In segmented markets such as these, workers' earnings depend upon the nature of the market, and on the characteristics of their employer, in addition to their own productive attributes.

Figure 7.2, which is adapted from Wachtel and Betsey (1972), illustrates this *bilateral segmentation* of the labour market. On the supply side, workers are divided into what J. E. Cairnes termed, over a century ago, 'non-competing groups', distinguished by their possession of varying quantities and types of education, formal training and job experience. In the figure this is shown by the three supply curves, S_1S_1, S_2S_2 and S_3S_3, which indicate increasing human capital endowments. Labour demand is also segmented, as is shown by the three demand curves, D_1D_1, D_2D_2 and D_3D_3. The earnings of any specified group of workers depend in part on their ownership of human capital, which determines the position of their supply curve. But pay is also influenced by the position of the demand curve which faces them. Thus a worker with a large amount of human capital (on supply curve S_3S_3), but who is unfavourably placed with respect to demand (on D_1D_1), will earn less (at W_{31}) than one with less human capital but a more advantageous demand curve (for example, W_{13}). According to this model, human capital theory explains some, but by no means all, of the dispersion in earnings between individuals.

In Figure 7.2 there are nine market segments. The theory of *dual labour markets* reduces this number to two, distinguishing the *primary* (or core) sector from *secondary* (or peripheral) employment. The two sectors are defined in terms of segmented labour demand. (Note that the dichotomy is an analytical simplification: it is not claimed to provide a literal description of reality.) There are three conceptually distinct, but overlapping, accounts of segmentation on the demand side of the labour market. The first is that of Doeringer and Piore (1985), who focus upon the operation of internal labour markets. For them the primary market is defined by the existence of highly-structured internal labour markets which provide 'good jobs' with security of employment, relatively high pay and prospects of advancement. The secondary labour market, characterised by the absence of internal labour markets, offers only 'bad jobs'. Here labour turnover is high and insecurity rife, job tenure rates are low, internal training and promotion prospects poor, and wages (for any given level of human capital endowment) low. The limited number of ports of entry into internal labour markets impedes mobility between the two sectors. This is further restricted by the adverse effects of unstable employment on the behavioural traits and work habits of those trapped in the secondary market, who become increasingly unsuitable for stable primary jobs.

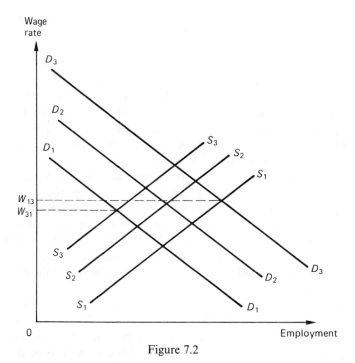

Figure 7.2

As we saw in Section 3, there may also be segmentation by industrial structure, since earnings are positively related to such factors as the capital–labour ratio, firm or plant size, profitability and product market power. These characteristics of the industry or firm can be interpreted as indices of the employer's 'ability to pay' relatively high wages. They are often taken as reflecting the existence of a dual economy, as with Galbraith's (1973) essentially institutionalist distinction between the 'planning system', which is dominated by giant corporations, and the 'market system', where the impersonal forces of supply and demand continue to control the allocation of resources. A very similar point is made by radical-Marxian economists when they distinguish the oligopolistic and competitive sectors of the US economy (Gordon, Edwards and Reich, 1982). To the extent that internal labour markets are widespread in the big business sector and uncommon in small companies, this represents simply an elaboration of Doeringer's and Piore's analysis. However, if it is the case that many low-wage, competitive firms provide stable employment, while giant corporations employ temporary and casual labour, the two accounts are less readily compatible.

A third dimension is demographic segmentation, in which racial minorities, women or teenagers are treated less favourably than the ethnic majority, men, or mature adults. As we saw in Chapter 6, this may involve overt wage discrimination between workers performing identical jobs or the segregation of the labour force by race, sex or age, 'crowding' the disadvantaged groups into a limited range of inferior occupations or industries. Demographic dualism exists if it can be demonstrated that women or blacks are placed in a completely separate labour market from men, and whites. Again, this version is not necessarily inconsistent with the other two explanations of segmentation, since access to good jobs, in both the internal labour market and the industrial structure senses, is generally much easier for prime-age white males than for less favoured groups. Indeed, it was their research into the operation of ghetto labour markets which first led Doeringer and Piore to formulate the dualist hypothesis.

There is strong empirical support for the existence of a dual labour market in the United States. Earnings are higher in the primary sector than in the secondary market, whether the market segments are separated in terms of internal labour markets or ability to pay. Rates of return to education and experience are significantly lower in the secondary market, suggesting that there are different earnings functions in the two sectors. And primary jobs are rationed, in the sense that there are generally many more workers able and willing to work there than there are jobs available (Dickens and Lang, 1985). There is some evidence that the gap between the two sectors is widening, with an increasing polarisation in wage levels and a tendency for growth in employment to display a 'pattern of the shrinking middle', with more highly-paid managerial and professional jobs at one extreme and an increase in low-wage secondary employment at the other (Bluestone and Harrison, 1988). These conclusions are, however, challenged by Dickens and Lang (1987), whose findings confirm the widening of the earnings gap between the two sectors but indicate a more rapid growth in primary than in secondary employment. Cutting across this debate, Piore and Sabel (1984) have identified a crisis in the mass-production industries which constitute the stronghold of primary employment, but anticipate a revival of family- and community-based craft production instead of a shift towards casual secondary jobs.

How far can the theory of labour market dualism be exported from its country of origin, the United States? Something very similar has long been observed in the poor countries of the Third World, where the gulf between the two sectors plays an important part in green economists' criticisms of Western models of development (Schumacher, 1973, part III). Dual labour markets have been uncovered in several parts of Western Europe (Berger and Piore, 1980) and also in Britain, although the evidence here is much sparser than for the United States. Mayhew and Rosewell (1979) found upward mobility in Britain to be considerable, and to be influenced by human capital endowments in a way which seemed inconsistent with the dualist claim that qualified workers are confined in the secondary sector for their entire working lifetimes. As they themselves point out, however, this is not necessarily incompatible with restrictions on the mobility of particular demographic groups. McNabb and Psacharopoulos (1981b) replicated the findings of US researchers concerning the existence of different earnings functions in the two markets, the rates of return on both schooling and experience being significantly lower for those in secondary jobs. Finally Atkinson (1985) highlights the increasing polarisation which has occurred in the course of the 1980s between *core* employees, who are offered secure employment in return for flexibility in the tasks which they perform, and several categories of less-favoured *peripheral* labour. These include workers on short-term and temporary contracts; part-timers; employees whose 'permanent' contracts nevertheless permit their dismissal at very short notice; 'temps' hired from outside agencies; self-employed outworkers; and independent sub-contractors. For Atkinson the crucial distinction is now between workers rather than employers, since peripheral or secondary jobs are increasingly found in firms which also offer significant numbers of primary jobs. Although these developments are by no means entirely new, there is little doubt that they have accelerated in recent years and reinforce the relevance to Britain of a (slightly modified) analysis of dual labour markets.

There remains the question of the theoretical implications of dualism. The concept originated with institutionalist writers, as we have seen, and was initially treated with deep suspicion by neoclassical economists (Cain, 1976). Piore (1983) suggests several reasons for the 'scorn and disdain' which dualism aroused on the part of orthodox theorists. First, it had been discovered through participant observation instead of econometric techniques. Second, it introduced sharp discontinuities which were displeasing to those brought up in the Marshallian tradition that – to quote the frontispiece of his *Principles* – 'natura non facit saltum' (nature does not make jumps). Third, dualism stresses the socio-economic causes of variations in behaviour between different demographic groups, which gives it an historical orientation which is quite alien to neoclassical theory.

Although himself opposed to radical-Marxian theory, Piore also notes that 'segmentation is much more consistent with the aesthetics of Marxian economics, and it is, therefore, no accident that many of its chief exponents are radical economists' (Piore, 1983, p. 250). Radical-Marxian theorists were very quick to adapt dual labour market theory to their own purposes. They identify segmentation and the earlier process of 'homogenisation' as the two strategies of labour control which have been used by corporate capitalism at different periods in its history. According to Edwards (1979) and Gordon, Edwards and Reich (1982), segmentation was adopted by big business as a conscious policy after 1920, in reaction to the high turnover rates and collective effort restrictions which had been engendered by the Taylorite 'scientific management' techniques in use during the homogenisation phase from the 1870s onwards. For radical-Marxian economists, the 'divide and conquer' strategy, which we considered as a theory of discrimination in Chapter 6, can be extended into a more general theory of labour management and labour market dualism. Some relevant empirical evidence is discussed by Reich (1984).

Dualism is also readily assimilable into post-Keynesian theory. Annable (1980) sets out a model of wage determination in the spirit of the *General Theory*, in which workers' utility depends less on the absolute level of real wages than on relative earnings, both in comparison with the pay of others and in relation to the individual's own past experience. The notion of 'satisfactory' wage rates, and of 'a fair day's work for a fair day's pay', condition the individual's supply of effort, and encourage primary employers to pay a wage rate in excess of the market-clearing level in order to maintain morale. Small owner-managed firms, which find it easier to monitor and control job performance, pay systematically lower wages to labour of equal quality.

The observation that 'in any economy in which firms cannot monitor workers perfectly, they will pursue policies which will cause workers to value their jobs', leads Bulow and Summers (1986, p. 389) to propose a model of dualism which is remarkably similar to that of Annable, but without any explicit post-Keynesian connotations. Indeed, Dickens and Lang (1985, pp. 801–2) argue that dualism is in fact consistent with neoclassical economics, once efficiency wage considerations are invoked to justify high wages in the primary labour market and the need for flexibility in costs is used to explain the low wages and instability of secondary jobs. Most orthodox theorists, however, remain profoundly suspicious of dual labour market analysis.

8

The Distribution of Individual Incomes

1 Evidence on the distribution of incomes

The need for a separate analysis of personal income distribution
became apparent in the previous two chapters. In Chapter 7, Section
2, it was noted that differences in overall earnings between occupations accounted for only a small part of the dispersion of employment incomes among individuals, and that wage differentials within
occupations were responsible for the bulk of earnings inequality.
Subsequent sections identified some of the reasons. There exist
systematic discrepancies in pay, for any given occupation, depending on the industry or region in which the individual works, on the
characteristics of the employer, and, finally, on whether the individual works in the primary or secondary sector; and there is the
additional influence of labour market discrimination, which was
discussed in Chapter 6.

Information on the distribution of individual earnings has been
collected for very many countries, often over considerable periods of
time. In Britain, for example, comprehensive statistics for manual
workers date from the Board of Trade's wages census in 1886. The
evidence, surveyed in the classic work of Lydall (1968), is remarkably consistent across time and space. The distribution of the
bottom 80 per cent of incomes from employment is not symmetrical
and bell-shaped, but positively skewed: it is *lognormal* rather than

normal. In addition, the top 20 per cent of incomes are distributed according to *Pareto's law*, tracing out a hyperbola which approximates to the formula:

$$N = AX^{-\alpha} \tag{8.1}$$

where N is the number of incomes above X, and A and α are constants. These two characteristics of the earnings distribution are shown in Figure 8.1, where they are contrasted with the normal distribution, shown by the dotted curve. Only if the logarithm of income is measured along the horizontal axis is the distribution symmetrical, as in Figure 8.2; and even this does not apply to the top 20 per cent of incomes.

Some idea of the magnitude of dispersion in earnings can be obtained from Table 8.1, which shows the earnings of the highest and lowest decile, and the upper and lower quartile, in relation to the median. In a representative sample of 1000 men or women, these are the individuals in 901st, 101st, 751st, 251st and 501st positions. At least where manual workers are concerned, the distribution seems to change very little over long periods of time. In 1974 the lowest and highest deciles and the lower and higher quartile were almost the same, as a percentage of the median, as they had been in 1886

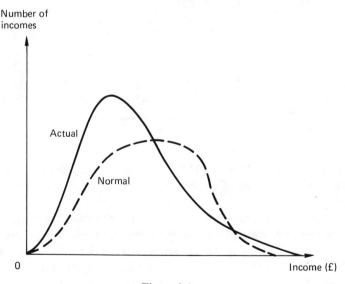

Figure 8.1

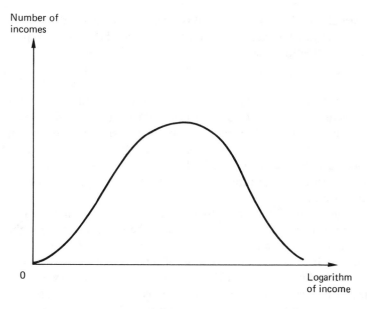

Figure 8.2

Table 8.1   *Gross weekly earnings of full-time employees on adult rates, April 1988 (£)*

	Lowest decile	Lower quartile	Median	Upper quartile	Highest decile
Men	127.1	162.7	215.5	288.7	384.2
Women	92.2	112.1	145.3	198.5	258.0

Source: HMSO (1988a), Table 1.

(Phelps Brown, 1977, p. 319). By 1988, however, there had been an appreciable widening of earnings differentials, as can be seen from Table 8.2.

Differences in earnings are responsible for most of the inequality in income as a whole. This is so for two main reasons. First, wages and salaries make up by far the largest part of the national income; the labour share is two-thirds, or three-quarters, or even more, in most advanced capitalist countries (see Chapter 9, Section 1).

Table 8.2 *Earnings of full-time male manual workers in Great Britain, 1886–1988*

	Median earnings (£ per week)	Lowest decile	Lower quartile	Upper quartile	Highest decile
		(as per cent of median)			
1886	1.2	68.6	82.8	121.7	143.1
1906	1.5	66.5	79.5	126.7	156.8
1938	3.4	67.7	82.1	118.5	139.9
1960	14.2	70.6	82.6	121.7	145.2
1968	22.4	67.3	81.0	122.3	147.8
1974	41.8	68.6	82.2	121.0	144.1
1988	188.0	63.5	79.0	126.2	157.1

Source: 1886–1974: Phelps Brown (1977, Table 9.1, p. 319); 1988: HMSO (1988a, Table 1). Figures for 1988 refer only to workers on adult rates.

Second, the average income derived from ownership of property is quite modest. Along with the Queen and the Duke of Westminster – respectively the wealthiest woman and the richest man in Britain – are millions of pensioners, widows and orphans. The relative importance of employment, self-employment, property and state benefits, classified by income level, is shown in Table 8.3. It can be seen that an increase in the share of employment income, and a corresponding decline in the property share, would indeed reduce overall inequality, but the effect would be small (Nolan, 1987). In at least one country – Australia – it would actually be negative (Kakwani, 1986). This is not to defend large fortunes, but rather to place them in perspective.

The contribution of differences in earnings to overall economic inequality is further emphasised by a comparison of the United Kingdom and the Soviet Union, where there is almost no private ownership of the means of production. In 1967, the poorest 20 per cent of non-farm households in the Soviet Union received 10.4 per cent of all household income, as against 8.3 per cent in Britain (in 1973). The top 20 per cent obtained 33.8 per cent of income in the

Table 8.3   *Distribution of pre-tax income by source in 1984–5 (%)*

		Employ-ment	Self-employment	Invest-ment	Occupational pensions	State benefits
Top	1%	57	26	14	2	2
Top	25%	75	10	8	3	5
Next	25%	69	7	6	6	12
Next	25%	38	4	7	7	45
Bottom	25%	23	1	8	3	64
All		64	8	7	4	9

Source: HMSO (1987b), Table D, p. 97.

Table 8.4   *Percentage shares of income before tax received by various groups*

		1978–9	1981–2	1984–5
Top	1%	5.3	6.0	6.4
Top	10%	26.1	28.3	29.5
Top	20%	42.6	45.0	46.3
Bottom	20%	5.9	5.5	5.8
Bottom	10%	2.4	2.0	2.3

Source: HMSO (1987b), Table A, p. 94.

USSR, and 39.9 per cent in the UK (Bergson, 1984, Table 6, p. 1070; see also Estrin, 1981). Including farm incomes would probably increase the degree of inequality recorded for the Soviet Union. Making allowance for its relatively low degree of economic development, however, would require an adjustment in the opposite direction, since the *Kuznets curve* suggests that industrialisation increases inequality in the early stages, reducing earnings dispersion only much later on (for a sceptical view of the Kuznets curve, see Lee and Koo, 1988).

There has been a pronounced widening of earnings differentials in Britain since the late 1970s. This is illustrated, in general terms, in

Table 8.4. To what extent this reflects only the depressed conditions of the early 1980s, and is therefore reversible, remains to be seen. In the case of the top 1 per cent, though, it does seem to have marked the end of a long-standing decline, from 11.2 per cent of income in 1949 to 5.3 per cent by 1978–9; in 1984–5 their share had recovered to 6.4 per cent (HMSO, 1987b, Chart 2, p. 96).

2   Inequality and the 'ability to work'

Since they explain the earnings of individual workers in terms of their productivity at work, it is only natural for neoclassical economists to account for the distribution of employment incomes as a whole in the same way: that is, in terms of the distribution of productive abilities. Profoundly conservative conclusions can be drawn from this, as in the following statement attributed to the father of the IQ test, Sir Cyril Burt: 'The wide inequality of personal income is largely, though not entirely, an indirect effect of the wide inequality in innate intelligence' (Cerny, 1985–6, p. 12). This is quite incorrect. After allowing for its correlation with family background and the level of schooling, the independent influence of IQ on earnings is actually very small (Bowles and Nelson, 1974; Atkinson, 1983, pp. 122–5).

Few, if any, neoclassical economists would regard genetic endowments as the major determinant of individual productivity. While some abilities are indeed inherited, most, as we saw in Chapter 3, Section 4, are acquired through education and training. Hence the individual's earnings depend upon the choices made, and the opportunities encountered, over the whole course of his or her working life (Phelps Brown, 1977, pp. 298–310; Canterbery, 1979). Significantly, the characteristic lognormal distribution of earnings can be derived from human capital theory in a quite straightforward manner. We may write the individual's earnings in period j as:

$$Y_j = X_j + \sum_{t=0}^{t=j-i} r_t C_t - C_j, \qquad (8.2)$$

where X_j represents the earnings attributable to 'raw uneducated ability', and r_t and C_t are respectively the rate of return to human capital and the amount of human capital acquired in each of the preceding periods. C_j is the investment made in period j, measured in terms of the income forgone. The fact that r_t and C_t enter multiplicatively into the earnings function means that the resulting distribution of incomes is likely to be lognormal, even if the distribution of human capital is itself negatively skewed. This point is reinforced if innate ability (represented by X_j) is positively correlated with either r or C (Sahota, 1980, pp. 11–14).

Becker (1967) distinguished between the 'egalitarian' and 'elite' versions of the analysis. In the former, illustrated in Figure 8.3, everyone is supposed to have the same capacity to benefit from human investment but opportunities are unequal, principally because of differences in family wealth and hence in the ability to borrow. There is a common demand curve for human capital, but different supply curves; the least privileged make the smallest investments, and obtain the highest marginal return. In Figure 8.4 all individuals have the same opportunities, but their abilities differ. There is a common supply curve and a range of demand curves, with

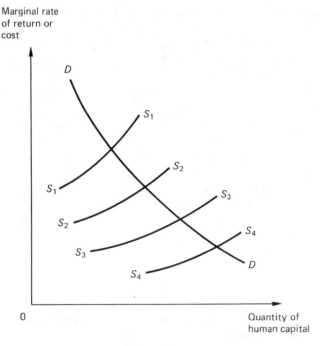

Figure 8.3

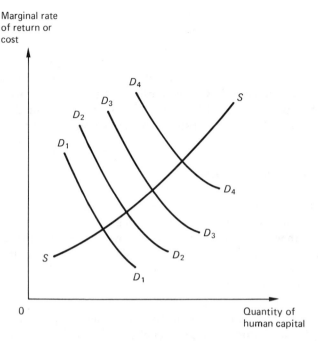

Figure 8.4

the most able people – the 'elite' – investing most and enjoying the highest returns. In reality, Becker suggests, both opportunities and abilities vary between individuals; the actual distribution of earnings reflects the operation of both factors.

Some of the problems inherent in this analysis were discussed in Chapter 3, Section 5(ii). Rates of return to human capital in general, and to schooling in particular, differ markedly between individuals, and these differences themselves must be explained. Only a small proportion of the dispersion in earnings is accounted for by differences in schooling. Moreover, increasing equality in the amount of schooling has not always been accompanied by a reduction in the inequality of earnings (Thurow, 1976, Chapter 3). Thus human capital arguments have come to rely heavily on the effect of (post-school) training. The difficulty here is that only the returns to formal training can be estimated directly; informal or on-the-job training is much more elusive. It is generally measured indirectly, using years of work experience as a proxy. But the link between length of service and the acquisition of skills is more than a little tenuous. What evidence there is suggests no correlation between experience and productivity (Medoff and Abraham, 1980), and we shall see in the following section that the undoubted relationship between experience and earnings can be derived from a non-neoclassical analytical framework. One final objection to human capital theory in this context is that it has very little to say concerning the top 20 per cent of the earnings distribution, the so-called 'Pareto tail'.

3   Alternative approaches

Despite the strength of these criticisms, no single coherent alternative to human capital theory has yet emerged. Indeed, radical-Marxian writers tend to accept its underlying premise – the relationship between income and productive ability – and simply emphasise the inequalities of opportunity depicted in Figure 8.3. If anything, it is the institutionalists who have been more ambitious in denying that higher earnings necessarily reflect higher productivity, especially in the Pareto tail. A distribution corresponding to equation (8.1) can be generated from a simple model of organisational hierarchy in which superiors always earn more than their subordinates, but without any presumption that they are necessarily more productive (Simon, 1957; Beckmann, 1971).

Imagine a bureaucratic pyramid with N levels. Except at the very bottom, each employee supervises a fixed number of workers in the level below. Call this the span of control, assume it to be constant at all levels of the organisation, and denote it by M. Finally, introduce a constant ratio g (> 1) by which the salary of each supervisor exceeds that of those for whom he or she is responsible. Then the number of employees at any level k is

$$N_k = M^{N-k}, \tag{8.3}$$

and the salary paid to those at level k is

$$Y_k = Y_1 g^{k-1} \tag{8.4}$$

where Y_1 is the salary applying to the bottom level. For an organisation with 10 levels, a span of control equal to 2, and a salary ratio of 1.2, the distribution of earnings is shown in Table 8.5. When plotted, it traces out a parabola conforming to Pareto's law.

Table 8.5 *Hierarchy and the distribution of salaries*

Level	Income per head (Y_k)	Number employed (N_k)
1	$Y_1 = 100$	$N_1 = 512$
2	$Y_2 = 120$	$N_2 = 256$
3	$Y_3 = 144$	$N_3 = 128$
4	$Y_4 = 173$	$N_4 = 64$
5	$Y_5 = 207$	$N_5 = 32$
6	$Y_6 = 249$	$N_6 = 16$
7	$Y_7 = 299$	$N_7 = 8$
8	$Y_8 = 358$	$N_8 = 4$
9	$Y_9 = 430$	$N_9 = 2$
10	$Y_{10} = 516$	$N_{10} = 1$ (The Boss!)

Source: See text.

Many large organisations, in both the public and private sectors, do seem to resemble this model, though the determinants of N, M and g remain to be established. It can be argued that there is nothing here which is inconsistent with neoclassical analysis: the salary ratio (g), orthodox economists might maintain, reflects the increasing marginal revenue productivity of employees at successively higher levels, itself presumably the result of their increasing human investments in the acquisition of skills. There is, however, little evidence to support this interpretation.

Institutionalists would describe the pattern of earnings illustrated in Table 8.5 as proof that there exists a highly structured internal labour market (see Chapter 4, Section 3). The salary distribution in such markets is determined by the imperatives of the organisation itself – and in particular by the perceived unfairness or impropriety of paying a supervisor less than the staff she supervises – rather than by the marginal products of the individuals (or even groups) involved. Many radical-Marxian economists would agree with this, adding a twist of their own to the effect that hierarchy serves to divide the workforce and perpetuate capitalist domination, rather than to promote economic efficiency as conventionally defined (Reich and Devine, 1981; Bowles, 1985). This has implications which extend well beyond the top 20 per cent of employment incomes. If promotion within the internal labour market is by seniority, at all occupational levels, then the relationship between experience and earnings may have little connection with human capital, and much more to do with the imperatives of the organisation of work.

Cutting across all this is the role of random elements: fortune, chance, good old-fashioned luck. Statisticians have long delighted in generating lognormal distributions by stochastic processes:

> Chance effects can lead to a lognormal distribution if the size of an income increase, or the probability of its occurrence, is a function of the previous size of the variable. For example, if we take a group of people and in successive periods give $1 to individuals selected at random, we will eventually approach a normal distribution. But if, instead of giving the fortunate individuals $1 each, we give them, say, 1 per cent of their previous income, we can get a lognormal distribution   (Mayer, 1960), p. 189.

This lends itself to a neoclassical interpretation, in which the dispersion of incomes is explained by chance in conjunction with differing attitudes to risk: there are successful gamblers, unsuccessful gamblers, and those who never place a bet but patronise insurance companies (Friedman, 1953b).

Adam Smith notwithstanding (see Chapter 7, Section 2), this is of very limited relevance to employment incomes. But luck does play an important part in the determination of earnings through the effect of labour market imperfections, especially the impact of trade unions and the effect of employer characteristics (reflecting the capacity to pay) on the earnings of individuals with very similar productive abilities. The research discussed at length in the previous chapter is pertinent here. Differences in wages between industries, between firms within the local labour market, and between primary and secondary segments of the dual labour market, reveal that individual earnings are only in part the outcome of individual choice. Luck also plays a part, as institutionalist – and, to a lesser extent, radical-Marxian – economists have always argued.

4 Poverty and the labour market

The least fortunate, presumably, are those at the very bottom of the income distribution, in the left-hand tail in Figure 8.1. There are many definitions of poverty, and many ways of measuring the numbers of poor people (Sawhill, 1988). The crucial issue is the choice between *absolute* and *relative* concepts of poverty. If the criterion for being poor is an inability to sustain life at some physiologically-given minimum subsistence level, then the percentage of poor people is almost certain to decline in the longer term as general living standards rise. However, poverty may more reasonably be defined as exclusion, on the grounds of low income, from the daily life of the community – buying newspapers, giving birthday presents to relatives, going on holiday, sending children on school trips. There is then no reason why growing per capita incomes cannot be associated with a constant, or even increasing, proportion of the population living in poverty.

A. K. Sen (1979) specifies a relative *poverty line*, $Z(\beta)$, in the following terms:

$$Z(\beta) = Z_0 + \beta(m - Z_0). \tag{8.5}$$

Here Z_0 is the absolute poverty line, m is the median income, and β is a coefficient between zero and unity which depends upon social values. Suppose that the absolute poverty line for a single person in 1990 is set (after housing costs) at £40 per week, and median income is £240. Then, if $\beta = \frac{1}{4}$, Sen's poverty line is $40 + \frac{1}{4}(240 - 40) = £90$ per week. Since the precise value of β is contentious, the prevailing minimum level of social welfare benefit – Income Support, formerly Supplementary Benefit or SB – is often used instead of this formula. This may be taken at face value or raised by some arbitrary proportion (40 per cent is common) in recognition of the miserable standard of life which SB permits. This is, in effect, an absolute poverty line, albeit not a physiological one: SB is tied to movements in the Consumer Price Index. and has therefore declined appreciably in relation to average earnings. The proportion living in poverty, thus defined, has fallen. But this is due to a decline in β, indicating that social attitudes have become less and less favourable to the poor.

To establish the nature of the connection between poverty and the labour market, information is required on its incidence among people of different economic status. In broad terms, people are either employed; self-employed; unemployed; or out of the labour force due to ill-health, old age or family responsibilities. The data in Table 8.6 (derived from Piachaud, 1982, Table 3.4, p. 39) refer to 1977, when both unemployment and part-time employment were very much less widespread than they are now. It is clear from the table, however, that on both measures of poverty – family income below 100 per cent, and 140 per cent, of SB level – employment at low wages and unemployment are major sources of poverty. Thus more than half of all households headed by an unemployed person were very poor, compared with one in nine of all households. On the more generous measure, non-participants (especially the 'unoccupied', who were mainly single mothers) were even more prone to poverty than the unemployed, but one-third of families headed by part-time workers, and one-ninth of those with a full-time worker at their head, were also poor. (Employment and self-employment were also the only significant routes to affluence, defined as family income over 300 per cent of the SB level.) Moreover, some of those recorded as 'retired' or 'unoccupied' will have been numbered among the *hidden unemployed* (see Chapter 10, Section 1), having left the labour force only because of the non-availability of jobs. Poverty, then, is not simply a problem of social welfare, nor is it confined to the elderly and disabled. Participation in the labour market is one of the most important ways in which people become, and remain, poor.

5   Anti-poverty policy

In this section, only those measures are discussed which impinge directly on the labour market; little is said concerning social security benefits for those poor people who are incapable of participation in the labour force. Subject to this qualification, it is evident from Table 8.6 that a return to full employment would be by far the most effective means of reducing poverty. In Australia in 1975–6, for example, 'The most severe poverty was observed among households whose head was unemployed. About 65 percent of persons in these households are poor, the percentage of children in poverty being over 80 percent' (Kakwani, 1986, p. 257). A similar story could be

Table 8.6   *Income level by economic status of head of family, 1977*

Economic status of head	Percentage of families with normal income			Number of families
	Less than 100% of SB level (Very poor)	*Less than 140% of SB level (Poor and very poor)*	*More than 300% of SB level (Prosperous)*	
Full-time employees	1.2	11.0	20.7	5232
Part-time employees	8.7	33.5	15.3	379
All employees	1.8	12.5	20.7	5827
Self-employed and employers	17.5	34.5	23.9	531
Unemployed	54.5	68.3	7.6	356
Disabled	29.2	64.6	1.2	161
Retired	16.8	68.0	4.1	1414
Unoccupied	38.7	87.3	1.8	825
All non-participants	25.2	74.4	3.1	2400
All	11.1	32.5	15.7	9152

Source: See text. For full details, see Piachaud (1982, chapter 3).

told for most advanced capitalist economies, and for the 1980s. The prospects for restoring the unemployment levels which prevailed between 1950 and 1975 are discussed in chapter 10. They are not, to put it mildly, very bright. This has led green economists especially, but also some writers from other schools, to call for a *basic income* to be guaranteed to all citizens, irrespective of their labour market status; that is, to workers, unemployed people and non-participants alike (Purdy, 1988, chapters 9–11). We shall return to this proposal in Chapter 10, Section 5. Some less far-reaching income support schemes, including a negative income tax and a tax credit system, are discussed by Atkinson (1983, chapter 11). All involve the supplementation of low incomes by state benefits. They are intended to apply to both the working and non-working poor, and to reduce the severity of the *poverty trap*. This term describes the very high effective marginal rates of taxation levied on low wage-earners by the withdrawal of means-tested benefits as their incomes from employment rise.

Turning to the labour market itself, most neoclassical economists argue that the working (work-seeking) poor have low incomes because of their low productivity, which results from inadequate human capital. This is why the unskilled are much more prone to unemployment and low pay than those who have made larger human investments. Poverty could be greatly reduced, orthodox economists suggest, by subsidies aimed at increasing the amount of education and training undertaken by the poor.

It must be said in defence of this approach that there has never been anything approaching full equality of opportunity in education, let alone the positive discrimination which would be needed to overcome disadvantages in family background. (Imagine higher spending per pupil in South Yorkshire comprehensives than at Eton, or a preponderance of working-class northerners at Oxford and Cambridge.) Since 1979, indeed, the trend has been in the opposite direction. Nevertheless, the objections to the human capital approach are numerous and well-founded (see Chapter 3, Section 5(i); Chapter 7, Section 6; and Section 2 above). Dual labour market theorists in particular argue that the supply of good jobs is only slightly elastic with respect to changes in the human capital endowments of the labour force. All that was achieved by President Johnson's 'Great Society' programme in the mid-1960s was to 'reshuffle the queue' a little, moving some better-educated and better-trained black and women workers into primary jobs at the expense of other groups (Doeringer and Piore, 1985, chapter 8). This was no bad thing from the viewpoint of social justice, but extremely large state-funded human investment programmes did not significantly reduce the incidence of poverty in the United States.

Institutionalist and radical-Marxian economists favour much more direct intervention in the labour market, either through the creation of jobs in the public sector, or by statutory regulation of wages in private industry, or some combination of both (see Bowles, Gordon and Weisskopf, 1984 for an unusually comprehensive package of proposals). The privatisation mania of the 1980s put the former policy into reverse, with the elimination of hundreds of thousands of jobs in central and local government. One might, however, question the notion that the state invariably offers 'good' jobs, in view of the very substantial incidence of low pay in what remains of public sector employment. Indeed, there is a real danger for the 1990s that any government 'job' creation will involve nothing more than compulsory labour in exchange for benefits, or 'Workfare', to use a term current in the United States.

An alternative, which is most strongly supported by dual labour market theorists, is to exert pressure on secondary employers in the private sector by forcing up wages for lower-paid workers in relation to those on average or above-average earnings. This might be achieved by 'solidaristic' trade union wage bargaining or direct intervention by the state, perhaps through the introduction of a *national minimum wage* (Brosnan and Wilkinson, 1988). Two immediate objections to this concern the reactions of employers and of the majority of (non-poor) workers. As regards the former, increased wage rates for the working poor will not necessarily lead to reductions in employment if low pay is associated with either monopsony power or X-inefficiency (see Chapter 2, Sections 2 and 5(ii)). The US evidence on this is mixed. The greatest impact of the federal minimum wage is on the earnings of teenagers, whose employment does appear to have been reduced in consequence, if only slightly; but the effect on adult employment is uncertain (Brown, Gilroy and Kohen, 1982). There is a further complication. If those affected by minimum wages are concentrated in the secondary labour market, where job tenure is limited and labour turnover is very rapid, any decline in employment may be quite evenly spread over the entire workforce. There will be no separate category of (newly and permanently unemployed) losers; and if the demand for labour is inelastic all workers will gain, since the aggregate wage bill will rise despite a contraction in the number of hours worked each year (A. G. King, 1974).

Potentially more serious is the response of other workers to policies which are designed to reduce their advantage over the low-paid. The experience of incomes policy is relevant here. On more than one occasion in the 1970s, national wage increases were applied on a flat-rate rather than a percentage basis. While this reduced the dispersion of earnings for a while, the effect was only temporary, with customary differentials soon restored in what tended to become a vigorously inflationary 'wage–wage spiral' (see Chapter 11, Section 3). To use an analogy which was popular at the time, it was as if a concertina had been suddenly compressed, only for it to regain its previous shape by an inexorable process of expansion once the pressure was removed. Institutionalists had always warned that inequality can be reduced only when popular attitudes favour it (Thurow, 1976, pp. 191–3), and this appears to be confirmed by the failure of these attempts at an egalitarian manipulation of the wage structure.

It is possible that similar results can be obtained, without these adverse and potentially inflationary repercussions, through a policy of subsidising low-wage jobs in the private sector. Two variants can be distinguished, according to the principal aim of the proposal. If the objective is primarily to reduce unemployment then the subsidy need apply only at the margin, to newly-created jobs. A tax concession geared to this result operated briefly in the United States, in 1977–8, with some success (Hamermesh and Rees, 1984, pp. 98–9). If, however, the chief purpose of the scheme is the broader one of supplementing the incomes of the working poor, it must also apply to those already employed at low wages (and will be correspondingly more expensive). Where w is the wage paid by the employer; w_b is the 'break-even' wage, below which no subsidy is paid; s is the rate of subsidy; and w^* is the sum actually received by the worker from the employer and the state; then w^* is determined in the following way:

$$
\begin{aligned}
w^* &= w & \text{if } w \geqslant w_b \\
w^* &= w + s(w_b - w) & \text{if } w < w_b.
\end{aligned}
\tag{8.6}
$$

The operation of the subsidy is illustrated in Figure 8.5, which assumes a perfectly competitive labour market (Blinder, 1974, pp. 149–55). It has the effect of shifting the labour supply curve out to the right, at all wage levels below OW_b, so that the new supply curve is $S'AS$ rather than SAS. This is because the quantity of labour supplied by the worker depends on the total income he or she receives, and no longer solely on the amount paid by the employer. There is both an increase in employment (of N_0N_1) and a reduction in the wage paid by the employer (by W_0W_1). A subsidy of W_1W^*, equal to $s(W_b - W_1)$, is paid to the worker by the state, at a total cost

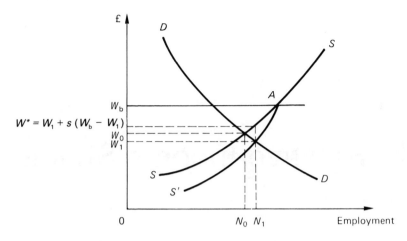

Figure 8.5

of $ON_1 \times W_1 W^*$. Note that the proposal widens the differential in the wage rate paid by employers who are covered by the scheme and those who, because they pay more than w_b, are not covered. This will give the covered employers a further cost advantage over their higher-paying competitors, and will tend to force down wages in the uncovered sector. To that extent this proposal, too, may be opposed by better-paid workers.

9

Relative Income Shares

1 Introduction

This and the next two chapters form a unity, since they all deal with those macroeconomic issues which have been largely ignored up to now. As will become apparent, there is an intimate relationship between the problems of relative income shares, wage inflation and unemployment; so intimate, in fact, that any attempt to separate them can be justified only on the grounds of convenience.

The present chapter concentrates on the distribution of income between labour and the owners of property. Before the competing theories of relative income shares can be considered, it is necessary to define terms and to establish some broad empirical tendencies. *Labour income* is defined as total wages, plus salaries, plus the labour component of incomes from unincorporated businesses and self-employment. *Property income* consists of corporate profits, interest and rent, together with the property element of self-employment income. Data on wages, salaries, corporate profits, interest and rent can be derived without too much difficulty from the national accounts, though there is considerable scope for disagreement over the treatment of inflation in the measurement of property incomes (especially in the context of inventory appreciation and real, as against money, interest rates).

Self-employment income can be divided into its labour and

172

property components on three criteria. First is the *asset basis*, whereby the average rate of profit in the corporate sector is imputed to the capital stock used by the self-employed, and the residual is treated as labour income. Second is the *labour basis*, with self-employed people being credited with average earnings in the industry in which they are engaged and their remaining income regarded as a return to their property. As returns to both capital and labour tend to be lower than in the corporate sector, these two methods of calculation yield significantly different results. A third rule, the *proportional basis*, simply allocates self-employment income according to the shares of labour and property in the rest of the economy. Alternatively, statistics may be drawn from the corporate sector alone; this carries the additional advantage that it excludes government activities, where property incomes are, by definition, zero (King and Regan, 1976, chapter 1).

Some evidence for the United Kingdom is presented in Tables 9.1 and 9.2, which offer little support for the notion that relative income shares are constant in the long run, like 'the velocity of light and the incest taboo' (Solow, 1958, p. 618). In Table 9.1 Feinstein's calculations for the period from 1860 to the early 1960s reveal a distinct upward tendency in the labour share, the rise taking place very largely in and around the two world wars. When the income of the self-employed is allocated between labour and property on the labour basis, the share of employment income is found to increase from 55 per cent in 1910–13 to 74 per cent in 1960–63, with the property share declining from 45 per cent to 26 per cent (Feinstein, 1968, Table 1, pp. 116–17 and Table 5, p. 126). The labour share accounts for between 60 per cent and 80 per cent of national income in many other advanced capitalist countries. For the relatively few where really long statistical series are available, very broadly similar trends can be identified in the cases of the United States and Germany; only in Sweden have relative shares remained roughly constant (King and Regan, 1976, pp. 18–26).

Two further empirical regularities have been observed in many advanced capitalist countries. The first is the very well-documented phenomenon of fluctuations in relative income shares over the trade cycle, with the labour share rising in the downswing and declining in the boom while the share of property income follows the opposite course. Second is the recent increased volatility of relative shares in the short-run. The property share – and especially its corporate

Table 9.1 Income shares as a percentage of gross national product at factor cost, United Kingdom, 1860–9 to 1960–3

| Years | Employee compensation | Income from self-employment | | Corporate profits | Rent | Total domestic profits | Gross domestic product | Net property income from abroad | Gross national product |
| | | Farmers | Others | | | | | | |
	(1)	(2)	(3)	(4)	(5)	(6)	(7)	(8)	(9)
1860–9	45.2	6.4		30.6	14.8		97.0	3.0	100
1870–9	45.2	4.5		32.1	13.7		95.5	4.5	100
1880–9	46.2	2.7		31.4	13.9		94.2	5.8	100
1890–9	48.0	2.4		30.8	12.5		93.8	6.2	100
1900–9	47.7	2.3		31.3	12.1		93.4	6.6	100
1910–14	47.3	2.5	13.7	17.1	11.0	28.1	91.6	8.4	100
1921–4	58.5	2.1	15.1	13.0	6.8	19.8	95.5	4.5	100
1925–9	58.1	1.3	14.8	12.5	7.5	20.0	94.2	5.8	100
1930–4	59.3	1.6	13.4	12.5	9.0	21.5	95.8	4.2	100
1935–8	58.9	1.6	11.6	15.0	8.8	23.8	95.9	4.1	100
1946–9	65.3	2.9	9.4	16.8	4.0	20.8	98.3	1.7	100
1950–4	65.3	2.8	7.8	18.0	3.9	21.9	97.9	2.1	100
1955–9	67.0	2.3	6.9	18.0	4.5	22.5	98.7	1.3	100
1960–3	67.4	2.1	6.3	17.9	5.1	23.0	98.8	1.2	100

Source: Feinstein (1968, Table 1, pp. 116–17).

profit component – was squeezed severely between the early 1960s and the mid-1970s, only to recover dramatically in the 1980s. This latter tendency is revealed very clearly in Table 9.2. Once again, the UK experience is not at all untypical (for a discussion of the United States, Australia and Japan, see King and Regan, 1988).

Why should it matter whether the labour share increases, remains constant, or declines? The answer to this question depends upon the theoretical perspective of the respondent. Some orthodox economists deny that relative income shares do constitute a significant practical or analytical problem. Most neoclassical writers, however, disagree, on the grounds that movements in the labour share indicate changes in the relationship between labour costs and labour productivity. If we write W as the aggregate wage and salary bill; Y is net national income; w represents the average annual wage and salary payment; and L stands for the number of persons employed; then we can write:

$$\frac{W}{Y} = \frac{w.L}{Y} = w \left/ \frac{Y}{L} \right. \qquad (9.1)$$

That is, the labour share is equal to the ratio of average earnings (w) to net output per worker (Y/L). Conversely, if P denotes aggregate property income, and given that $Y = P + W$, we have:

$$\frac{P}{Y} = 1 - \frac{W}{Y} = 1 - w \left/ \left[\frac{Y}{L} \right] \right. . \qquad (9.2)$$

Any increase in w, relatively to (Y/L), results in a declining property share. Now assume that there is some 'natural' or equilibrium level of relative income shares. Any squeeze on the property share will then, according to neoclassical analysis, induce a decline in the level of employment (see Chapter 10, Section 3).

Post-Keynesian and radical-Marxian economists deny that there is any automatic link between 'excessive' real wage growth and rising unemployment, but none the less take the question of relative income shares very seriously indeed. They tend to regard wage inflation as the outcome of conflict between labour and property-owners, whose respective claims on total output imply relative shares which add up to more than unity and are therefore mutually incompatible (see Chapter 11, Section 2). Radical-Marxian theorists make this clash of interests the core of their analysis of relative shares (see Section 4 below), while post-Keynesians assert the need

Table 9.2	*Income shares as a percentage of gross domestic product (after stock appreciation), 1946–87*

	Corporate profits	Rent	Self-employment income	Employee compensation
1947	13.4	5.1	13.3	67.1
1948	14.3	4.4	12.9	66.0
1949	15.1	4.2	12.9	66.6
1950	13.1	4.8	12.5	67.4
1951	13.8	4.4	11.6	67.4
1952	16.3	4.3	11.0	66.5
1953	16.2	4.5	10.6	65.4
1954	16.1	4.7	10.3	65.9
1955	16.2	4.7	10.1	67.2
1956	15.2	4.7	9.6	67.4
1957	15.3	4.7	9.4	67.5
1958	15.1	5.3	9.1	67.2
1959	15.5	5.5	9.2	67.3
1960	16.2	5.5	9.1	67.8
1961	14.2	5.5	8.8	68.5
1962	13.8	5.8	8.7	69.5
1963	14.5	5.8	9.5	66.9
1964	14.6	5.9	9.2	66.9
1965	14.1	6.0	9.4	67.1
1966	12.9	6.2	9.5	68.1
1967	12.9	6.3	9.5	67.7
1968	12.5	6.5	9.7	67.4
1969	12.3	6.0	9.6	67.2
1970	11.3	6.3	9.4	68.6
1971	12.2	6.4	9.8	67.4
1972	12.2	6.3	10.4	67.1
1973	11.6	6.3	11.4	66.6
1974	7.2	7.1	10.9	70.2
1975	6.6	6.8	9.7	72.5
1976	7.3	6.9	9.9	70.6
1977	11.5	6.8	9.4	67.3
1978	12.4	6.7	9.3	66.9
1979	11.9	6.9	9.3	67.6

Table 9.2 *Income shares as a percentage of gross domestic product (after stock appreciation), 1946–87*

	Corporate profits	Rent	Self-employ- ment income	Employee compensation
1980	11.2	7.1	8.8	68.9
1981	10.8	7.5	8.9	68.3
1982	12.5	7.5	8.9	66.5
1983	13.7	7.2	9.2	65.5
1984	15.3	7.1	9.6	64.4
1985	16.8	7.1	9.1	63.8
1986	15.4	7.2	9.4	65.0
1987	17.4	7.0	9.2	64.3

Note: Shares add up to less than 100 per cent because of (i) profits of public enterprises; (ii) statistical discrepancy; (iii) imputed charge for consumption of non-trading capital.
Sources: 1946–65: HMSO (1969, Table 1, pp. 2–3); 1966–87: HMSO (1988b, Table 1.3, pp. 12–13).

for a permanent incomes policy to reconcile these conflicting claims (this question is discussed in Chapter 11, Section 3). Both schools think of the marginal propensity to save out of labour income as being close to zero, so that property-owners are the only savers. This means that the property share sets the limit to the aggregate savings ratio. If s_p is the (constant) propensity to save out of property income, then:

$$\frac{S}{Y} = s_p \cdot \frac{P}{Y},$$
(9.3)

where S is total savings and S/Y approaches P/Y as s_p tends to unity and (as Marx once put it) capitalists manage to 'live on air'. With the direction of causality reversed, equation (9.3) forms the basis of post-Keynesian explanations of relative income shares (see Section 3 below). Radical-Marxian analysis is discussed in Section 4. First, however, neoclassical explanations must be assessed.

2 The neoclassical theory of relative income shares

The neoclassical theory of relative income shares is derived from the fundamental microeconomic principle that in competitive equilibrium the wage rate equals the marginal product of labour, and the rate of return on capital (the rate of profit) equals its marginal product. In the simplest possible one-commodity model, with only two inputs and perfect competition in both product and input markets, the tedious distinctions which were drawn in Chapter 2 between physical productivity and various concepts of revenue productivity can be neglected, and orthodox theory can be reduced to the statement that:

$$1 = \frac{W}{Y} + \frac{P}{Y} = \frac{MPPL.L}{Y} + \frac{MPPK.K}{Y}. \tag{9.4}$$

Here *MPPL* and *MPPK* are the marginal physical products of labour and capital, while *L* and *K* are the quantities of the two inputs which are employed.

Equation (9.4) requires that the shares of labour and property sum to unity. This 'adding-up problem' can be solved if either one of two conditions holds. The first is that the production function relating output (Y) to the inputs of L and K is linear and homogeneous, with constant returns to scale. In this case a mathematical proposition known as *Euler's theorem* ensures that the two shares add up to one.[1] The second condition is that – irrespective of the nature of returns to scale in production – the economy is in long-run perfectly competitive equilibrium. This means that all firms are operating at the bottom of their long-run average cost curves, where, for very small variations in output, returns to scale actually are constant. In the absence of these (somewhat unlikely) circumstances, the marginal productivity principle will give rise to income claims which either exceed, or fall short of, total output (Robinson, 1934).

One special case in which there are constant returns to scale is that

---

[1] Euler's theorem states that, for a linear homogeneous function

$$z = f(x, y), \quad x \cdot \frac{\delta z}{\delta x} + y \cdot \frac{\delta z}{\delta y} = z$$

Thus, for the production function $Y = f(K, L)$, it is true that

$$K \cdot \frac{\delta Y}{\delta K} + L \cdot \frac{\delta Y}{\delta L} = Y \text{ or}$$

$$Y = K.MPPK + L.MPPL$$

of the *Cobb–Douglas production function*, which relates output to inputs of capital and labour in the following way:

$$Y = AK^{\alpha}L^{1-\alpha} \qquad (9.5)$$

Here A and α are technically-determined constants, and a doubling of both inputs leads to a doubling of output.[2] It is easily demonstrated that, on neoclassical assumptions, α and $1 - \alpha$ are respectively the capital and labour shares in aggregate income.[3] Evidently they will remain constant, whatever the capital-labour ratio may be.

It follows from this that the elasticity of substitution of the Cobb–Douglas function is unity (Heathfield and Wibe, 1987, pp. 80–1). As we saw in Chapter 2, Section 3, the elasticity of substitution is defined as:

$$\sigma = \frac{\%\ \text{change in}\ K/L}{\%\ \text{change in}\ w/p_K}. \qquad (9.6)$$

If $\sigma = 0$, substitution is technically impossible and isoquants are L-shaped. When $\sigma = \infty$, the two inputs are indistinguishable and the isoquants are linear. Between these two extremes, if $\sigma < 1$ any alteration in the relative price of labour will be associated with a less than proportionate change in the capital-labour ratio. When $\sigma > 1$, the capital–labour ratio will change by a larger percentage than the ratio of input prices. If $\sigma = 1$, the relative quantities and prices of the two inputs will vary in the same proportion.

This has direct implications for relative income shares. In the

[2] Replace K and L in equations (9.5) by $2K$ and $2L$; call the corresponding level of output Y'. Then:
$$\begin{aligned} Y' &= A(2K)^{\alpha}(2L)^{1-\alpha} \\ &= A\,2^{\alpha}K^{\alpha}2^{1-\alpha}L^{1-\alpha} \\ &= A\,2^{\alpha}2^{1-\alpha}K^{\alpha}L^{1-\alpha} \\ &= 2Y \end{aligned}$$

[3] Since the price of capital equals its marginal product, we have
$$p_K = MPPK = \frac{\delta Y}{\delta K} = \frac{\delta}{\delta K}(AK^{\alpha}L^{1-\alpha})$$
$$= \alpha(AK^{\alpha-1}L^{1-\alpha})$$
$$= \alpha\frac{Y}{K}.$$

Thus $\dfrac{P}{Y} = \dfrac{P_K}{Y} \cdot K = \alpha\dfrac{Y}{K}\dfrac{K}{Y} = \alpha$

An equivalent argument shows that:
$$\frac{W}{Y} = 1 - \alpha$$

long-run the relative price of labour has tended to rise with the secular growth in real wages; and the ratio of capital to labour has also increased over time. Since the labour share has also tended to rise, neoclassical economists conclude that the elasticity of substitution is in fact less than unity, with the declining relative quantity of labour being more than offset by the increase in its relative price. A unitary elasticity of substitution, as with the Cobb–Douglas, would entail constant shares; and, if $\sigma > 1$, the labour share would have fallen.

Two complications should be noted. First, it is not necessarily the case that the elasticity of substitution will be the same for all values of the capital–labour ratio. Such *Constant Elasticity of Substitution* (CES) functions are, however, favoured by orthodox theorists on the grounds of simplicity and convenience (Heathfield and Wibe, 1987, chapter 5). Second, and more significantly, the production function itself is likely to shift over time as a result of technological change. Holding the capital–labour ratio constant, Hicks (1932, p. 121) distinguished three types of technical progress. *Neutral* or *unbiased* changes increase the marginal products of capital and labour by the same proportion, and thus have no effect on relative income shares. Biased technical change does, however, alter relative shares. *Labour-saving* innovations increase the marginal product of capital relative to the marginal product of labour, and reduce the labour share. Conversely, *capital-saving* technical change reduces the marginal product of capital, relative to that of labour, and increases the labour share.

Abstracting from technical change, neoclassical analysis suggests that relative shares will change only slowly in response to the accumulation of capital. This is because income shares are rather insensitive to quite substantial alterations in the capital-labour ratio. This can be seen from a formula derived by Bronfenbrenner (1960, p. 285):

$$\frac{\% \text{ change in } (W/Y)}{\% \text{ change in } (L/K)} = \frac{(1 - W/Y)(\sigma - 1)}{\sigma}. \qquad (9.6)$$

The significance of this relationship can be seen by inserting realistic values for the labour share (W/Y) and the elasticity of substitution. With $W/Y = \frac{3}{4}$, and $\sigma = \frac{1}{2}$, the right-hand side of equation (9.6) is $(\frac{1}{4})(-\frac{1}{2})/(\frac{1}{2}) = -\frac{1}{4}$. This means that a 5 per cent increase in W/Y (from 75 per cent to 78.75 per cent) would require a 20 per cent fall in L/K or, more familiarly, a 20 per cent increase in the capital–labour ratio. Much the same is true, *mutatis mutandi*, for $\sigma > 1$. Unless the elasticity of substitution is close to zero, or very much greater than unity, relative shares will be fairly stable so long as the economy is in equilibrium (disequilibrium is another matter: see Morley, 1979).

Since, in orthodox theory, changes in the capital–labour ratio are associated with changes in relative input prices, this can be thought of in another way. An increase in the relative price of labour will raise the labour share only if $\sigma < 1$ (otherwise the share of employment income will remain constant or, if $\sigma > 1$, it will fall). Even then, however, large increases in wages relatively to the return on capital lead to only small shifts in relative shares.

But this conclusion is only as strong as the analysis from which it is derived. There are, in fact, numerous and compelling objections to the neoclassical theory of relative income shares. One, the adding-up problem, has already been mentioned in this section, and the many microeconomic difficulties which arise with the marginal productivity principle were discussed in detail in Chapter 2, Section 5. There are, in addition, very serious problems with the application of marginal productivity theory at the level of the entire economy, since there is no reason to suppose that aggregate production functions either exist or are 'well-behaved' in the manner which is required if orthodox analysis is to succeed. There is a large and highly technical literature on the question, dating from the 1960s and casting very great doubt on the coherence of the theory (Fisher, 1969; Harcourt, 1972; Howard, 1979, chapter 4).

3 Post-Keynesian theory

Pioneered by Kalecki (1954) and Robinson (1956), post-Keynesian opposition to the orthodox treatment of relative income shares grew out of these technical criticisms, reinforced by two further considerations. One is the failure of neoclassical distribution theory to deal with imperfect competition, and in particular with oligopoly. The other is its neglect of the macroeconomic dimensions of the problem, especially the relationship between relative shares and saving, investment and the rate of economic growth (Sawyer, 1985, chapters 2 and 4).

Consider first the connection between capital accumulation and relative income shares. Equation (9.3) in Section 1 expressed the savings ratio as a function of the property share and the propensity to save out of property income, on the simplifying assumption that the propensity to save out of employment income is zero. Since, in macroeconomic equilibrium, planned saving must equal planned investment, this can be written as:

$$\frac{I}{Y} = s_p \frac{P}{Y}. \tag{9.7}$$

It is, however, more consistent with the spirit of the *General Theory* to reverse the direction of causation, treating investment as the exogenous factor and rearranging the terms of equation (9.7) to give:

$$\frac{P}{Y} = \frac{1}{s_p} \cdot \frac{I}{Y}. \tag{9.8}$$

This explains the profit share in terms of the ratio of planned investment to income (I/Y) and the propensity to save out of profits (s_p). The investment ratio depends upon capitalists' 'animal spirits', that is, on the state of their confidence in the economic future. For a given value of s_p, it determines the share of national income which must accrue to property in order to generate the appropriate ratio of savings to income. The higher the proportion of income which entrepreneurs plan to invest, the higher the property share must be.

The argument is illustrated in Figure 9.1, where the 45-degree line shows all the possible combinations of the two income shares. The equilibrium profit share is imposed by the horizontal line giving the value of $(1/s_p) \cdot (I/Y)$ and the corresponding share of employment income can be read off along the horizontal axis. An increase in the planned investment ratio to $(I/Y)'$ increases the equilibrium profit share. The slopes of OA and OB show the ratios of the property share to the labour income in each case.

A link can also be established between relative income shares and the rate of economic growth. In *steady-state* growth the relationship between output and the capital stock does not change, and the capital–output ratio (K/Y) is constant. Thus the rate of growth of output (g) is equal to the rate of growth of the capital stock. But the latter is simply the ratio of net investment to capital (I/K). This makes it possible to express the investment–income ratio in terms of the capital–output ratio and the rate of economic growth:

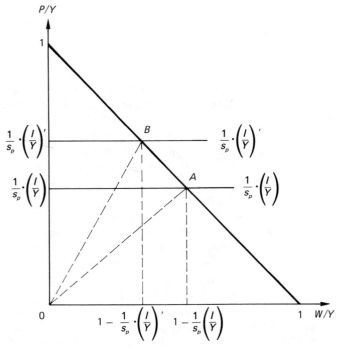

Figure 9.1

$$\frac{I}{Y} = \frac{I}{K} \cdot \frac{K}{Y} = g \cdot \frac{K}{Y}. \tag{9.9}$$

By substituting this value of (I/Y) into equation (9.8), we obtain:

$$\frac{P}{Y} = \frac{g}{s_p} \cdot \frac{K}{Y}, \tag{9.10}$$

which reveals that the profit share is positively related to the rate of growth and the capital–output ratio, and negatively related to the propensity to save out of profits. The faster the planned rate of growth, the more capital which is needed to produce each extra unit of output, and the smaller the proportion of their incomes that capitalists save, the larger the equilibrium share of property income must be.

There is in principle no reason why this macroeconomic theory of relative income shares could not be combined with neoclassical

microeconomics. Indeed, this potential compatibility is sometimes
seen as a major weakness of post-Keynesian analysis (Howard,
1979, pp. 157–67). Almost all post-Keynesian economists, however,
reject the orthodox theory of price determination as irrelevant to
oligopoly (see Chapter 2, Section 5(i), above). Their alternative is a
model of administered pricing, in which the firm sets its prices by
adding a margin, or mark-up, to its variable costs of production to
cover overheads and provide a net profit. On this question there is an
important difference in emphasis among post-Keynesian writers.
For Kalecki, mark-ups are conditioned by the strength of the
competition which is faced by the firm, and thus reflect the *degree of
monopoly*. More recently, Eichner (1985, chapter 3) has argued that
the corporation's pricing policy is dominated by the need to finance
its planned expansion internally, through retained profits, so that, in
aggregate, mark-ups depend directly on the investment ratio.

In both cases the profit share is higher, the greater the average
mark-up over variable cost.[4] It is also influenced by the level of
effective demand, as illustrated in Figure 9.2 for a representative
post-Keynesian corporation which faces constant average variable
costs (AVC) up to full capacity output (OQ_c). Since average fixed
costs (AFC) decline continuously as output increases, average total
costs (ATC) follow a similar path. Price is set at OP by the addition
of a margin to average variable cost. The firm will sell as much as it
can, up to OQ_c, at that price; sales vary with demand, but price does
not. Profits per unit of output, net of overheads, are given by the
vertical distance between ATC and the horizontal line PP. They
increase rapidly as output rises from OQ_1 (which the firm regards as
unusually low), through OQ_n (its anticipated normal level of output)
to OQ_c. (See King and Regan, 1988, pp. 82–5, and King, 1988,
chapter 9, for a fuller discussion.)

---

[4] The firm sets its price (p) by applying a constant mark-up ($k>1$) to its average
variable cost. Thus $p=k.AVC$. Its total revenue (R) is the product of price and
quantity (Q), so that $R=p.Q=k.AVC.Q=k.TVC$, where TVC ($=Q.AVC$) is total
variable cost. TVC is the sum of wage costs (W) and raw material costs (M). Hence
$R=k(W+M)$. Gross profits (Π) can be written as $\Pi=R-TVC=k.TVC-TVC=(k-1)TVC=(k-1)(W+M)$. For the economy as a whole, $Y=W+\Pi=W+(k-1)(W+M)$, and the wage share is:

$$\frac{W}{Y}=\frac{W}{W+(k-1)(W+M)}=\frac{1}{1+(k-1)(1+j)}$$

where $j=M/W$ is the ratio of raw material costs to wage costs. The higher the mark-up (k), the lower, given j, is the wage share.

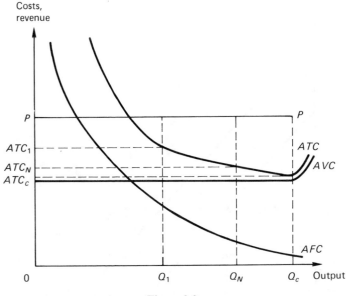

Figure 9.2

For the individual firm effective demand is exogenous, but this is not the case for the economy (or even the 'fix-price' corporate sector) as a whole. The possibility exists that mark-ups are too high to permit full capacity utilisation and full employment of labour. This is illustrated in Figure 9.3, which resembles Figure 9.1 except that total real profits and total real wages, not P/Y and W/Y, are measured along the two axes. The horizontal line now represents the level of real profits needed to generate savings equal to the level of planned investment, given s_p; and the rays OA and OB show two different ratios of P to W, and hence two different relative income shares. (Note that they give exactly the same information as in Figure 9.1, since $P/W = (P/Y)/(W/Y)$.) The slopes of OA and OB depend upon the average mark-up and hence, in Kalecki's analysis, upon the average degree of monopoly. Finally, the 45-degree lines Y_1Y_1 and Y_fY_f indicate all possible combinations of P and W for the real income levels Y_1 and Y_f, the latter corresponding to full employment.

If I and s_p are given, full employment is possible only if the degree of monopoly is represented by OA. If mark-ups are higher, and

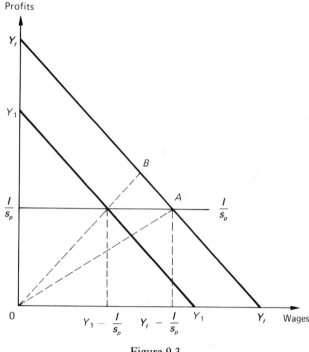

Figure 9.3

relative shares are shown by the slope of OB, effective demand will
be sufficient only for an output of Y_1. Any higher level of property
income will generate planned savings greater than the planned level
of investment, and output will fall. In this version of post-Keynesian
theory it is the degree of monopoly which fixes relative income
shares; the macroeconomic variables, I and s_p, influence the degree
of capacity utilisation (see also Goodwin, 1983).

Post-Keynesian theory avoids many of the problems associated
with the neoclassical analysis of relative income shares. It makes no
use of aggregate (or indeed any) production functions; repudiates
both the assumption of universal perfect competition and the
marginalist equilibrium theory of price determination; and allows
for the macroeconomic repercussions of changes in income distribution. The class nature of capitalist society is explicitly recognised,
and account is taken of the possibility that trade unions might
influence relative shares through their ability to constrain price

mark-ups (Kalecki, 1971; Sawyer, 1985, chapter 6). The fundamental weakness of the model is its silence concerning the forces which affect several key magnitudes: the investment ratio, the rate of capital accumulation, the capitalists' savings propensity, and the capital–output ratio, are all exogenously-determined. To this extent post-Keynesian theory fails to provide a full explanation of relative income shares, even in the core oligopoly sector to which it is, necessarily, confined.

4 The radical-Marxian approach

The Marxian *rate of exploitation* (also known as the rate of surplus value) bears a rough resemblance to the ratio of property income to employment income. It is defined, in terms of the labour theory of value, as follows. The working day is divided into two parts, which Marx termed necessary and surplus labour. *Necessary labour* is the time required to produce the goods consumed by the worker and his or her family each day, and the remainder of the working day is *surplus labour*. The rate of exploitation is the ratio of surplus to necessary labour. Since only necessary labour is paid for, and surplus labour is unpaid, it may also be described as the ratio of unpaid to paid labour, Moreover, since unpaid labour is the source of *surplus value*, and paid labour represents the *variable capital* which is employed in production, the rate of exploitation is also equivalent to the ratio of surplus value to variable capital.
To summarise:

$$\text{rate of exploitation} = \frac{\text{surplus labour}}{\text{necessary labour}} = \frac{\text{unpaid labour}}{\text{paid labour}}$$

$$= \frac{\text{surplus value}}{\text{variable capital}}. \qquad (9.11)$$

In Marx's words:

> The rate of surplus value, all other circumstances remaining the same, will depend on the proportion between that part of the working day necessary to reproduce the value of the labouring-power and the surplus time or surplus labour performed for the capitalist. It will, therefore, depend on the ratio in which the

working day is prolonged over and above that extent, by working which the working man would only reproduce the value of his labouring power, or replace his wages (Marx, 1865, p. 428; original stress deleted).

Marx pointed to three determinants of the rate of exploitation. First is the level of *real wages*. Second is the *productivity of labour* used, directly or indirectly, to produce wage-goods. This, in turn, depends both on the level of technical development and on the social processes which regulate the intensity of work. These factors establish the amount of necessary labour which must be performed in order to maintain the working class. The third variable is the *length of the working day*, which fixes the total amount of labour performed. Surplus labour is simply the difference between total and necessary labour.

Marx argued that competition would tend to equalise the rate of exploitation in all sectors of the economy, since neither hours of work nor real wages would differ greatly, for workers with an equivalent level of skill. In this he was only partly correct. Differences in the standard work week are indeed quite small. However, as we saw in Chapter 7, Sections 3 and 5, the same cannot be said of intra-occupational wage variations. Marx's human capital theory of long-run wage determination is not adequate, and rates of exploitation do differ significantly between classes of workers (Roemer, 1979).

Setting these problems aside, a radical-Marxian theory of relative income shares begins with the recognition that, in aggregate, surplus value is the source of property income, while labour incomes are derived from variable capital. Thus, in broad terms:

$$\text{rate of exploitation} = \frac{\text{surplus value}}{\text{variable capital}} = \frac{P}{W}. \tag{9.12}$$

There are two important qualifications to this. First, there are several reasons why the market prices at which commodities are sold will not be proportional to their labour values. This drives a wedge between surplus value and property income; between variable capital and employment income; and, finally, between the rate of exploitation and P/W (Howard and King, 1985, chapters 8–9). Second, Marx distinguished *productive* from *unproductive labour*. The precise criteria which he employed remain controversial, but most radical-Marxian economists would at least agree upon extreme cases: a factory worker employed by a capitalist for profit performs productive labour, while domestic servants carry out unproductive labour (for further discussion see Howard and King, 1985, pp. 128–32).

This is important, because only productive labourers create surplus value, and it is only their wages and salaries which constitute variable capital. The incomes of unproductive workers represent expenditure out of (in effect, deductions from) surplus value. Hence surplus value is greater than total property income, and variable capital is less than aggregate labour income. It follows that, other things being equal, the rate of exploitation is greater than the ratio of P to W. Many radical-Marxian economists believe it to be a fundamental law of advanced capitalist society that unproductive activities grow relative to productive work. If this is so, the gap between the rate of exploitation and P/W will widen continuously, and the measure of relative income shares used by orthodox – and post-Keynesian – theorists will be increasingly misleading (Baran and Sweezy, 1968, pp. 83–4).

These difficulties are not insuperable, and with sufficient care the rate of exploitation can be calculated from the national accounts. This has been done for the United States (Wolff, 1987), but not yet for Britain. A radical-Marxian theory of relative shares starts from the three determinants of the rate of exploitation which were identified above: the length of the working day, the real wage, and the general level of labour productivity. There is a close analogy here with equations (9.1) and (9.2), so long as w and Y/L are thought of as hourly magnitudes. Marx's own writings on relative income shares are not entirely consistent. He regarded real wages as being constrained by high and rising unemployment, and argued that productivity would grow as a result of both technological progress and increasing intensity of work effort, the latter reflecting the capitalist's absolute power over the worker at the point of production. The working class could, however, exercise sufficient political power to reduce the working day (Howard and King, 1985, pp. 119–23).

Marx believed that there were counter-cyclical fluctuations in the rate of exploitation. In the upswing of the trade cycle unemployment falls, real wages rise, work effort declines and, as labour becomes scarcer, the working day may be reduced. The reverse occurs in the downswing. In the long run, Marx seems to have expected the rate of exploitation to rise, though in some of his numerical examples he holds it constant. Moreover, Marx sometimes argued that relative shares are indeterminate, since there is no floor to profits in the way that a minimum real wage is set by the physical subsistence requirements of workers and their families. The rate of exploitation then becomes a function of the class struggle over wages, work intensity and the standard working day. In Marx's own words, 'The matter resolves itself into a question of the respective powers of the combatants' (Marx, 1865, p. 443).

In the 1970s this neo-institutionalist strand in Marx's thought was used to explain the world-wide 'profit squeeze', in which the property share was reduced by aggressive bargaining on the part of organised labour in a 'hard' product market environment where increasing international competition made it impossible for corporations to raise prices fully to compensate for higher wage levels (Glyn and Sutcliffe, 1972). For the United States, Weisskopf concluded that

> the long-term decline in the rate of profit from 1949 to 1975 was almost entirely attributable to a rise in the true share of wages, which indicates a rise in the strength of labour. This rise, however, was largely defensive in nature. The working class did not succeed in making true real wage gains commensurate with the growth of true productivity; it merely succeeded in defending itself somewhat more successfully against a long-term deterioration in the terms of trade than did the capitalist class (Weisskopf, 1979, p. 370).

Radical-Marxian writers regard the productivity of labour as also affected by class conflict (see Chapter 4, Section 4, above). The influential French 'regulation school' argue that the slowdown in productivity growth from the late 1960s represented a major crisis for 'Fordist' methods of labour management, in which the alienation induced by mass-production technologies found its expression in increasing absenteeism and indiscipline at work, and in a withdrawal of cooperation and commitment on the part of manual labour (Lipietz, 1986; Howard and King, 1991, chapter 16). Similarly, Bowles, Weisskopf and Gordon (1984) suggest that there was a serious decline in the motivation of industrial workers in the United States in this period. This was exacerbated by a reduction in the effectiveness of employer control over the labour force, which was the result of a diminution both in the costs to the worker of dismissal for shirking and in the intensity of supervision and surveillance at work (see also Bowles and Boyer, 1988).

Returning to equations (9.1) and (9.2), radical-Marxian analysis makes both w and Y/L dependent upon the outcome of a class struggle between workers and capitalists. (Indeed, they tend to emphasis this factor much more strongly than Marx himself had done.) There is a significant overlap here with institutionalist writings on income distribution. Institutionalists, though, are inclined to reject the Marxian notion of a totally polarised two-class society, and to attribute considerable power to the self-employed, and to other groups of small property-owners. They also pay more attention than the radical-Marxians to the influence of the state. The institutionalist theory of relative income shares is, however, still relatively undeveloped (Marchal and Ducros, 1968).

5 Theories and evidence

In Section 1 it became apparent that four principal questions were posed by the evidence. First, the labour share in many advanced capitalist countries lies between 60 per cent and 80 per cent of national income. Second, it has tended to increase in a number of these economies in the very long run, that is, over a century or more. Third, there are pronounced counter-cyclical fluctuations in the labour share, and corresponding pro-cyclical changes in the share of income from property. The fourth problem concerns the profit squeeze and its subsequent reversal. What light can the three theories considered in earlier sections – neoclassical, post-Keynesian and radical-Marxian – shed on these phenomena?

Why, firstly, should the property share fall so generally in the range 20–40 per cent of national income? Why not 2–4 per cent or, for that matter, 70–90 per cent? Cobb and Douglas claimed, at the very outset, that this was due to technology. In the production function of equation (9.5), α tended to lie between $\frac{1}{4}$ and $\frac{1}{3}$, and $(1-\alpha)$ between $\frac{3}{4}$ and $\frac{2}{3}$ (Douglas, 1948). However, as we saw in

Section 2, there are strong theoretical reasons for believing that these and all subsequent econometric estimates of the parameters of aggregate production functions are unreliable.

One element of post-Keynesian thought would instead invoke equation (9.3), on the argument that the property share reflects the size of the investment–income ratio (which is between 10 and 20 per cent in most circumstances) and s_p (which is perhaps around 0.5). The problem is that these magnitudes are unexplained. Furthermore, the direction of causality can easily be reversed, with relative income shares constraining the investment ratio, or placing limits on the capitalists' propensity to consume, or both. This would nevertheless be consistent with post-Keynesian analysis if relative shares were themselves determined by the degree of monopoly, through the mark-up pricing mechanism described in Section 3 above. A theory of mark-ups then becomes crucial.

This might be derived from radical-Marxian analysis, on the presumption that profits are best regarded as a residual. The aggregate wages bill which is required to preserve social harmony can be viewed as a first charge on net output – whether or not this involves a concept of 'subsistence' wage levels is a matter of semantics – with the remaining 20–40 per cent available for distribution to property-owners. Firms' gross profit margins are made to conform to this property share by the combined effects of product market competition and trade union wage pressure, which also restrain the investment ratio and the propensity to save out of profits to an appropriate range.

Turning to the second question, most orthodox economists interpret the long-run increase in the labour share as the outcome of 'capital deepening' – that is, an increase in the quantity of capital per worker – with an elasticity of substitution which is less than unity. Capital-saving technical progress would have the same effect. Quite apart from the general objections to neoclassical theories of relative shares, there is a particular problem in this context. Capital accumulation and technological change tend to be gradual, continuous processes, while the alterations in relative income shares revealed by Tables 9.1 and 9.2 were sudden and confined to particular, quite brief, periods.

In principle this represents no real difficulty for the macroeconomic dimension of post-Keynesian theory, since there is no obvious reason why a reduction in the investment ratio or in profit mark-ups, or an increase in the propensity to save out of profits, could not occur very rapidly. Precisely why such changes might have taken place is another matter. Once again, post-Keynesian analysis needs to be supplemented by radical-Marxian arguments. The sustained full employment which accompanied the two world wars greatly strengthened the bargaining position of the working class in both Britain and the United States, almost certainly increasing the minimum tolerable real wage. In the British case, the sharp reduction in working hours which was conceded in 1919 also cut the amount of surplus labour performed by the typical worker, lowering the rate of exploitation and diminishing mark-ups, the property share of net output and – eventually – the investment ratio (Dowie, 1975).

The third question concerns the existence of pro-cyclical fluctuations in the property share and counter-cyclical changes in the share of labour income. One entrant falls at the first fence: radical-Marxian theory predicts the opposite of this, since the rate of exploitation is supposed to vary directly, not inversely, with the level of unemployment (see Section 4 above). These cyclical swings pose no great problem for neoclassical theory (King and Regan, 1988, p. 56), but are most easily explained by the microeconomic variant of post-Keynesian analysis, in which price and unit variable costs remain roughly constant over the cycle while average fixed costs fall as capacity utilisation increases.

What, finally, of the profit squeeze? Short, sharp changes in relative income shares are not easy to reconcile with neoclassical reasoning, at least so long as equilibrium is assumed to prevail. As explained in Section 1, on almost any plausible value for the elasticity of substitution, no short-run change in the capital–labour ratio or in the relative prices of labour and capital will have a major impact on shares. Some orthodox economists would, however, object that the period after 1973, in particular, was one of pronounced disequilibrium, and that the ultimate restoration of something close to equilibrium in product and input markets was associated with the elimination of the profit squeeze.

Post-Keynesian theory is at its weakest on this issue, since the evidence connecting the increase in the labour share in the late 1960s and 1970s to a decline in the investment–income ratio is weak and contradictory (King and Regan, 1988, pp. 64–82). There is much more to be said for the radical-Marxian story, in which class conflict plays a central role. Working-class power was first increased by two decades of full employment and then undermined by the return of mass unemployment. In the first phase, productivity growth tended to slow down at the same time as the 'target' real wage accelerated; in the second, wage expectations were depressed and labour's ability to resist the intensification of work was greatly diminished.

As will be seen in Chapter 10, there is considerable common ground on these questions between radical-Marxian writers and one influential strand of neoclassical thought, which attributes the growth in unemployment after 1970 to the emergence and widening of a gap between real wages and unemployment (Bruno and Sachs, 1985). To return to a point made at the beginning of the present chapter: there is an intimate relationship between relative income shares, unemployment, and the general rate of wage inflation.

10

Unemployment

1 The evidence

Unemployment is a surprisingly slippery concept. One crucial distinction is between *recorded* and *hidden unemployment*. Since 1982 the Department of Employment's statistics have covered only those workers who draw unemployment benefit, excluding the many – especially married women – who do not draw benefit, and rendering the count sensitive to alterations in the system of administering payments. The numbers of hidden unemployed undoubtedly increased as a result of the new recording arrangements, which were only one of the 19 changes introduced between 1979 and 1986. Of these, 18 reduced the recorded unemployment rate, so that the official British statistics give a misleading impression of trends in unemployment during the 1980s (Unemployment Unit, 1986).

The Organisation for Economic Cooperation and Development (OECD) defines as unemployed all those who are without work, are currently available for work, and are actively seeking work. All three criteria are problematical. In the case of the first condition, very meagre part-time activities such as casual baby-sitting or running a mail-order club may qualify as 'work' (D. Taylor, 1986, p. 17), and those who have only very recently lost their jobs may also be excluded. As regards the second, there would certainly be an increase in the number of women counted as currently available for work and thus unemployed if child care facilities were improved and there were more day centres for elderly parents. The third condition raises obvious questions as to what qualifies as job search, and whether it is reasonable to require it from those whose prospects of actually finding work are very small. Estimates of non-searchers who want work, and are available for it, range from 800 000 to 1 250 000 (Johnson, 1987, p. 3; D. Taylor, 1986, p. 17).

Four alternative definitions of unemployment are presented in Table 10.1, together with the relevant numerical estimates for 1986 (Johnson, 1987, Table 1, p. 2; cf. Department of Employment, 1988). On the widest definition the true unemployment rate was 14.3 per cent of the labour force (which is itself defined as the sum of those employed, self-employed and unemployed). For comparative purposes, the more restrictive OECD concept is indispensable. Table 10.2 shows how unemployment in Britain rose from less than 2 per cent of the labour force in the 1960s, to approximately 5 per cent at the end of the 1970s, and then to more than 11 per cent by the mid-1980s (there has since been a significant decline). A similar, but less pronounced, upward tendency is apparent for the OECD countries as a whole, while for the United States the long-term increase is smaller still. In Table 10.3 unemployment rates are reported for thirteen individual countries, for 1963 and the third quarter of 1988. In every case the figure is higher in 1988, but the increases vary from moderate (Norway, Japan) to severe (the Netherlands, Belgium, West Germany, Spain, the UK). The remarkable dispersion in unemployment rates, and the speed at which they have increased, is an interesting problem with significant theoretical implications (see Section 4 below).

A longer-term perspective may also be useful. In the British case the earliest unemployment statistics, for 1858–1914, are those derived from trade union records. (Since they refer primarily to craftsmen, the data almost certainly underestimate the general level of unemployment.) These show an annual average unemployment rate which ranges from 0.9 per cent (in 1872) to 11.9 per cent (in 1858); the worst year after 1880 was 1886, with an unemployment rate of 10.2 per cent. With the extension of state unemployment benefits to the great majority of the labour force in the early 1920s much more comprehensive statistics became available, based on the numbers registered as unemployed and looking for work. Between 1923 and 1929 the unemployment rate thus defined varied from 10.6

Table 10.1 *Criteria for being unemployed, and alternative definitions of unemployment, 1986*

Criterion	Claiming benefit	Sought work last week	Sought work within last 4 weeks	Available for work	Worked last week	Worked within last 4 weeks	Number (000s)
1	Yes	Yes	—	Yes	No	—	2002
2	No	Yes	—	—	No	—	826
3	Yes	—	Yes	Yes	—	No	101
4	No	—	Yes	Yes	—	No	47
5	Yes	—	No	Yes	—	No	859
6	Yes	—	No	Yes	—	No	206
			000s	%			
UK Labour Force Survey		1 + 2 =	2828	10.6			
OECD estimate		1 + 2 + 3 + 4 =	2976	11.2			
UK official definition (claimants)		1 + 3 + 5 + 6 =	3168	11.7			
Widest definition		1 + 2 + 3 + 4 + 5 + 6 =	4041	14.3			

Source: Johnson (1987, Table 1, p. 2).

Table 10.2   *Unemployment rates 1963–88*

	UK	US	All OECD
1963	2.0	5.5	3.2
1964	1.4	5.0	3.0
1965	1.2	4.4	2.9
1966	1.1	3.7	2.7
1967	2.0	3.7	3.1
1968	2.1	3.5	3.1
1969	2.0	3.4	2.9
1970	2.2	4.8	3.4
1971	2.8	5.8	3.8
1972	3.1	5.5	3.9
1973	2.2	4.8	3.5
1974	2.1	5.5	3.9
1975	3.2	8.3	5.4
1976	4.8	7.6	5.5
1977	5.2	6.9	5.5
1978	5.1	6.0	5.4
1979	4.6	5.8	5.4
1980	5.6	7.0	6.0
1981	9.0	7.5	6.9
1982	10.4	9.5	8.3
1983	11.2	9.5	8.8
1984	11.2	7.4	8.4
1985	11.5	7.1	8.3
1986	11.6	6.9	8.2
1987	10.3	6.1	7.4
1988	8.3	5.4	6.8

Sources: 1963: OECD (1988), Table 5.1, pp. 30–1; 1988: OECD (1989), p. 22.

to 12.7 per cent of the total workforce (excluding the self-employed). It rose to 22.5 per cent in 1932, before falling equally rapidly to 11.3 per cent in 1937 (Mitchell, 1962, pp. 64–5, 67).

The interwar period compares most unfavourably with later decades. In the period 1947–65 unemployment varied from 1.1 to 2.1 per cent of the labour force (again omitting the self-employed), with

Table 10.3 *Unemployment rates by country 1963 and 1988*

	1963	1988
Canada	5.1	7.8
US	5.5	5.4
Japan	1.2	2.5
Australia	2.1	7.2
Belgium	1.7	10.2
Finland	1.5	4.5
France	1.5	10.3
Netherlands	0.6	9.5
Norway	1.2	3.2
Portugal	2.5	5.7
Spain	1.9	19.1
UK	2.0	8.3
West Germany	0.7	6.2
All OECD	3.2	6.8

Sources: 1963: OECD (1988), Table 5.1, pp. 30–1; 1988: OECD (1989), p. 22.

no discernible trend (Sinclair, 1987, Table 1.11, p. 18). Then came the long increase, accelerating after 1979, which has already been documented. In the 1980s unemployment was very much greater than it had been during the thirty years after 1945. While accurate comparisons are impossible, it seems likely that the unemployment rate in 1986 was as high as at any time since records began, excepting only the early 1930s and one or two exceptionally depressed years in the late nineteenth century.

Before we turn to consider the competing theories of unemployment, something should be said about its incidence, which is extremely uneven. There are, first of all, persistent and pronounced regional differences, which have existed for more than a century (Armstrong and Taylor, 1985, chapter 8; Southall, 1988). Moreover, it is true as a broad generalisation that the unemployed 'come disproportionately from fringe groups' such as young people, racial minorities and the unskilled, while 'white, well-educated, prime-age males are relatively immune' (Sinclair, 1987, p. 30; for detailed

Table 10.4   *Unemployment rates (%) by occupation, Great Britain,*
                  Spring 1987

	Men	Women	All
Non-manual			
Managerial and Professional	3.2	3.6	3.3
Clerical and related	4.5	5.2	5.0
Other non-manual	5.9	7.9	7.0
All non-manual	3.7	5.0	4.4
Manual			
Craft and similar	7.5	9.7	7.8
General labourers	21.3	20.3	21.2
Other manual	11.1	8.1	9.8
All manual	9.7	8.3	9.3
All occupations	11.0	10.1	10.6

Source: Department of Employment (1988), Table 8, p. 541.

discussion of youth unemployment see Junankar, 1987 and Hart,
1988). Unemployment rates by occupation in 1987 are shown in
Table 10.4.

2   Radical-Marxian and green theories of unemployment

For radical-Marxian economists there are two principal types of
unemployment. The first is associated with excess capacity and low
profits, and results from a cyclical decline in the aggregate demand
for labour. This *crisis unemployment*, which is closely related to what
both neoclassical and post-Keynesian writers term 'Keynesian
unemployment', will be discussed in Sections 3–4. Marx believed the
second category of unemployment to be a normal feature of
capitalist economic life, and to be consistent with both full capacity
utilisation and high profits. Indeed, since it held down real wages,
this *technological unemployment* was a major precondition for the
maintenance of profitability. It was the outcome of an inexorable
tendency for technical progress to increase the constant capital
required in production (raw materials, buildings and – especially –

machinery) faster than the variable capital (human labour-power) which was needed (Howard and King, 1985, pp. 195–9).

Marx's analysis of technological unemployment was presented in terms of labour values, and is therefore open to all the criticisms which can be made of the labour theory of value (Howard and King, 1985, part III). It can, however, be recast in such a way as to avoid these problems. In fact a broadly similar argument can be set out using the familiar isoquant analysis of neoclassical theory. In Figure 10.1, the L-shaped isoquants $Q_0 A Q_0$ and $Q_1 B Q_1$ show the various combinations of homogeneous machines and identical workers which are required to produce Q_0 and Q_1 units of output. The cost-minimising ratio of machines to workers is given by the prevailing technology, and does not depend upon the relative prices of the two inputs. It is equal to OK_0/OL_0 ($=OK_1/OL_1$), and is shown by the slope of the ray OAB from the origin. If there are OK_0 machines, only OL_0 workers will be employed (and only Q_0 units of output can be produced). With a labour force of OL_1, technological unemploy-

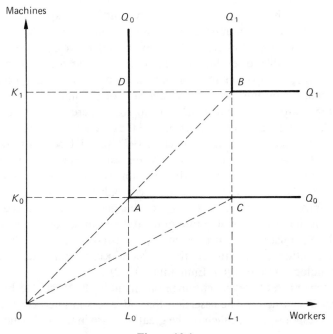

Figure 10.1

ment is L_0L_1. Note that this could also be regarded as *capital-shortage unemployment*, since all OL_1 workers could be employed if there were OK_1 machines instead of OK_0.

This is a static argument, but a dynamic element can easily be introduced. Assume that Marx was right about the labour-saving bias of technical change, and that the previous technology is represented by the ray OC, with a machine-worker ratio of OK_0/OL_1. (This is derived from an isoquant, Q_1BCQ_0, which for the sake of convenience has not been drawn in Figure 10.1, indicating all the possible combinations of machines and workers capable of producing an output of Q_0.) Under this technology OK_0 machines would require the employment of OL_1 workers, and so long as Q_0 was produced there would be no technological unemployment. With the technical innovation represented by the shift to the ray OAB, however, workers are displaced by machines. For Marx the history of production techniques in advanced capitalist economies could be summarised as a continuous leftward pivoting of the machine–worker ray.

Even essentially neoclassical economists have often been prepared to concede that Third World unemployment can be explained in this way. The green economist E. F. Schumacher also argued that the use of inappropriate Western technology in underdeveloped countries was responsible for excluding the majority of their people from any effective participation in economic activity. Schumacher became internationally famous for his advocacy of an 'intermediate technology' with a machine–worker ratio somewhere between that of traditional methods of production and the excessive capital-intensity of Western techniques (Schumacher, 1973, part III; see also McRobie, 1981). Somewhat ironically, his sternest critics have come from the ranks of the Marxists, with the claim that economic backwardness can best be overcome by the use of advanced methods which maximise the production of surplus value per worker employed and permit the fastest possible rate of capital accumulation. This essentially Stalinist argument does entail, if it is correct, a faster rate of job creation in the future than would occur with intermediate technology (Dobb, 1960; Emmanuel, 1982).

How much of the current unemployment in the West is technological in character? The assertion that advances in microelectronics were responsible for much of the great increase in unemployment in the decade after 1973 unites many radical-Marxians (Gorz, 1983) and most, if not all, green economists (Ekins, 1986), in addition to less theoretically-minded trade union leaders (Jenkins and Sherman, 1979) and management experts (Handy, 1984). If the 'new technology' does indeed have a pronounced and continuing labour-displacing bias, then no return to the full employment conditions of the post-war decades is possible. Such a 'miniaturisation of the proletariat', to use John Quail's striking phrase, would entail fundamental changes in the structure, functioning and even the ideology of capitalism. It would, for example, necessitate a rupture in the age-old relationship between employment and income. These wider issues are discussed in Section 5 below.

There are three principal difficulties with the radical-Marxian and green analysis. The first is theoretical. The argument set out above and illustrated by Figure 10.1 is much too simple. In aggregate, 'capital' must be measured in monetary, not physical, units, so that changes in the prices of machines are every bit as important as the quantity employed. Technical progress in machine-making industries tends to reduce machine prices, allowing a given sum of money to purchase a larger number of machines. Thus a rapid increase in the (physical) ratio of machines to workers may be consistent with no change whatever in the capital–labour ratio, measured in money.

The second and third problems are empirical, and concern the effects and timing of technological change. A major burst of labour-saving technical progress should make the productivity of labour grow more rapidly. In fact productivity growth decelerated after 1970 (Layard 1986, pp. 76–80; cf. Chapter 9 above, Section 5). Productivity did grow somewhat faster in the 1980s, at least in the UK. However, this was not on a scale sufficient to justify claims about a 'technological revolution', and is more likely to have resulted from a sharp reduction in X-inefficiency due to the severity of the depression. This leads into the third objection. Even a genuine revolution in technology is a continuous and relatively slow process, since existing machines which embody the old methods of production are not all scrapped at once. But the rise in unemployment after 1979 was sudden and violent, and was associated with a significant decline in capacity utilisation; both indicate a crisis in the aggregate demand for labour.

Several related pieces of evidence point to the possibility that there may, after all, be something in the technological unemployment thesis. One is the failure of unemployment to fall sharply as output levels recovered in the mid-1980s, in very marked contrast to the experience of 1933–7. Another is the strong recovery of profits in the same period, implying that the crisis was soon overcome. Moreover, productivity growth did accelerate in the early years of the decade. Finally, there is the emergence of capacity constraints in a number of sectors at a time when unemployment remained very high (J. Taylor, 1986). Very schematically, in terms of Figure 10.1, it is possible that the British economy has moved from B to D and then to A. Although the new technology was not responsible for the original increase in unemployment, it may very well be a major barrier preventing it from returning to its original level.

3   Unemployment in neoclassical theory

Precisely what does and what does not qualify as a 'neoclassical' theory of unemployment is problematical, since orthodox economists not only disagree among themselves but are sometimes unable to agree as to whether they are in agreement! (Compare Nickell, 1984, with Minford, 1984, p. 958.) There exists a plethora of labels, including 'Keynesian', 'classical', 'neo-Keynesian', 'bastard Keynesian' and 'neoclassical-Keynesian', in addition to plain neoclassical. In consequence no attempt is made in this section to set out a definitive neoclassical analysis of unemployment, since there is no such animal. All the arguments which are assessed here are, however, within the broad tradition of orthodox economics as described in Chapter 1. All can be contrasted, more or less clearly, with the views held by the other schools of thought which were outlined there. There is one further complication. In neoclassical theory there is a very close connection between the theories of unemployment and of wage inflation, and this makes the dividing line between the subject-matter of this chapter and the next very difficult to draw.

   A useful starting-point is the distinction between *non-demand-deficient* and *demand-deficient* unemployment. There are two ways of defining non-demand-deficient unemployment, U_{nd} (Solow, 1986, pp. S30–S32). One is in terms of the overall balance between aggregate labour supply and labour demand, and the other is by reference to the rate of wage inflation. In the first specification,[1] demand-deficient unemployment (U_d) is zero so long as there is at least one unfilled job vacancy for each unemployed worker. All unemployment is then non-demand-deficient, and exists only because jobs and workers are not matched, for either *frictional* or *structural* reasons. Structural unemployment refers to a long-term mismatch, in which the distribution of vacancies and of unemployment differs either geographically, or occupationally, or both. The jobs, that is, are in the wrong regions, or require the wrong skills, for them to be filled by the unemployed workers. Workers are frictionally unemployed, on the other hand, when there exist for them vacancies in the appropriate region and occupation, but they are still engaged in *job search* (on which see Chapter 3, Section 3(iv)). Note that there corresponds to this a process of *worker search* by employers.

On these definitions, non-demand-deficient unemployment is equal to total vacancies; that is, $U_{nd} = V$. Demand-deficient unemployment is either zero or equal to the excess of total unemployment over vacancies; that is, $U_d = 0$ when $U \leqslant V$ and $U_d = U - V$ when $U > V$. (See Perlman, 1969, chapter 8, for a detailed discussion.) A hyperbolic relationship between U and V can then be plotted, as in Figure 10.2, where the unemployment and vacancy rates are measured along the two axes. On UV_1, vacancies and unemployment are equal at A, so that $U_{nd} = OU_1$ and $U_d = 0$; at B, unemployment exceeds vacancies and $U_d = U_1 U_2$. If for some reason the UV

---

[1] Where S_L and D_L denote the aggregate supply and demand for labour; N is employment; V is total vacancies; and U is total unemployment, with U_{nd} and U_d representing its non-demand-deficient and demand-deficient components, we can write:

$$S_L = N + U$$

and

$$D_L = N + V.$$

Labour supply consists of those at work and looking for work; labour demand is the sum of jobs filled and jobs unfilled. Hence:

$$U_d = S_L - D_L = (N + U) - (N + V) = U - V,$$

which is subject to the restriction that it can never meaningfully be negative; and

$$U_{nd} = U - U_d = U - (U - V) = V.$$

Unemployment (%)

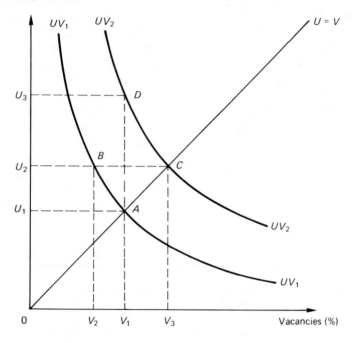

Figure 10.2

relationship shifts outwards, to UV_2, then U_{nd} rises (to OU_2, at C). Demand-deficient unemployment exists at D, where it equals U_2U_3. Note that a movement from A to C, or from B to D, involves an increase in the vacancy rate (of V_1V_3, or V_2V_1) in addition to a higher unemployment rate.

Non-demand-deficient unemployment can be divided into its frictional and structural elements by comparing the geographical and occupational composition of job vacancies with the corresponding characteristics of the unemployed (Armstrong and Taylor, 1981). There are significant problems with this procedure, as indeed with the use of UV analysis more generally. The official data invariably understate the true level of vacancies, since many employers fill jobs without reference to the Department of Employment; in 1987 notified vacancies constituted only one-third of total unfilled vacancies (Smith, 1988). The measurement of frictional and structural unemployment is also extremely sensitive to the regional and skill classifications which are used. Nevertheless, certain general conclusions can safely be drawn from the *UV* method. First, if unemployment is greatly in excess of vacancies, then it has a significant demand-deficient component. Second, if the observed *UV* relationship has shifted outwards over time, part at least of any increase in unemployment will have been due to factors other than deficient demand for labour.

The alternative method of classifying unemployment makes no use of data on job vacancies, but concentrates instead on the rate of growth of money wages. It defines non-demand-deficient unemployment as the minimum level consistent with a steady inflation rate. (This is generally expressed in terms of prices; however, as we saw in Chapter 9, Section 1, if relative income shares are constant then the rates of price inflation and of wage inflation differ only by the rate of productivity growth.) This is the *natural rate* of unemployment or, as it is also often termed, the *non-accelerating-inflation rate of unemployment*, or NAIRU. Only unemployment in excess of the NAIRU is regarded as demand-deficient (Layard, 1986). The thinking behind this approach is much the same as that which underpins the *UV* method, since, in neoclassical theory, equilibrium in the labour market is both a necessary and a sufficient condition for non-acceleration of money wages. Indeed, in a celebrated article in 1968 Milton Friedman defined the natural rate as

the level that would be ground out by the Walrasian system of general equilibrium equations, provided there is imbedded in them the actual structural characteristics of the labor and commodity markets, including market imperfections, stochastic variability in demands and supplies, the cost of gathering information about job vacancies and labor availabilies, the costs of mobility, and so on   (Friedman, 1968, p. 8).

This seems to imply a sort of *UV* relationship, with the natural rate determined by the frictional and structural imperfections which have already been discussed.

In practice, however, the natural rate/NAIRU is calculated in a fundamentally different way, from a model of aggregate wage determination which is then used to estimate the unemployment rate required if money wages were not to grow at an increasing rate. A full account of this 'reverse-Phillips curve' procedure must be deferred until the following chapter. It is sufficient to note, at this point, that the *UV* and NAIRU methods imply numerically quite contrasting results. The most authoritative estimate of the NAIRU for Britain in 1980–3 puts it at slightly over 9 per cent, compared with 2 per cent in 1956–66 (Layard and Nickell 1986, Table 10, p. S158). Estimates of non-demand-deficient unemployment on the *UV* basis are inevitably somewhat speculative, since (recorded) *U* has exceeded (recorded) *V* in every month for over thirty years, so that there exist no recent data on the lower section of the *UV* curve. While the curve does seem to have shifted outwards, repeatedly and quite substantially, since 1966 (J. Taylor, 1986, Figure 3, p. 265), it is difficult to believe that a vacancy rate of 9 per cent would be needed to equate *U* and *V*. Such a vacancy level has never been recorded, even in the tightest post-war labour market and even if allowance is made for massive under-reporting of vacancies.

In a sense these disputes matter very little, since non-demand-deficient unemployment has increased significantly on either definition. Some writers of a 'new classical' persuasion appear to believe that *all* unemployment is frictional, and occurs because unemployed workers freely choose to spend their time in labour market search (or in leisure) rather than taking up the job offers which are always available to them (Lucas, 1987, chapter V). But this is an extreme view. The majority of neoclassical economists agree that demand-deficiency played an important role in the growth of unemployment in the early 1980s. The weakness in labour demand may be *Keynesian*, reflecting a deficiency in the aggregate demand for commodities, or *classical*, due to an excessive real wage level (Malinvaud, 1985). This crucial distinction is illustrated in Figure 10.3, which has been adapted from Coen and Hickman (1988). Here *LDP* is the aggregate labour demand schedule when full capacity output is being produced, and *LD* is that relevant to the actual output level. OL is the total labour force, derived from the aggregate labour supply curve LS_L (which for simplicity is assumed to be inelastic with respect to the real wage rate). ON_1 workers would be employed, at full capacity output, if the real wage were at its equilibrium level OW^*; hence N_1L is non-demand-deficient unemployment. Actual employment is ON_3, so that demand deficient unemployment is N_3N_1. This has two components. N_2N_1 is Keynesian unemployment, which would exist even at a wage of OW^* because actual output is less than the full

Real wage

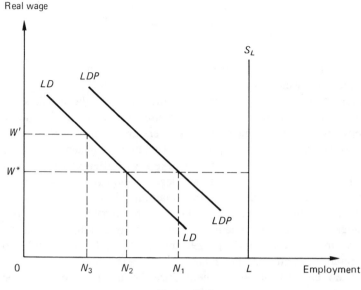

Figure 10.3

capacity level. N_3N_2 is classical unemployment, which occurs since the actual wage rate $O'W$ is above the equilibrium level.

Using a two-sector model like that outlined in Chapter 5, Section 4, Minford (1983) claims that there was a sharp increase in classical unemployment in the late 1970s and early 1980s. According to Minford, growing trade union power forced up real wages in the union sector and reduced the number of jobs available there. But wages did not fall in the non-union sector, because an increase in the real value of social security payments made benefit-financed leisure a more attractive alternative to employment at low wages. In terms of Figure 5.8 on p. 101, the $N_u'N_u$ workers displaced from the union sector chose to remain unemployed rather than work in the non-union sector, where the wage remained constant at OW_n. Minford concluded that weaker unions and lower benefits would be required if unemployment were to be significantly reduced.

Minford's specific proposals relied on hotly-disputed estimates of the union/non-union wage differential, on the generosity of actual as against notional benefit levels, and on the sensitivity of unemployment to changes in benefits (Nickell, 1984). Similar reasoning is however employed by many neoclassical writers. Thus Layard (1986, chapter 3) posits an inverse relationship between the unemployment rate and workers' target real wage, as shown by the curve TRW_1 in Figure 10.4. Given labour productivity, the maximum feasible real wage is set (at OW^*) by the size of the mark-up over prime cost which is applied by the average firm: ignoring raw materials, the real wage w/p is simply the inverse of p/w, which is one plus the mark-up (see Chapter 9, Section 3, for a very similar model). Between them the behaviour of workers and firms establishes the NAIRU, which equals OU_1. If the actual unemployment rate is less than this, for example at OU_2, workers will attempt to obtain a higher real wage ($O'W$). This will lead to increased money wages and, assuming that the mark-up is maintained, to accelerated price inflation. 'The only reason we have unemployment', Layard concludes, 'is that governments are using it to contain, or reduce, inflation' (Layard, 1986, p. 29; this presumably refers only to demand-deficient unemployment).

The increase in unemployment since the late 1970s can then be accounted for in two ways. Either there was a decline in the feasible real wage, because of the OPEC oil price rises and the productivity slowdown; or the target real wage increased, relatively to labour productivity, due to growing trade union power. In both cases the NAIRU rises. This can be seen from Figure 10.4, where a decline in the feasible real wage from OW^* to OW^{**} raises the NAIRU from OU_1 to OU_3, while a *ceteris paribus* increase in the target real wage from OW^{**} to OW^* involves a shift from TRW_1 to TRW_2 and a higher NAIRU of OU_4. Layard (1986) stresses both factors, and also accepts that the actual unemployment rate exceeded that necessary to stabilise wage-inflation. In their influential account of the international stagflation of the early 1980s, Bruno and Sachs (1985) emphasised the OPEC-induced decline in the feasible real wage. In the late 1960s and early 1970s, especially, the increase in marginal tax rates brought about by fiscal drag may have increased the (pre-tax) target wage, with similar implications for unemployment.

Some of the ideas involved in this – mark-up pricing, target real wages, unemployment as a disciplinary device – have a distinctly unorthodox ring to them. So, too, does the final contribution from neoclassical economics. This is the concept of *hysteresis*, which is derived from a Greek word meaning 'lagged adjustment' and is borrowed from the physical sciences. In an economic context,

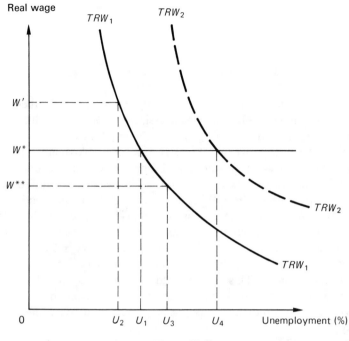

Figure 10.4

hysteresis refers to the dependence of the NAIRU in any given period on the actual unemployment rate in the past, and hence on previous levels of (Keynesian or classical) demand-deficient unemployment. This might occur if wages are fixed with reference only to the interests of 'insiders' currently in employment, while the wishes of unemployed 'outsiders' are ignored. Continuously increasing unemployment would have no moderating effect on the wage demands of those remaining in employment, so that the NAIRU (as defined earlier) would itself increase continuously. Or it may be the case that the skills and motivation of the long-term unemployed atrophy, rendering them more and more unemployable (Sinclair, 1987, chapter 13; Blanchard and Summers, 1987). From a neoclassical viewpoint, hysteresis is a thoroughly subversive concept, which dissolves the distinctions between demand-deficient and non-demand-deficient unemployment, and between the classical and Keynesian variants of the former, and raises the prospect that the

NAIRU could be reduced permanently and dramatically by an increase in aggregate demand (Blanchard and Summers, 1988).

4   Post-Keynesian and institutionalist analysis

There is nothing in the concept of hysteresis which makes it necessarily unacceptable to non-neoclassical schools of thought, any more than radical-Marxian or green economists, for example, would deny the existence of frictional or structural unemployment. There remains the question of the initial impulse which set off the unemployment rate on its upward course. The two events stressed by neoclassical writers, the OPEC oil shocks and the productivity slowdown, are generally treated as exogenous influences which were magnified in their effects by anti-inflationary government policies. But orthodox economists have generally been very reluctant to concede that there may be endogenous sources of instability in capitalist economies. This has rendered the synthesis of neoclassical theory and the ideas of Keynes a distinctly precarious one, since 'Keynesian' unemployment sits uneasily with orthodox economic analysis.

The idea that capitalism is inherently crisis-prone is, however, central to post-Keynesian economics, and also of course to radical-Marxian theory. A brief digression is in order here on the Marxian analysis of crisis unemployment, which was touched upon in Section 2. For stable economic growth, Marx maintained, it was not enough that workers be compelled to produce surplus value. There must also be sufficient effective demand for capitalists to be able to sell commodities at a profit; the surplus value which was produced had to be 'realised' on the market. If capitalists came to believe that this was impossible, they would defer purchases of machinery and raw materials, and lay off workers. By so doing they would precipitate the very realisation difficulties which they had feared. Recurrent economic crises were thus, for Marx, an intrinsic and inescapable feature of capitalism (Howard and King, 1985, chapter 16). These crises cause periodic bursts of crisis unemployment, which results from deficient aggregate demand for labour and therefore has much in common with the notion of 'Keynesian' unemployment which was developed in the previous section.

Modern radical-Marxian writers interpret Marx's own unfinished theory of crisis in conflicting ways, some of them more coherent and empirically plausible than others (see Howard and King, 1991, chapter 16). Post-Keynesian crisis theory draws on two important elements in radical-Marxian thought: the market power of the giant corporations, and the differences in savings propensities between workers and corporate capitalists. One version of the resulting model, which originated with Kalecki (1954) and Steindl (1952) and was refined by Eichner (1985), was set out in Chapter 9, Section 3, using Figure 9.3. If the degree of monopoly is too high, and the inducement to invest is too weak, the equilibrium level of output (Y_1) will be below that required to give full employment (Y_f, defined broadly as the level of employment which exists when there is only non-demand-deficient unemployment, calculated according to the *UV* method). This analysis can be used to derive a theory of long-term or secular stagnation, which is not convincing. Suitably modified, however, it can be used to generate a model of cyclical fluctuations in output and employment (Sawyer, 1985, chapter 3). Unemployment in the post-Keynesian framework is certainly 'crisis unemployment' in radical-Marxian terms. Interestingly enough, it is probably also consistent with some of the supposedly neoclassical models which were discussed in the previous section, especially that of Layard. Whether it can legitimately be termed 'Keynesian' unemployment is debatable, since Keynes himself assumed perfect competition and rejected mark-up pricing.

There is no government in this simple post-Keynesian model, and hence no way of confronting Layard's provocative contention – which is intuitively appealing to radical-Marxian and post-Keynesian economists – that mass unemployment is a disciplinary weapon in the arsenal of the capitalist state. Strong support for Layard comes, however, from the international evidence presented in Table 10.3. There is a close relationship between the 1986 unemployment rate (and the increase in unemployment over the previous twenty years), and the social, political and labour market institutions of the various advanced capitalist countries. This can be linked in the first instance to the macroeconomic policies adopted by the respective governments: the tighter is fiscal and monetary policy, the higher, *ceteris paribus*, the 1986 unemployment rate. But this in turn bears an inverse relation to the intensity of class conflict, since 'a country's economic performance in the 1980s is well explained by two factors: the degree of social consensus/corporatism and the degree of constraint in the exercise of policies of restraint' (McCallum, 1986, p. 943; cf. McCallum, 1983, Glyn and Rowthorn, 1988, and Newell and Symons, 1987). In Europe, at least, the countries with low unemployment are those where *corporatism* prevails; that is, where wage determination is controlled by centralised, powerful but conciliatory trade union and employer federations in close collaboration with the state. The Scandinavian nations, above all Norway and Sweden, are the most notable examples. Where social cohesion is weaker, as in Britain, draconian demand deflation has been deemed necessary to safeguard capitalism against wage inflation and the associated prospect of a renewed profit squeeze (Crouch, 1979; Therborn, 1986).

5 Policies on unemployment

Those neoclassical economists who believe most of the current unemployment to be 'classical' in nature argue that cuts in real wages and reductions in benefit levels are required to combat it. This, they suggest, would involve further attacks on trade union power, perhaps through the complete removal of union immunity from civil liability for the losses caused to employers by strikes (Minford, 1983). Some go so far as to hint at the abolition of state unemployment benefits (Lucas, 1987).

Post-Keynesian, institutionalist and – with some reservations – neoclassical writers of a 'Keynesian' persuasion reject these proposals on the grounds that they rest on an exaggerated view of the effects of unions and of benefits. As to the latter, the crucial statistic is the *replacement ratio*, defined as the benefit income of a household with an unemployed head, divided by its post-tax income if the head were in employment. At any point in time, replacement ratios vary according to family circumstances, and in particular the number of dependent children. They are also affected by the take-up rate for means-tested benefits, so that notional benefit entitlements give only a very rough guide to incomes actually received. For most unemployed people, replacement ratios are quite low. In 1982 two-fifths of all unemployed people had a replacement ratio of less than 50 per cent, and for another two-fifths the ratio was between 50 and 80 per cent; only one in five had a replacement ratio above 80 per cent (Layard, 1986, Table 5, p. 48). It is unclear whether average replacement ratios remained stable after 1979 (Sinclair 1987, pp. 273–4) or rose a little (Layard, 1986, Figure 16, p. 49), but they certainly did not rise fast enough to account for much of the great increase in unemployment in the early 1980s.

Similar scepticism is in order concerning the effects of trade unions. It is quite possible that a growth in union power in the mid-1970s did lead to an increase in real wages. Since the end of that decade, however, the power of trade unions has declined considerably on almost every conceivable measure, whether it be membership as a proportion of the total labour force, legal rights, political influence, or the frequency of strikes (especially of successful strikes). Real wages did grow rapidly in the mid-1980s, but more as a result of employer policy – perhaps on 'efficiency wages' grounds – than through union pressure (see Chapter 4 above and Chapter 11, Section 2, below).

Thus the 'Keynesian' wing of neoclassical economics denies the value of a frontal assault on unemployment benefit or on trade unions, arguing instead for an expansion in aggregate demand through a less stringent fiscal policy. This, Layard suggests, should be targeted towards the unemployed and backed up by an incomes policy (Layard, 1986, chapters 6 and 10). Layard proposes an increase in public sector employment, centred on higher infrastructure investment and supplemented by wage subsidies in the private sector to encourage increased employment of low-skilled workers in long-term unemployment (see also Johnson and Layard, 1986 and Sinclair, 1987, pp. 279–93; Sinclair however is ambivalent about demand stimulation and hostile to incomes policy). The 'Keynesian' neoclassicals believe that any sustained reduction in unemployment carries a very real danger of accelerating wage inflation, since hysteresis has lifted the NAIRU to 9 per cent or more. Hence they urge the adoption of a permanent tax-based incomes policy, along lines to be discussed in Chapter 11, Section 3, below.

Little of this would be opposed by post-Keynesian writers, and the concept of tax incentives as an alternative to conventional incomes policy actually originated with the US post-Keynesian Sidney Weintraub (Wallich and Weintraub, 1971). Many radical-Marxian economists also look to a revived public sector for large-scale growth in employment (Aaronovitch, 1981). They tend to be more suspicious of incomes policy, and to envisage both a higher degree of intervention in the private sector, and a much more rapid fall in unemployment, than neoclassical and most post-Keynesian economists think prudent. Andrew Glyn's projected 'million jobs a year', for example, is decidedly ambitious by comparison with Layard's (rather vague) unemployment target of 'well below two million' (Glyn, 1985; Layard, 1986, p. 4). But these are differences of degree rather than of kind. On policy questions, if not underlying theory, there is much to be said for Layard's contention that 'on unemployment issues there is, in fact, wide agreement among British economists, and I believe the majority would share the general line of argument in this book' (Layard, 1986, p. 12).

Opposition to these remedies comes from some radical-Marxian and nearly all green economists. The radical-Marxian dissenters claim either that crisis unemployment cannot be reduced significantly by 'Keynesian' methods (Howard and King, 1991, chapters 5, 16), or that these solutions are irrelevant since most unemployment is technological in nature. On either argument, full employment and capitalism are fundamentally incompatible. Green economists tend to be unimpressed by the radical-Marxian concept of crisis unemployment but, as we saw in Section 2, accept the essence of Marx's analysis of technological unemployment. They have been much more imaginative than most radical-Marxians in devising alternative cures. At their most modest, these include the encouragement of self-employment and small business activity, and the establishment of worker cooperatives which operate with relatively low capital–labour ratios and therefore represent a form of 'intermediate technology'. Green economists also call for work-sharing, in one version through the acceptance of '50,000-hour jobs' (32 hours per week for 45 weeks in 35 years), in place of the traditional 100 000 hours, made up of 47 hours – including overtime – in each of 47 weeks in 47 working years (Handy, 1984, p. 57).

Many green economists go much further than this, to urge that the connections between work and employment, and between employment and income, be severed. If people were able to work for the sake of work, because the job market was no longer their principal source of income, alienation would be greatly reduced or eliminated (see Chapter 3, Section 5(i)). And the very concept of unemployment as a social evil would disappear. The introduction of a *basic income*, payable to all citizens as of right, would make it possible for people without large private wealth to opt out of the labour market altogether, devoting themselves to creative activities, voluntary work, childcare, looking after elderly relatives, or plain idleness, without suffering dire poverty or being stigmatised as 'scroungers' (Purdy, 1988, chapters 9–11). This is a more far-reaching proposal than anything else considered in this section. The idea of a basic income is profoundly anti-capitalist, and was inspired by the Utopian visions of early socialists like Paul Lafargue, advocate of the 'the right to be lazy', and of Major C. D. Douglas with his plans for a 'social dividend' (Keane and Owens, 1986, chapter 9; King, 1988, chapter 7).

11

Wage Inflation and Incomes Policy

1 Introduction

This chapter deals with two important, distinct but very closely related macroeconomic problems: the determinants of the aggregate levels of real and money wages. Table 11.1 shows the annual rates of increase in both magnitudes between 1949 and 1988. It is evident from the table that changes in money wages are very much more volatile than variations in real wage growth. Note, too, the very sharp acceleration of money wage inflation between 1969 and 1970, again in 1974–5, and once more in 1979–80, each followed by a period of deceleration. As for real wage levels, the most noticeable feature is their continued growth throughout the 1980s, despite persistent heavy unemployment.

As was pointed out earlier, there is an intimate connection between aggregate wage determination and the subject-matter of Chapters 9 and 10. Thus questions of relative income shares, and of unemployment, will arise at various points in the discussion. The relationship between unemployment, real wages and money wage inflation will feature prominently in Section 2, along with recent controversies over the concept of wage flexibility. The pertinence of relative income shares is apparent from equation (9.2), on p. 175 above, which revealed the share of property income to be related positively to average labour productivity, and negatively to the wage

218

Table 11.1 *Annual rates of increase in average weekly earnings,
retail prices and real weekly earnings 1949–88 (%)*

	Average weekly earnings	Retail prices	Real weekly earnings
1949	3.4	2.8	0.6
1950	5.5	2.7	2.7
1951	10.4	9.6	0.7
1952	7.4	7.7	− 0.3
1953	6.1	3.1	2.9
1954	8.0	1.8	6.1
1955	9.0	4.5	4.3
1956	6.8	1.4	5.3
1957	5.7	3.7	1.9
1958	2.1	3.0	− 0.8
1959	5.4	0.6	4.8
1960	7.3	1.0	6.2
1961	5.5	3.4	2.0
1962	3.4	4.3	− 0.9
1963	5.6	2.0	3.5
1964	7.7	3.3	4.3
1965	7.1	4.8	2.2
1966	6.6	3.9	2.6
1967	3.6	2.5	1.1
1968	7.8	4.7	3.0
1969	7.8	5.4	2.3
1970	12.1	6.4	5.4
1971	11.3	9.4	1.7
1972	13.0	7.1	5.5
1973	13.4	9.2	3.8
1974	17.8	16.2	1.4
1975	26.6	24.2	1.6
1976	15.6	16.5	− 0.7
1977	9.0	15.8	− 5.9
1978	13.0	8.3	4.3
1979	15.5	13.4	1.9
1980	20.7	18.0	2.3
1981	12.9	11.9	0.9
1982	9.4	8.6	0.7

Table 11.1 *cont.*

	Average weekly earnings	Retail prices	Real weekly earnings
1983	8.4	4.6	3.6
1984	6.1	5.0	1.0
1985	8.5	6.1	2.3
1986	7.9	3.4	4.4
1987	7.9	4.2	3.6
1988	8.7	4.9	3.6

Sources: earnings: 1949–63, HMSO (1971); 1964–88, *Economic Trends*, various issues; prices: 1949–63, *Annual Abstract of Statistics*, various issues; 1964–88, *Economic Trends*, various issues.

rate. In the simple one-sector model employed in Chapter 9 it was not necessary to distinguish real and money wages, but here it is essential. The link between money wage changes and alterations in the real wage rate is an important theme in Section 2 of this chapter. It is also prominent in Section 3, where it is central to an assessment of proposals for reducing the rate of money wage inflation.

Throughout this chapter reference will be made to four of the five schools of thought identified in Chapter 1 (green economists have contributed little or nothing on the topics under review). The demarcation lines between them are however harder to draw than elsewhere in the book. This is because there are sharp divisions within the contending traditions (especially inside the neoclassical camp), and also due to the unusually high degree of cross-fertilisation which has occurred between them.

2   Theories of aggregate wage determination

(i)   Neoclassical theory

As far as the real wage level is concerned, neoclassical theory is a straightforward extension of the microeconomic analysis set out in Chapter 2. Leaving aside the complications posed by monopoly and monopsony, the equilibrium real wage is given by the marginal product of labour, and the maximum sustainable rate of growth of real wages is equal to the rate at which productivity increases. If real wages run ahead of productivity – perhaps as a result of aggressive bargaining by trade unions – employment declines, with a corresponding increase in unemployment, until equilibrium is re-established. A similar argument applies in the case of exogenous changes in productivity growth (for example, the 1970s productivity slow-down), and to a deterioration in the terms of trade, which reduces the international purchasing power of domestic output. The more flexible the real wage level, the faster the adjustment mechanism and the more transient the increase in unemployment.

Thus orthodox economists link changes in the real wage level to the degree of excess supply of labour. On the assumption that unemployment is a good proxy for the latter (on which see Chapter 10, Section 1), this gives an inverse relation between the rate of change of real wages and the unemployment rate. What does this imply for the determinants of the money wage level? There have been three stages in the neoclassical response to this question. In the first, Phillips (1958) and Lipsey (1960) argued that the rate of change of money wages ($\dot{w}$) would be a negative function of the unemployment rate (U):

$$\dot{w} = f(U). \qquad (11.1)$$

The *early Phillips curve* specified by equation (11.1) rested on the implicit supposition that neither workers nor employers anticipated future price inflation, and therefore behaved as if money wage and real wage increases were identical. This does not entail that economic actors suffered from 'money illusion', or that they failed to expect the price level to increase, only that their expectations were too small to affect their behaviour (on the important distinction between *expectation* and *anticipation* see Rowthorn, 1977, pp. 215, 225–6).

The second stage involved an *expectations-augmented Phillips curve* (Friedman, 1968), in which money wage changes were affected both by the unemployment rate and by economic agents' expectations of future price inflation, upon which they acted. These expectations were presumed to be formed 'adaptively' in the light of past inflationary experience. Thus:

$$\dot{w} = g(U) + \dot{p}^e \qquad (11.2)$$

where

$$\dot{p}^e = \dot{p}^e_{-1} + \alpha(\dot{p}_{-1} - \dot{p}^e_{-1}). \tag{11.3}$$

Here the expected rate of price inflation in the current period ($\dot{p}^e$) equals expected inflation in the previous period ($\dot{p}^e_{-1}$) plus some fraction ($0 < \alpha < 1$) of the difference between expectation and reality in the previous period. On this argument the negative relationship between money wage inflation and unemployment exists only in the short run, when price inflation is imperfectly anticipated. In the long run the Phillips curve is vertical.

The third stage came with the hypothesis of *rational expectations*, which replaced the adaptive expectations model of equation (11.3) (Maddock and Carter, 1982). A significant minority of neoclassical economists – perhaps for a time the majority – now claimed that employers and workers did not make the persistent errors which were implied by adaptive expectations, but fully anticipated price inflation from the outset. On this *new classical* argument there are no grounds for distinguishing short-run and long-run Phillips curves, since both are vertical at the 'natural' rate of unemployment, or NAIRU (see Chapter 10, Section 3). There is no trade-off between unemployment and wage inflation, even in the short run, and equation (11.2) can be replaced by:

$$\dot{w} = \dot{q} + \dot{p} \tag{11.4}$$

where $\dot{q}$ is the rate of growth of (marginal) labour productivity, and $\dot{p}$ is the actual rate of price inflation, which depends on the government's monetary policy.

These – no doubt familiar – arguments are treated at length in all orthodox macroeconomic textbooks (Gordon, 1987, part IV; Dornbusch and Fisher, 1984, chapters 13–14). The econometric evidence is mixed, and its reliability hotly disputed (see Holden, Peel and Thompson, 1987, chapter 2). In their survey of the literature Beckerman and Jenkinson (1986a, p.31) found no sign of a significant relationship between wage inflation and unemployment. This casts doubt on both the early and the expectations-augmented Phillips curves, but does not necessarily favour the new classical theory (as will be seen in the next sub-section, Beckerman's and Jenkinson's own explanation of the deceleration in money wages in the early 1980s is easier to reconcile with post-Keynesian analysis).

However, a recent international study came to a quite different conclusion:

> Averaging across OECD countries and over the whole postwar period, a one-point increase in unemployment has been associated with falls of two per cent per annum in wage inflation for the first year or two, with further falls of one per cent or so for the next few years ... for a change in unemployment in one country alone the coefficients are only half or two-thirds as great, but for changes in unemployment in all countries together the coefficients are larger. (Grubb, 1986, p. 75).

This implies both that the Phillips curve is indeed negatively sloped in the short run, and that the short run is a period of considerable length. Grubb's model of aggregate wage determination is a rather complex one. In addition to the two variables identified in equation (11.2) it includes a third factor, the difference between the rate of growth of real wages $(\dot{w} - \dot{p})$ and the underlying rate of productivity growth. Simplifying somewhat, it can be written as:

$$\dot{w} = h(U) + \dot{p}^e + a(\dot{w} - \dot{p} - \dot{q}) \tag{11.5}$$

where a is a constant and $\dot{q}$ now denotes the long-run or trend rate of growth of productivity. Similar models are frequently used by neoclassical researchers (Holden, Peel and Thompson, 1987, chapter 2). But what is the term $(\dot{w} - \dot{p} - \dot{q})$? On one interpretation it is merely a more elaborate version of the $\dot{q}$ which appears in equation (11.4), and reflects the possibility that real wages may lag behind the growth of productivity before eventually catching up. Equation (11.5) would then be fully consistent with neoclassical analysis.

It could however be argued that the *real wage frustration* which is measured by $(\dot{w} - \dot{p} - \dot{q})$ reflects a more fundamental social conflict over relative income shares, which cannot be assimilated into even the most sophisticated orthodox model (see sub-section (ii) below). Nor can neoclassical theory readily explain the 'world-wide wage explosion' of 1968–70: after allowing for all the variables in equation (11.5), money wage inflation was more than two percentage points higher after 1970 than it had been before (Grubb, 1986). Finally, there remains the puzzle of real wage behaviour in the 1980s. It is not at all clear how orthodox theorists can explain the coexistence of mass unemployment and rapid growth in the average real wages of those in employment.

(ii) Post-Keynesian, institutionalist and radical-Marxian theories

Post-Keynesian theory differs sharply from neoclassical analysis at several points. Money wage rates are set by collective bargaining, while real wages depend on movements in prices, and these are determined in the product market. Oligopolistic firms fix prices by a mark-up procedure in which the gross profit margin varies according to the degree of monopoly power which they enjoy. The money supply is an endogenous variable, which responds to changes in aggregate demand rather than vice versa (on this last question see Moore, 1988).

A formal model of real wages, derived from the work of Michał Kalecki, is presented by Sawyer (1988, pp. 54–5). As in Chapter 9, Section 3, prices are formed by the addition of a fixed percentage mark-up (k) to the firm's average variable costs (AVC):

$$p = (1+k)AVC \tag{11.6}$$

Average variable costs are the sum of labour and raw material costs per unit of output. Unit wage costs equal the money wage (w) multiplied by the amount of labour required to produce each unit of output (L/Q, the inverse of the average product of labour). Material costs per unit of output are the product of material prices (f) and unit input requirements (M/Q). Thus

$$AVC = w \left[\frac{L}{Q} \right] + f \left[\frac{M}{Q} \right] \tag{11.7}$$

A tedious set of substitutions gives the following expression for the real wage, defined in terms of product prices rather than the consumer price level:

$$\frac{w}{p} = \frac{1}{(1+k)} \cdot \frac{Q}{L} - \frac{f}{p} \cdot \frac{M}{L} \tag{11.8}$$

Thus the real wage is higher, the lower the mark-up (k); the higher the average – not the marginal – product of labour (Q/L); and the lower are raw material usage (M/L) and material prices relative to those of manufactured goods (f/p). Holding labour productivity growth constant, real wages will increase more rapidly if the degree of monopoly declines (reducing k) or raw materials become relatively less expensive (reducing f/p).

On the determination of the money wage level post-Keynesian theorists have less to say, beyond an insistence that collective bargaining is much more important than atomistic competition in the labour market. They do, however, emphasise the importance of relative wages, with the implication that any disturbance to the wage structure may initiate a leapfrogging process which will lead to accelerating wage inflation. Moreover, in at least some versions of post-Keynesian theory a variable similar to $(\dot{w} - \dot{p} - \dot{q})$ in equation (11.5) is used to incorporate wage-earners' anticipation of a steady and continuous increase in their living standards over time.

Institutionalists accept most of this, attaching even more significance than the post-Keynesians to collective wage bargaining. In addition they invoke some of the factors which were discussed in Chapter 4 above. For institutionalists the insulation of the internal labour market from the external market greatly reduces the influence of unemployment on both real and money wage levels. This gives rise to a sharp distinction between 'insiders' and 'outsiders', with the (unemployed) outsiders unable to compete effectively with the (employed) insiders even if they are prepared to work for considerably lower wage rates (Lindbeck and Snower, 1986). The Balkanisation of the labour market is what permits real wages to rise in the face of sustained high unemployment.

This conclusion is totally at odds with more traditional variants of radical-Marxian theory. Marx himself had very little interest in money wages, but argued forcefully that fluctuations in the average level of real wages were dominated by changes in the size of the 'industrial reserve army' of the unemployed; trade unions played a very minor role (Marx, 1867, part VIII; cf. Hyman, 1971). In this respect his views were consistent with neoclassical economic theory. Insider–outsider distinctions are implicit in the models of labour market segmentation adopted by later radical-Marxian writers (see Chapter 7, Section 6, above), but such models do not of themselves yield any precise theory of aggregate wage determination. The most fully-developed radical-Marxian analysis is that of Rowthorn (1977), which combines elements of post-Keynesian and institutionalist theory with the basic Marxian notion that class conflict over relative income shares lies at the heart of the inflationary process.

In Rowthorn's model, workers negotiate money wage increases

which are designed to provide a tolerable level of real wages, or, alternatively, an acceptable share of total output. Firms set prices, after the style of post-Keynesian economics, to achieve a target rate of profit on capital. After external balance has been achieved and the requirements of the state have been met, the remainder of the national product is available to satisfy the demands of workers and capitalists. If the aspirations of the two classes are inconsistent, price stability is impossible. Negotiated increases in money wages are passed on in higher prices, and inflation serves to redistribute income from workers to capitalists. Rowthorn derives a form of expectations-augmented Phillips relation similar to equation (11.2), which shifts whenever workers become more aggressive in their wage bargaining or firms attempt to raise profit margins. His model also contains a NAIRU, defined as that unemployment rate at which 'the total claims on the private sector are just compatible with what is available to meet them' (Rowthorn 1977, p. 223; cf. Layard, 1986, chapter 3, and Chapter 10, Section 3 above).

Recent research lends some support to these non-neoclassical streams of thought. Sharp fluctuations in relative income shares have on occasion (as in the mid-1970s) been associated with equally pronounced changes in the rate of money wage growth, suggesting the existence of class conflict over the distribution of income. This is confirmed by international comparisons, which reveal that inflation rates vary inversely with the degree of social cohesion, the latter measured either by the level of strike activity or by the degree to which wage bargaining is centralised (McCallum 1983, 1986). Real wages seem to grow fastest in periods of booming profits, while the relationship between real wage growth and unemployment is relatively weak (Carruth and Oswald, 1987). This is consistent with an insider–outsider perspective, from which the employer's ability to pay is expected to exert more influence on wage determination than conditions in the external labour market, and may explain the rise in real wages in the 1980s.

The significance of the insider–outsider distinction is reinforced by another piece of evidence:

An increase in the proportion of long-term unemployed strongly attenuates the downward pressure on wages exerted by any given level of unemployment. This arises because the long-term unemployed are less active in the labour market and are, in any event, less desirable to prospective employers (Nickell, 1987, p. 126; see however Carruth and Oswald, 1987, where this is denied).

Beckerman and Jenkinson (1986b) go further, arguing that the decline in money wage inflation after 1980 in the OECD countries owed little or nothing to increasing unemployment, but resulted instead from the decline in raw material prices. Finally, Perry interprets the experience of the last three decades in terms of 'a norm rate of [money] wage increase that is relatively stable in the face of typical cyclical variations in the economy and typical fluctuations in the actual inflation rate'. The norm increased 'as a result of the historic expansion of the 1960s and the sustained low unemployment rates that the expansion had produced during the last half of that decade'. It subsequently declined, but only 'after a similarly historic period of recession and high unemployment' (Perry, 1986, pp. 129, 141).

These findings are disparate and not always easy to reconcile with each other. They do not obviously lend themselves to the formulation of any single coherent theory of real or money wage determination. But they do cast considerable doubt on the relevance of neoclassical analysis, and indicate that the alternative approaches considered in this sub-section have much to commend them. Few if any of the authors cited in the previous two paragraphs would consider themselves to be post-Keynesians or institutionalists, still less radical-Marxians. Most would claim to be working within the tradition of orthodox economic analysis. There is in fact a substantial gap between neoclassical theory and practice where questions of aggregate wage determination are involved.

3 Incomes policy

Economists' attitudes towards incomes policy are conditioned by their broader philosophical and political concerns, so that they correspond only rather loosely to their theoretical affiliations. Post-Keynesians and institutionalists are most likely to favour incomes policies, since they have little faith in the automatic operation of competitive market forces and tend to view wage inflation as the outcome of a process of inter-group conflict which must be managed in the interest of society as a whole (Eichner, 1985, pp. 135–48).

They emphasise, too, the truism that any government must have a policy on the wages and salaries of its own employees, who account for a large (and until recently a growing) proportion of the total labour force. Radical-Marxian theorists share many of these ideas, but are often hostile to incomes policy on political grounds, fearing the emasculation of militant trade unionism and a redistribution of income away from labour (a classic text in this vein is Cliff and Barker, 1966). Orthodox economists are divided on the issue. Some see wage inflation as a market failure which can be corrected only through government intervention (Layard, 1986). Others regard the proposed cure as significantly worse than the disease. Many neoclassical writers are opposed in principle to any extension of the economic power of the state, and also resist incomes policies because they expect a loss in microeconomic efficiency and the suppression (rather than the eradication) of inflationary pressure (Brittan and Lilley, 1977).

The more narrowly economic case for an incomes policy assumes that the short-run Phillips curve is negatively inclined, and that it can be shifted inwards by a successful policy. From a neoclassical perspective this is possible if the policy reduces the inflationary expectations of workers and employers, reducing the value of the variable $\dot{p}^e$ in equation (11.2). In post-Keynesian and institutionalist theory the elimination of the wage–wage spiral will have the same effect. Finally, in radical-Marxian terms, an incomes policy may serve to diminish class conflict over the relative shares of labour and property incomes by weakening the independence and combativity of the trade unions. In all three cases the short-run Phillips curve shifts, as shown by the movement from SPC_1 to SPC_2 in Figure 11.1. Since the NAIRU remains constant at OU_n, this offers the long-run prospect of moving from A to B, with a reduced rate of money wage growth of $\dot{w}_1\dot{w}_2$. In the short run the range BC is available, with the possibility of both lower unemployment and a reduced rate of wage inflation.

A different situation is shown in Figure 11.2. Here, in the absence of an incomes policy, the short-run Phillips curve would shift outwards from SPC_1 to SPC_2. This might occur because of an increase in the 'wage norm' discussed in the previous section, perhaps because of a sustained increase in the tightness of the labour market such as that which is supposed to have been produced in the late 1960s by the Vietnam war. Or it may be due to a supply shock

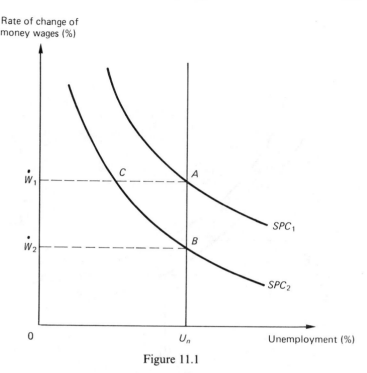

Figure 11.1

like the OPEC oil price rises, the productivity slowdown of the 1970s, or a sudden upsurge in trade union militancy. With an unchanged NAIRU, this would imply a move from A to B, with a long-run increase in the rate of wage inflation of $\dot{w}_1\dot{w}_2$ and the possibility of higher unemployment as the government attempts to lower the rate of wage inflation. This involves a movement along SPC_2 from B towards C, with unemployment rising towards OU_2. A successful incomes policy would either prevent the initial outward shift in the short-run Phillips curve or reverse it once it had occurred, permitting a lower level of unemployment (for a given NAIRU) than would otherwise be the case. Here an incomes policy is proposed as an alternative to savage deflation and to the other ways in which the curve might be shifted inwards, including direct attacks on trade union bargaining power.

Incomes policies are currently employed in a number of advanced capitalist countries. They were frequently used in Britain between 1948 and 1979, almost continuously so in the final fifteen years of

Rate of change of
money wages (%)

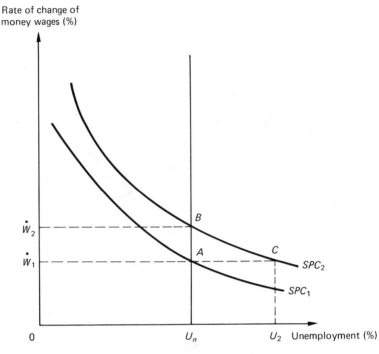

Figure 11.2

this period; since 1979, however, there has been no formal policy
(Holden, Peel and Thompson, 1987, chapter 1). Two elements are
involved: a general wage norm, and a set of exceptions or 'loop-
holes'. At least five different wage norms can be identified. To assess
their implications, assume that there is no change in the terms of
trade, or in the ratio of taxation to national income. We can then
distinguish:

(i)   A *wage freeze*, in which $\dot{w}=0$. This was in force for six
        months in 1966 and, on a selective basis, in 1948–50. If $\dot{p}>0$
        (as is probable), a wage freeze reduces real wages; if $\dot{q}>0$ it
        will in any case lower the labour share.

(ii)   *Wage indexation*, with $\dot{w}=\dot{p}$ (see Holden, Peel and Thomp-
        son, 1987, chapter 5). Partial indexation was in effect in
        1973–4. With full indexation the labour share will fall if $\dot{q}>0$.

(iii)   A *productivity norm*, where $\dot{w}=\dot{q}$, with $\dot{p}=0$ and relative shares unchanged. This principle dominated the incomes policies of the 1960s.

(iv) An *external competitiveness norm*. Where $\dot{p}_{row}$ is the rate of price inflation in the rest of the world, this entails that $\dot{w} = \dot{q} + \dot{p}_{row}$, and aims to produce a rate of price inflation in Britain equal to that overseas, thereby protecting the balance of payments. This norm has never been explicitly stated, but similar thinking could be detected in the incomes policies of the 1970s.

(v) *De-escalation*, with $\dot{w} = \dot{w}_{-1} - a$. Here the norm is specified as the rate of wage inflation in the previous period ($\dot{w}_{-1}$), less some constant quantity (a). The 'n minus one' norm applied in 1971 was of this type. The effect on real wages, and on relative income shares, depends on the rate at which $\dot{p}$ declines.

Typically, four categories of exception have been recognised as providing grounds for wage increases in excess of the norm. The first involves the rectification of *anomalies*, in particular where an incomes policy was introduced immediately before the annual pay settlement date of the affected group, seriously disadvantaging them in relation to the great majority of wage-earners. *Low pay* has sometimes been accepted as justifying special treatment, but the interests of the working poor have more often been provided for by the inclusion of a flat-rate component in the wage norm itself (as in the '£1 plus 4 per cent' norm announced in 1973), or by replacing a percentage increase by a cash sum (for example, the £6 norm of 1975–6).

Increases above the norm have also been permitted in response to *labour shortages* in specific occupations or industries. Finally, there is the *productivity* loophole, allowing exceptional wage increases in return for clearly specified changes in working practices which lead to significant and demonstrable increases in the productivity of labour (for example by eliminating 'restrictive practices' and craft demarcations). In this case incomes policy is being used less to restrain wage inflation than to encourage the growth of produc-tivity. Where the gains from such 'productivity bargaining' spill over to the labour force as a whole, these two goals conflict with each other, as occurred in the late 1960s (Clegg, 1971).

Assume that money wage rates are effectively restrained by the policy. Would there also need to be controls over non-labour incomes, and on prices? The answer to this question depends upon the behaviour of relative income shares. At one extreme it can be argued that there is essentially no correlation between money wage growth and increases in real wages; mark-up pricing ensures that higher money wage rises flow on rapidly into higher prices, leaving the shares of labour and property unchanged. There is thus no economic rationale for price restrictions, or for limitation of profits, interest, rent or dividends (Whitehead, 1973). At the other extreme, recent research in the United States indicates that 'wage changes do not contribute statistically to the explanation of inflation. ... Deviations in the growth of labour cost from the path of inflation cause changes in labour's income share, and changes in the profit share in the opposite direction, but do not feed back to the inflation rate. ... The Phillips curve wage equation matters only for the distribution of income, and the mark-up pricing hypothesis is dead' (Gordon, 1988, p. 276). In this case an incomes policy directed solely at wages and salaries would redistribute income from labour to property, presumably incurring the vehement opposition of trade unionists.

In practice, political acceptability requires that attention be paid to profits and prices. The most common procedure has been the establishment of productivity-based price guidelines, similar to those governing the behaviour of recently privatised public utilities like British Telecom and British Gas. The maximum permissible price increase for any individual producer ($\dot{p}_i$) is calculated from the formula:

$$\dot{p}_i = \dot{w} - \dot{q}_i, \qquad (11.9)$$

where $\dot{q}_i$ is the trend rate of productivity growth in the sector concerned, and $\dot{w}$ is the general wage norm (there are assumed to be no exceptions). If the wage norm is itself productivity-based, so that $\dot{w} = \dot{q}$, then prices in the i^{h} sector are allowed to rise if its productivity growth is below the average, and must fall if $\dot{q}_i > \dot{q}$. There are serious difficulties with the operation of such price controls, especially in multi-product companies where the measurement of productivity growth for individual product lines may be impossible. The cyclical component in labour productivity is an added complication, along with the effects of fluctuations in the prices of imported raw materials. Replacing direct price controls with profit criteria would solve these problems, but raise a host of others. And, as neoclassical critics of incomes policy have always emphasised, both sets of restrictions represent a powerful disincentive to innovation, enterprise and technical change.

Traditional incomes policies can be administered in three ways. Reliance may be placed on *moral suasion* in the hope that the civic conscience of workers and employers will be sufficient to ensure their compliance. Only in societies with very strong cohesion, however, will public-spiritedness overcome the strong temptation to benefit from a free ride. Hence the use also of *paradigmatic behaviour in the public sector*, with wage and price norms being rigidly applied to government employees and the charges of state departments and public enterprises, in the expectation that restraint here will prove contagious. If, however, the impact on the private sector is weak and tardy, a substantial wage gap will open up between the two sectors, leading to inexorable pressure by public sector workers for the restoration of their position in the earnings league. This was how incomes policies broke down in 1974 and again in 1978–9. Finally, *sanctions* were enacted in the late 1960s, and indirectly (through the threatened loss of government contracts) in the mid-1970s, against employers whose wage or price increases exceeded the norm. However, difficulties of enforcement (especially against small firms) and fears of political unpopularity meant that prosecutions were rare.

The history of incomes policy in Britain before 1979 was a turbulent one. 'The general experience of these conventional incomes policies seems to be that they are effective for a short while and then, because of pressures to relax the controls, the policies are either abandoned completely or are modified to deal with new circumstances' (Holden, Peel and Thompson, 1987, p. 29). Opposition tended to emerge first of all from groups of workers whose relative earnings had decreased, often in the context of a more general groundswell of discontent with an apparent decline in labour's share of national output. In the early stages of each incomes policy, money wage growth undoubtedly decelerated, but in 1969–70, 1974–5 and 1979–80 the ending of the policy was accompanied by a brief but rapid acceleration in wage inflation (see Table 11.1). Whether the overall effect was significant remains doubtful, one recent survey of the econometric evidence leading to the conclusion that 'much of the work is flawed and the final results are not convincing' (Holden, Peel and Thompson, 1987, p. 54).

Dissatisfaction with the outcome of traditional incomes policies

has stimulated interest in the *tax-based incomes policy* (TIP) originally suggested by the post-Keynesian economist Sidney Weintraub in the belief that reliance on market incentives would produce
more effective wage restraint than regulation had been able to
achieve. Weintraub proposed that a surcharge on corporate profits
tax be imposed on employers who paid wage increases above the
norm. This would stiffen companies' resistance to excessive wage
claims by trade unions and, once unions adapted their own bargaining stance in response to the tax, would also induce them to
moderate their demands. Neither sanctions, nor unusually stringent
restraint on public sector earnings, nor even tiresome moralising by
the government, need be involved; wage inflation would decline
automatically as a consequence of rational behaviour on the part of
the employers and unions. Finally, the tax base could be defined in
such a way as to encourage increased employment of low-wage, low-
skilled workers who are unusually prone to unemployment (Wallich
and Weintraub, 1971). Layard (1986, chapter 10), maintains that
similar benefits would flow from the adoption of an 'inflation tax'
levied on the growth in company payrolls above a specified norm.
Other variants of TIP are discussed by Paci (1988).

The major criticisms of the Wallich–Weintraub plan are summarised by Rees (1978). The proposals would not apply to partnerships,
non-profit institutions and government agencies, who do not pay
corporate profit tax, and could not in practice to be enforced against
small companies. It is probable, too, that the suggested tax surcharge would be passed on to consumers, at least by firms which
enjoy substantial market power, thereby negating its dampening
effect on the inflation rate. Similar objections apply to a payroll-
based inflation tax. Moreover, the principal advantages which are
claimed for TIP – that it relies on market forces, and dispenses with
the politicisation and centralisation of wage determination required
by conventional policies – are 'much weakened if it is the norm
which is prominent and not the tax' (Bosanquet, 1983, p. 34). TIP is
not neutral with respect to the distribution of income, but favours
the strong, who can pass on the inflation tax (or afford to pay it) at
the expense of the weak. Bosanquet concludes that TIP is unlikely to
succeed when inflation results from fundamental conflict over income distribution (ibid., pp. 46–8). The same may be said of incomes
policies in general, reinforcing the stress placed on social conflict in
the institutionalist and radical-Marxian analyses of aggregate wage
determination.

12

Conclusion

On many of the basic issues in labour economics there are very marked contrasts between the competing theoretical traditions which were identified in Chapter 1. The neoclassical treatment of the firm's demand for labour, for example, is quite distinct from the post-Keynesian analysis (Chapter 2). Orthodox assumptions about the meaning of work differ fundamentally from those of green and radical-Marxian economists (Chapter 3). The institutionalist literature on collective action, trade unionism and the social foundations of labour market discrimination is clearly opposed to neoclassical analysis (Chapters 5–6). Post-Keynesian and radical-Marxian theories of relative income shares cannot be reconciled easily – if indeed at all – with marginal productivity theory (Chapter 9). Similar remarks apply to the discussion of wage differentials (Chapter 7) and the sources of economic inequality (Chapter 8). In all these cases, pronounced differences of perspective and emphasis separate the rival schools of thought.

In some areas, however, it has proved much more difficult to draw sharp lines of demarcation between them. Where the internal labour market and the organisation of work are concerned, there often appears to be little to choose between institutionalist, radical-Marxian and orthodox analysis (Chapter 4). This theoretical convergence is most striking on the question of aggregate wage determination (Chapter 11). Not only do institutionalists, post-Keynesians and radical-Marxian writers broadly agree on the importance of social conflict in the generation of wage inflation, but their concerns are shared by a large (and growing) number of neoclassical economists. While the green and radical-Marxian theory of technological unemployment stands alone, there is considerable common ground between post-Keynesian, radical-Marxian and many orthodox theorists concerning the role of demand deficiency and its relation to conflict over the distribution of income (Chapter 10).

To some extent this rather confusing situation results from the incompleteness and imprecision of all four non-neoclassical schools, which was alluded to in Chapter 1. But it also reflects a militant 'imperialism' on the part of orthodox economists, who are always eager to expand their analytical range by demonstrating the ability of neoclassical theory to deal with an ever-increasing number of problem areas. This is combined with an opportunistic willingness to appropriate concepts and modes of reasoning from rival traditions, frequently in apparent ignorance of their origins, which almost invariably go unacknowledged. The efficiency wage hypothesis discussed in Chapter 4 provides a particularly glaring example of the 're-invention of the wheel' by neoclassical writers, in unknowing imitation of an earlier generation of institutionalists (Segal, 1986). The same could be said of insider–outsider theory (Chapter 10, Section 3) and of the increasing emphasis on demand factors in the explanation of inter-industry wage differentials (Chapter 7, Section 3). Even the radical-Marxian concept of class struggle has been borrowed by orthodox writers. In this case, however, the compliment has been returned, with some radical-Marxians defining key notions such as class and exploitation in terms of the rational behaviour of self-seeking individuals (Howard and King, 1991, chapter 17; cf. Chapter 6, Section 3, above).

What, then does the future hold for labour economics? It is unlikely that any one school of thought will completely dominate its rivals. The green, post-Keynesian and even the radical-Marxian traditions simply have too little to say on too many important issues for them to be able to triumph over all opposition. In the 1940s and early 1950s institutionalists did mount a comprehensive challenge to the prevailing orthodoxy. They failed equally comprehensively, largely because they 'dealt bit by bit with pieces of the puzzle and never assembled them into an integrated statement, let alone into a model or a consistent theory' (Kerr, 1983, p. 307). The orthodox counter-attack was in the long run no more successful, since its chief weapon – human capital theory – proved unable to meet the demands which were made on it. This had become evident to its more perceptive supporters by the mid-1970s (Blaug, 1976). Since then, no single theory has been able to claim hegemonic status, nor has anything approaching a coherent synthesis emerged.

The history of economics in general is an untidy one, lacking any sign of the unsteady but cumulatively overwhelming progress which is sometimes supposed to characterise the natural sciences. Instead, interest wanes in what were formerly regarded as major analytical advances, while old heresies become respectable and ideas which had been discarded as fallacious resurface (King, 1988, chapter 1; Goodwin, 1980). Labour economics conforms to this pattern, or lack of pattern, perhaps to a greater degree than almost any other branch of the discipline. It is inevitable that this should be so, given the intractable nature of so many of its problems. Preference formation, the concept of power, the rationality of collective behaviour, are all central concerns, and none of them can be easily resolved. Theoretical pluralism is the only honest answer, and in all probability the only practicable solution too.

Bibliography

Aaronovitch, S. (1981) *The Road from Thatcherism: the Alternative Economic Strategy* (London: Lawrence & Wishart).

Addison, J. T. and Barnett, A. H. (1982) 'The Impact of Unions on Productivity', *British Journal of Industrial Relations*, vol. 20, pp. 145–62.

Akerlof, G. A. (1982) 'Labor Contracts As Partial Gift Exchange', *Quarterly Journal of Economics*, vol. 97, pp. 543–69.

Akerlof, G. A. and Yellen, J. L. (1988) 'Fairness and Unemployment', *American Economic Review*, vol. 78 (Papers and Proceedings), pp. 44–9.

Alchian, A. A. and Demsetz, H. (1972) 'Production, Information Costs, and Economic Organisation', *American Economic Review*, vol. 62, pp. 777–95.

Andrews, P. W. S. (1964) *On Competition In Economic Theory* (London: Macmillan).

Annable, J. E. Jr (1980) 'Money Wage Determination in Post Keynesian Economics', *Journal of Post-Keynesian Economics*, vol. 2, pp. 405–19.

Applebaum, E. (1979) 'The Labor Market', in A. S. Eichner (ed.), *A Guide to Post-Keynesian Economics*, pp. 100–119 (London: Macmillan).

Armstrong, H. W. and Taylor, J. (1981) 'The Measurement of Different Types of Unemployment', in J. Creedy (ed.), *The Economics of Unemployment in Britain*, pp. 99–127 (London: Butterworth).

Armstrong, H. W. and Taylor, J. (1985) *Regional Economics and Policy* (Deddington: Philip Allan).

Arrow, K. J. (1972a) 'Models of Job Discrimination', in A. H. Pascal (ed.), *Racial Discrimination in Economic Life*, pp. 83–102 (Lexington, Mass.: D. C. Heath).

Arrow, K. J. (1972b) 'Some Mathematical Models of Race in the Labor Market', in A. H. Pascal (ed.), *Racial Discrimination in Economic Life*, pp. 187–203 (Lexington, Mass.: D. C. Heath).

Ashenfelter, O. C. and Johnson, G. E. (1969) 'Bargaining Theory, Trade Unions and Industrial Strike Activity', *American Economic Review*, vol. 59, pp. 35–49.

Atkinson, A. B. (1983) *The Economics of Inequality* (Oxford: Clarendon Press).

Atkinson, J. (1985) *Flexibility, Uncertainty and Manpower Management* (Brighton: Institute of Manpower Studies, University of Sussex, Report No. 89).

Baily, M. N. (1982) 'Labor Market Performance, Competition and Inflation', in Baily (ed.), *Work, Jobs and Inflation*, pp. 15–44 (Washington, DC: Brookings Institution).

Baldamus, W. A. (1961) *Efficiency and Effort: an Analysis of Industrial Administration* (London: Tavistock).

Baran, P. A. and Sweezy, P. M. (1968) *Monopoly Capital* (Harmondsworth: Penguin).

Bean, C. R., Layard, P. R. G. and Nickell, S. J. (1986) 'The Rise in Unemployment: a Multi-Country Study', *Economica*, n.s., vol. 53, pp. S1–S22.

Becker, G. S. (1957) *The Economics of Discrimination* (Chicago: Chicago University Press).

Becker, G. S. (1964) *Human Capital* (New York: National Bureau for Economic Research).

Becker, G. S. (1965) 'A Theory of the Allocation of Time', *Economic Journal*, vol. 75, pp. 493–517.

Becker, G. S. (1967) *Human Capital and the Personal Distribution of Income* (Ann Arbor: University of Michigan Press).

Beckerman, W. (1979) 'Small is Stupid', *Times Higher Education Supplement*, 23 November.

Beckerman, W. and Jenkinson, T. (1986a) 'How Rigid are Wages Anyway?', in Beckerman (ed.), *Wage Rigidity and Unemployment*, pp. 21–42 (London: Duckworth).

Beckerman, W. and Jenkinson, T. (1986b) 'What Stopped the

Inflation? Unemployment or Commodity Prices?', *Economic Journal*, vol. 96, pp. 39–54.

Beckmann, M. J. (1971) 'Klassen, Einkommensverteilung und die Struktur Bürokratischer Organisationen', *Kyklos*, vol. 24, pp. 660–5.

Beechey, V. (1987) *Unequal Work* (London: Verso).

Bell, D. N. F. (1982) 'Labour Utilisation and Statutory Non-Wage Costs', *Economica*, vol. 49, pp. 335–43.

Bellante, D. (1979) 'The North-South Differential and the Migration of Heterogeneous Labor', *American Economic Review*, vol. 69, pp. 166–75.

Beller, A. H. (1979) 'The Impact of Equal Opportunity Laws on the Male/Female Earnings Differential', in C. B. Lloyd *et al.* (eds), *Women in the Labor Market*, pp. 304–30 (New York: Columbia University Press).

Bienefeld, M. A. (1972) *Working Hours in British Industry: an Economic History* (London: Weidenfeld & Nicolson).

Berger, S. and Piore, M. J. (1980) *Dualism and Discontinuity in Industrial Societies* (Cambridge: Cambridge University Press).

Bergson, A. (1984) 'Income Inequality Under Soviet Socialism', *Journal of Economic Literature*, vol. 22, pp. 1052–99.

Blackaby, D. (1986) 'An Analysis of the Male Racial Earnings Differential in the United Kingdom, Using the General Household Survey', *Applied Economics*, vol. 18, pp. 1233–42.

Blackaby, D. H. and Manning, D. N. (1987) 'Regional Earnings Revisited', *Manchester School*, vol. 55, pp. 158–83.

Blanchard, O. J. and Summers, L. H. (1987) 'Hysteresis in Unemployment', *European Economic Review*, vol. 31, pp. 288–95.

Blanchard, O. J. and Summers, L. H. (1988) 'Beyond the Natural Rate Hypothesis', *American Economic Review*, vol. 78 (Papers and Proceedings), pp. 182–7.

Blanchflower, D. (1986) 'What Effect Do Unions Have on Relative Wages in Great Britain?', *British Journal of Industrial Relations*, vol. 24, pp. 195–204.

Blaug, M. (1975) 'Kuhn Versus Lakatos, or Paradigms Versus Research Programmes in the History of Economics', *History of Political Economy*, vol. 7, pp. 399–433.

Blaug, M. (1976) 'The Empirical Status of Human Capital Theory: a Slightly Jaundiced Survey', *Journal of Economic Literature*, vol. 14, pp. 827–55.

Blaug, M. (1980) *The Methodology of Economics: or How Econo-mists Explain* (Cambridge: Cambridge University Press).

Blinder, A. S. (1974) *Toward an Economic Theory of Income Distribution* (Cambridge, Mass.: MIT Press).

Bloom, G. F. (1940–1) 'A Reconsideration of the Theory of Exploitation', *Quarterly Journal of Economics*, vol. 55, reprinted as pp. 413–42 of American Economics Association, *Readings in the Theory of Income Distribution* (Homewood, Ill.: R. D. Irwin, 1946).

Bluestone, B. and Harrison, B. (1988) *The Great U-Turn: Corporate Restructuring and the Polarizing of America* (New York: Basic Books).

Bonnell, S. (1981) 'Real Wages and Unemployment in the Great Depression', *Economic Record*, vol. 57, pp. 277–81.

Bonnell, S. M. (1987) 'The Effect of Equal Pay For Females on the Composition of Employment in Australia', *Economic Record*, vol. 63, pp. 340–51.

Booth, A. (1984) 'A Public Choice Model of Trade Union Behaviour and Membership', *Economic Journal*, vol. 94, pp. 883–98.

Bosanquet, N. (1983) 'Tax-Based Incomes Policies', *Oxford Bulletin of Economics and Statistics*, vol. 45, pp. 33–49.

Bowers, J., Deaton, D. and Turk, J. (1982) *Labour Hoarding in British Industry* (Oxford: Blackwell).

Bowles, S. (1985) 'The Production Process in a Competitive Economy', *American Economic Review*, vol. 75, pp. 16–36.

Bowles, S. and Boyer, R. (1988) 'Labor Discipline and Aggregate Demand: A Macroeconomic Model', *American Economic Review*, vol. 78 (Papers and Proceedings), pp. 395–400.

Bowles, S. and Gintis, H. (1975) 'The Problem With Human Capital Theory – A Marxian Critique', *American Economic Review*, vol. 65, pp. 74–82.

Bowles, S. and Gintis, H. (1988) 'Contested Exchange: Political Economy and Modern Economic Theory', *American Economic Review*, vol. 78 (Papers and Proceedings), pp. 145–50.

Bowles, S. and Nelson, V. I. (1974) 'The "Inheritance of IQ" and the Intergenerational Reproduction of Economic Inequality', *Review of Economics and Statistics*, vol. 56, pp. 39–51.

Bowles, S., Gordon, D. M. and Weisskopf, T. E. (1984) *Beyond the Wasteland: a Democratic Alternative to Economic Decline* (London: Verso).

Bradfield, M. (1976) 'Necessary and Sufficient Conditions to Explain Regional Wage Differentials', *Journal of Regional Science*, vol. 16, pp. 247–55.

Braverman, H. (1974) *Labor and Monopoly Capital: the Degradation of Work in the Twentieth Century* (New York: Monthly Review Press).

Brittan, S. and Lilley, P. (1977) *The Delusion of Incomes Policy* (London: Temple Smith).

Bronfenbrenner, M. (1960) 'A Note on Relative Shares and the Elasticity of Substitution', *Journal of Political Economy*, vol. 68, pp. 284–7.

Bronfenbrenner, M. (1971) *Income Distribution Theory* (Chicago: Aldine-Alderton).

Brosnan, P. and Wilkinson, F. (1988) 'A National Statutory Minimum Wage and Economic Efficiency', *Contributions to Political Economy*, vol. 7, pp. 1–48.

Brown, C., Gilroy, C. and Kohen, A. (1982) 'The Effect of the Minimum Wage on Employment and Unemployment', *Journal of Economic Literature*, vol. 20, pp. 487–528.

Brown, C. V. (1983) *Taxation and the Incentive to Work* (Oxford: Oxford University Press, second edition).

Brown, E. H. Phelps (1977) *The Inequality of Pay* (Oxford: Oxford University Press).

Brown, W., Hayles, J., Hughes, B. and Rowe, L. (1980) 'Occupational Pay Structures Under Different Wage-Fixing Arrangements: a Comparison of Intra-Occupational Pay Dispersion in Australia, Great Britain and the United States', *British Journal of Industrial Relations*, vol. 18, pp. 217–30.

Brown, W., Hayles, J., Hughes, B. and Rowe, L. (1984) 'Product and Labour Markets in Wage Determination: Some Australian Evidence', *British Journal of Industrial Relations*, vol. 22, pp. 169–76.

Bruno, M. and Sachs, J. B. (1985) *Economics of World-Wide Stagflation* (Oxford: Blackwell).

Buchanan, J. M. (1968) *The Demand and Supply of Public Goods* (Chicago: Rand McNally).

Bulow, J. I. and Summers, L. H. (1986) 'A Theory of Dual Labor Markets with Application to Industrial Policy, Discrimination, and Keynesian Unemployment', *Journal of Labor Economics*, vol. 4, pp. 375–414.

Cain, G. (1976) 'The Challenge of Segmented Labor Market Theories to Orthodox Theory', *Journal of Economic Literature*, vol. 14, pp. 1215–57.

Cain, G. C. (1986) 'The Economic Analysis of Labor Market Discrimination: a Survey', in O. Ashenfelter and R. Layard (eds), *Handbook of Labor Economics*, volume I, pp. 698–785 (Amsterdam: North-Holland).

Canterbery, E. R. (1979) 'A Vita Theory of the Personal Income Distribution', *Southern Economic Journal*, vol. 46, pp. 12–48.

Carruth, A. and Oswald, A. (1987) 'Wage Inflexibility in Britain', *Oxford Bulletin of Economics and Statistics*, vol. 49, pp. 59–78.

Carter, M. and Maddock, R. (1984) 'Working Hours in Australia: Some Issues', in R. Blandy and O. Covick (eds), *Understanding Labour Markets in Australia*, pp. 222–45 (London: Allen & Unwin).

Cerny, P. (1985–6) 'The Ugly Social Consequences of Elegantly Simple Formulae', *Solidarity*, no. 10, pp. 7–13.

Chamberlain, N. W. and Kuhn, J. W. (1965) *Collective Bargaining* (New York: McGraw-Hill).

Chamberlin, E. H. (1933) *The Theory of Monopolistic Competition* (Cambridge, Mass.: Harvard University Press).

Clark, K. B. and Freeman, R. B. (1980) 'How Elastic is the Demand for Labor?', *Review of Economics and Statistics*, vol. 62, pp. 509–20.

Clegg, H. (1971) *How To Run an Incomes Policy, and Why We Made Such a Mess of the Last One* (London: Heinemann).

Cliff, T. and Barker, C. (1966) *Incomes Policy, Legislation and Shop Stewards* (London: London Industrial Shop Stewards Defence Committee).

Coase, R. H. (1937) 'The Nature of the Firm', *Economica*, n.s., vol. 4, pp. 386–405.

Coen, R. M. and Hickman, B. G. (1988) 'Is European Unemployment Classical or Keynesian?', *American Economic Review*, vol. 78 (Papers and Proceedings), pp. 188–93.

Creedy, J. and Whitfield, K. (1988) 'The Economic Analysis of Internal Labour Markets', *Bulletin of Economic Research*, vol. 40, pp. 247–69.

Crouch, C. (1979) *The Politics of Industrial Relations* (Manchester: Manchester University Press).

Cyert, R. M. and March, J. G. (1963) *A Behavioral Theory of the Firm* (Englewood Cliffs, NJ: Prentice-Hall).

Darby, M., Haltiwanger, J. and Plant, M. (1985) 'Unemployment

Rate Dynamics and Persistent Unemployment Under Rational Expectations', *American Economic Review*, vol. 75, pp. 614–37.

Denison, E. F. (1974) *Accounting For United States Economic Growth, 1929–69* (Washington, DC: Brookings Institution).

Department of Employment (1988) 'Measures of Unemployment and Characteristics of the Unemployed', *Employment Gazette*, October, pp. 534–47.

Dickens, W. T. and Katz, L. F. (1987) 'Inter-industry Wage Differences and Industry Characteristics', in K. Lang and J. S. Leonard (eds), *Unemployment and the Structure of Labor Markets*, pp. 48–89 (Oxford: Blackwell).

Dickens, W. T. and Lang, K. (1985) 'A Test of Dual Labor Market Theory', *American Economic Review*, vol. 75, pp. 792–805.

Dickens, W. T. and Lang, K. (1987) 'Where Have All the Good Jobs Gone? Deindustrialization and Labor Market Segmentation', in K. Lang and J. S. Leonard (eds), *Unemployment and the Structure of Labor Markets*, pp. 90–102 (Oxford: Blackwell).

Dobb, M. H. (1960) *An Essay on Economic Growth and Planning* (London: Routledge & Kegan Paul).

Doeringer, P. B. and Piore, M. J. (1985) *Internal Labor Markets and Manpower Analysis* (New York: M. E. Sharpe, second edition; first published 1971).

Dore, R. (1973) *British Factory, Japanese Factory: the Origins of National Diversity in Industrial Relations* (Berkeley: University of California Press).

Dornbusch, R. and Fischer, S. (1984) *Macroeconomics* (London: McGraw-Hill, third edition).

Douglas, P. H. (1948) 'Are There Laws of Production?', *American Economic Review*, vol. 38, pp. 1–41.

Dowie, J. (1975) '1919–20 Is In Need Of Attention', *Economic History Review* n.s., vol. 28, pp. 429–50.

Dunlop, J. T. (1944) *Wage Determination Under Trade Unions* (New York: Macmillan).

Edgeworth, F. Y. (1881) *Mathematical Psychics* (London: Kegan Paul).

Edwards, R. C. (1975) 'Individual Traits and Organisational Incentives: What Makes a Good Worker?', *Journal of Human Resources*, vol. 11, pp. 51–68.

Edwards, R. C. (1979) *Contested Terrain: the Transformation of the Workplace in the Twentieth Century* (London: Heinemann).

Eichner, A. S. (ed.) (1979) *A Guide to Post-Keynesian Economics* (New York: M. E. Sharpe).

Eichner, A. S. (1985) *Toward A New Economics* (London: Macmillan).

Ekins, P. (1986) *The Living Economy: a New Economics in the Making* (London: Routledge).

Emmanuel, A. (1982) *Appropriate Or Underdeveloped Technology?* (Chichester: Wiley).

Estrin, S. (1981) 'Income Dispersion in a Self-Managed Economy', *Economica*, n.s., vol. 48, pp. 181–94.

Feinstein, C. H. (1968) 'Changes in the Distribution of the National Income in the United Kingdom Since 1860', in J. Marchal and B. Ducros, (eds), *The Distribution of National Income*, pp. 115–39 (London: Macmillan).

Fellner, W. J. (1960) *Competition Among the Few* (New York: Kelley; first published 1949).

Fisher, F. M. (1969) 'The Existence of Aggregate Production Functions', *Econometrica*, vol. 7, pp. 553–77.

Fisher, L. (1951) 'The Harvest Labor Market in California', *Quarterly Journal of Economics*, vol. 65, pp. 463–91.

Freeman, R. B. (1988) 'Evaluating the European View that the United States has No Unemployment Problem', *American Economic Review*, vol. 78 (Papers and Proceedings), pp. 294–9.

Freeman, R. B. and Medoff, J. L. (1984) *What Do Unions Do?* (New York: Basic Books).

Friedman, M. (1951) 'Some Comments on the Significance of Labor Unions for Economic Policy', in D. McCord Wright (ed.), *The Impact of the Union*, pp. 204–34 (New York: Harcourt, Brace).

Friedman, M. (1953a) 'The Methodology of Positive Economics', in Friedman, *Essays in Positive Economics*, pp. 3–43 (Chicago: University of Chicago Press).

Friedman, M. (1953b) 'Choice, Chance and the Personal Distribution of Income', *Journal of Political Economy*, vol. 61, pp. 277–90.

Friedman, M. (1968) 'The Role of Monetary Policy', *American Economic Review*, vol. 58, pp. 1–17.

Galbraith, J. K. (1952) *American Capitalism: the Concept of Countervailing Power* (Boston: Houghton Mifflin).

Galbraith, J. K. (1973) *Economics and the Public Purpose* (Boston: Houghton Mifflin).

George, K. D. and Shorey, J. (1985) 'Manual Workers, Good Jobs and Structured Internal Labour Markets', *British Journal of Industrial Relations*, vol. 23, pp. 425–47.

Gintis, H. (1972) 'A Radical Analysis of Welfare Economics and Individual Development', *Quarterly Journal of Economics*, vol. 86, pp. 572–99.

Gintis, H. (1976) 'The Nature of Labor Exchange and the Theory of Capitalist Production', *Review of Radical Political Economics*, vol. 8, pp. 36–54.

Glyn, A. (1985) *A Million Jobs a Year* (London: Verso).

Glyn, A. and Rowthorn, R. (1988) 'Western European Unemployment: Corporatism and Structural Change', *American Economic Review*, vol. 78 (Papers and Proceedings) pp. 194–9.

Glyn, A. and Sutcliffe, B. (1972) *British Capitalism, Workers and the Profits Squeeze* (Harmondsworth: Penguin).

Goodwin, C. D. (1980) 'Towards a Theory of the History of Economics', *History of Political Economy*, vol. 12, pp. 610–19.

Goodwin, R. M. (1983) 'A Note on Wages, Profits and Fluctuating Growth Rates', *Cambridge Journal of Economics*, vol. 7, pp. 305–9.

Gordon, D. M., Edwards, R. and Reich, M. (1982) *Segmented Work, Divided Workers: the Historical Transformation of Labor in the United States* (Cambridge: Cambridge University Press).

Gordon, R. J. (1987) *Macroeconomics* (Boston: Little, Brown; fourth edition).

Gordon, R. J. (1988) 'The Role of Wages in the Inflation Process', *American Economic Review*, vol. 78 (Papers and Proceedings), pp. 276–83.

Gorz, A. (1983) *Farewell to the Working Class* (London: Pluto).

Greenhalgh, C. (1980a) 'Participation and Hours of Work for Married Women in Great Britain', *Oxford Economic Papers*, vol. 32, pp. 296–318.

Greenhalgh, C. (1980b) 'Male-Female Wage Differentials in Great Britain: is Marriage an Equal Opportunity?' *Economic Journal*, vol. 90, pp. 751–75.

Greenhalgh, C. A. and Stewart, M. B. (1985) 'The Occupational Status and Mobility of British Men and Women', *Oxford Economic Papers*, vol. 37, pp. 40–71.

Greenwood, M. (1975) 'Research on Internal Migration in the United States: a Survey', *Journal of Economic Literature*, vol. 13, pp. 397–433.

Groshen, E. L. (1988) 'Why Do Wages Vary Among Employers?', *Federal Reserve Bank of Cleveland Economic Review*, vol. 24, pp. 19–38.

Grubb, D. (1986) 'Topics in the OECD Phillips Curve', *Economic Journal*, vol. 96, pp. 55–79.

Grubb, D., Jackman, R. and Layard, R. (1983) 'Wage Rigidity and Unemployment in OECD Countries', *European Economic Review*, vol. 21, pp. 11–39.

Gunderson, M. (1989) 'Male–Female Wage Differentials and Policy Responses', *Journal of Economic Literature*, vol. 27, pp. 46–72.

Hall, R. E. (1982) 'The Importance of Lifetime Jobs in the U.S. Economy', *American Economic Review*, vol. 72, pp. 716–24.

Hall, R. L. and Hitch, C. J. (1939) 'Price Theory and Business Behaviour', *Oxford Economic Papers*, vol. 2, pp. 12–45.

Hamermesh, D. S. (1986) 'The Demand For Labor in the Long Run', in O. Ashenfelter and R. Layard (eds), *Handbook of Labor Economics*, volume I, pp. 429–71 (Amsterdam: North-Holland).

Hamermesh, D. S. and Rees, A. (1984) *The Economics of Work and Pay* (New York: Harper and Row).

Handy, C. (1984) *The Future of Work* (Oxford: Blackwell).

Harcourt, G. C. (1972) *Some Cambridge Controversies in the Theory of Capital* (Cambridge: Cambridge University Press).

Harris, J. R. and Todaro, M. P. (1970) 'Migration, Unemployment and Development: a Two-Sector Analysis', *American Economic Review*, vol. 60, pp. 126–42.

Harris, N. (1971) *Beliefs in Society: the Problem of Ideology* (Harmondsworth: Penguin).

Hart, P. E. (1988) *Youth Unemployment in Great Britain* (Cambridge: Cambridge University Press).

Hashimoto, M. and Raisian, J. (1985) 'Employment Tenure and Earnings Profiles in Japan and the United States', *American Economic Review*, vol. 75, pp. 721–35.

Heathfield, D. F. and Wibe, S. (1987) *An Introduction to Cost and Production Functions* (London: Macmillan).

Hicks, J. R. (1932) *The Theory of Wages* (London: Macmillan).

Hicks, J. R. (1937) 'Mr Keynes and the Classics: a Suggested Interpretation', *Econometrica*, vol. 5, pp. 147–59.

Hieser, R. O. (1970) 'Wage Determination With Bilateral Monopoly in the Labour Market: a Theoretical Treatment', *Economic Record*, vol. 46, pp. 55–72.

Himmelweit, S. and Mohun, S. (1977) 'Domestic Labour and Capital', *Cambridge Journal of Economics*, vol. 1, pp. 15–31.

Hirsch, B. T. (1985) 'Comment', *Industrial and Labor Relations Review*, vol. 38, pp. 247–50.

Hirsch, F. (1977) *Social Limits to Growth* (London: Routledge & Kegan Paul).

HMSO (1969) *National Income and Expenditure 1969* (London).

HMSO (1971) *British Labour Statistics: Historical Abstract (1886–1968)* (London).

HMSO (1987a) *Social Trends* 17 (London).

HMSO (1987b) *Economic Trends* 409, November (London).

HMSO (1988a) *New Earnings Survey 1988* (London).

HMSO (1988b) *United Kingdom National Accounts 1988* (London).

HMSO (1989) *Social Trends* 19 (London).

Hodgson, G. (1982) 'Theoretical and Policy Implications of Variable Productivity', *Cambridge Journal of Economics*, vol. 6, pp. 213–26.

Hodson, R. (1983) *Workers' Earnings and Corporate Economic Structure* (New York: Academic Press).

Holden, K., Peel, D. A. and Thompson, J. L. (1987) *The Economics of Wage Controls* (London: Macmillan).

Hood, W. and Rees, R. D. (1974) 'Inter-Industry Wage Levels in U.K. Manufacturing', *Manchester School*, vol. 42, pp. 171–85.

Howard, M. C. (1979) *Modern Theories of Income Distribution* (London: Macmillan).

Howard, M. C. and King, J. E. (1985) *The Political Economy of Marx* (Harlow: Longman, second edition).

Howard, M. C. and King, J. E. (1991) *A History of Marxian Economics. Volume 2: 1929–1990* (London: Macmillan).

Hunt, E. H. (1973) *Regional Wage Variations in Britain, 1850–1914* (Oxford: Clarendon Press).

Hyman, R. (1971) *Marxism and the Sociology of Trade Unions* (London: Pluto Press).

Jackman, R. and Roper, S. (1987) 'Structural Unemployment', *Oxford Bulletin of Economics and Statistics*, vol. 49, pp. 9–36.

Jackson, R. V. (1987) 'The Structure of Pay in Nineteenth Century Britain', *Economic History Review* n.s., vol. 40, pp. 561–70.

Jenkins, C. and Sherman, B. (1979) *The Collapse of Work* (London: Eyre Methuen).

Johnes, G. (1985) 'Error Removal, Loss Reduction and External

Effects in the Theory of Strikes', *Australian Economic Papers*, vol. 24, pp. 310–25.

Johnson, C. (1987) 'The Meaning of Unemployment', *Lloyds Bank Economic Bulletin*, vol. 105, pp. 1–3.

Johnson, G. E. and Layard, P. R. G. (1986) 'The Natural Rate of Unemployment: Explanation and Policy', in O. Ashenfelter and R. Layard (eds), *Handbook of Labour Economics*, volume II, pp. 921–99 (Amsterdam: North-Holland).

Johnston, J. (1972) 'A Model of Wage Determination Under Bilateral Monopoly', *Economic Journal*, vol. 82, pp. 837–52.

Junankar, P. N. (ed.) (1987) *From School to Unemployment? The Labour Market for Young People* (London: Macmillan).

Kakwani, N. (1986) *Analyzing Redistribution Policies: a Study Using Australian Data* (Cambridge: Cambridge University Press).

Kalecki, M. (1954) *The Theory of Economic Dynamics* (London: Allen and Unwin).

Kalecki, M. (1971) 'The Class Struggle and the Distribution of National Income', *Kyklos*, vol. 24, pp. 1–9.

Keane, J. and Owens, J. (1986) *After Full Employment* (London: Hutchinson).

Kerr, C. (1950) 'Labor Markets: Their Character and Consequences', *American Economic Review*, vol. 40, pp. 278–91.

Kerr, C. (1977) *Labor Markets and Wage Determination: the Balkanisation of Labor Markets and Other Essays* (Berkeley: University of California Press).

Kerr, C. (1983) 'The Intellectual Role of Neorealists in Labor Economics', *Industrial Relations*, vol. 22, pp. 298–318.

Keynes, J. M. (1936) *The General Theory of Employment, Interest and Money* (London: Macmillan).

Killingsworth, M. R. (1983) *Labour Supply* (Cambridge: Cambridge University Press).

King, A. G. (1974) 'Minimum Wages and the Secondary Labor Market', *Southern Economic Journal*, vol. 41, pp. 215–19.

King, J. E. (1988) *Economic Exiles* (London: Macmillan).

King, J. E. and Regan, P. (1976) *Relative Income Shares* (London: Macmillan).

King, J. E. and Regan, P. (1988) 'Recent Trends in Labour's Share', in Y. S. Brenner, J. P. G. Reijnders and A. H. G. M. Spithoven (eds), *The Theory of Income and Wealth Distribution*, pp. 54–86 (Brighton: Wheatsheaf).

Klamer, A. (1983) *Conversations With Economists* (Totowa, N.J.: Rowman and Allanheld).

Kniesner, T. J. and Goldsmith, A. H. (1987) 'A Survey of Alternative Models of the Aggregate U. S. Labor Market', *Journal of Economic Literature*, vol. 25, pp. 1241–80.

Krejci, J. (1972) *Social Change and Stratification in Postwar Czechoslovakia* (London: Allen & Unwin).

Krueger, A. B. and Summers, L. H. (1987) 'Reflections on the Inter-industry Wage Structure', in K. Lang and J. S. Leonard (eds), *Unemployment and the Structure of Labor Markets*, pp. 18–47 (Oxford: Blackwell).

Lakatos, I. (1978) *The Methodology of Scientific Research Programmes* (Cambridge: Cambridge University Press).

Lane, D. (1982) *The End of Social Inequality?: Class, Status and Power Under State Socialism* (London: Allen & Unwin).

Langley, P. C. (1974) 'The Spatial Allocation of Migrants in England and Wales: 1961–66', *Scottish Journal of Political Economy*, vol. 21, pp. 259–77.

Latsis, S. (1976) *Method and Appraisal in Economics* (Cambridge: Cambridge University Press).

Laurence, P. (1981) 'A Squat Black Living', *Guardian* (London), 21 August.

Layard, R. (1986) *How To Beat Unemployment* (Oxford: Oxford University Press).

Layard, R., Barton, M. and Zabalza, A. (1980) 'Married Women's Participation and Hours', *Economica* n.s., vol. 47, pp. 51–72.

Layard, R. and Nickell, S. (1986) 'Unemployment in Britain', *Economica* n.s., vol. 53, pp. S121–S169.

Lee, J. W. and Koo, S. M. (1988) 'Trade-off Between Economic Growth and Income Equality', in Y. S. Brenner, J. P. G. Reinders and A. H. G. M. Spithoven (eds), *The Theory of Income and Wealth Distribution*, pp. 155–77 (Brighton: Wheatsheaf).

Leibenstein, H. (1987) *Inside the Firm: the Inefficiencies of Hierarchy* (Cambridge, Mass.: Harvard University Press).

Lester, R. A. (1946) 'Shortcomings of Marginal Analysis for Wage-Employment Problems', *American Economic Review*, vol. 36, pp. 63–82.

Lewis, H. G. (1986) 'Union Relative Wage Effects', in O. Ashenfelter and R. Layard (eds), *Handbook of Labor Economics*, volume II, pp. 1139–81 (Amsterdam: North-Holland).

Lindbeck, A. and Snower, D. J. (1986) 'Wage Rigidity, Union Activity and Unemployment', in Beckerman, W. (ed.), *Wage Rigidity and Unemployment*, pp. 97–126 (London: Duckworth).

Linder, S. B. (1970) *The Harried Leisure Class* (New York: Columbia University Press).

Lipietz, A. (1986) 'Behind the Crisis: the Exhaustion of a Regime of Accumulation. A "Regulation School" Perspective on some French Empirical Works', *Review of Radical Political Economics*, vol. 18, pp. 13–32.

Lipsey, R. G. (1960) 'The Relation between Unemployment and the Rate of Change of Money Wage Rates in the U.K. 1862–1957: a Further Analysis', *Economica n.s.*, vol. 27, pp. 1–31.

Lipsky, D. B. (1985) 'Comment', *Industrial and Labor Relations Review*, vol. 38, pp. 250–3.

Lucas, R. E. (1987) *Models of Business Cycles* (Oxford: Blackwell).

Lucas, R. E. B. (1985) 'Migration Among the Batswana', *Economic Journal*, vol. 95, pp. 358–82.

Lydall, H. F. (1968) *The Structure of Earnings* (Oxford: Oxford University Press).

Machlup, F. (1946) 'Marginal Analysis and Empirical Research', *American Economic Review*, vol. 36, pp. 519–54.

Maddock, R. and Carter, M. (1982) 'A Child's Guide to Rational Expectations', *Journal of Economic Literature*, vol. 20, pp. 39–51.

Malinvaud, E. (1985) *The Theory of Unemployment Reconsidered* (Oxford: Blackwell; second edition).

Marchal, J. and Ducros, B. (1968) 'Introduction', in Marchal, J. and Ducros, B. (eds), *The Distribution of National Income*, pp. xiii–xxx (London: Macmillan).

Marsden, D. (1986) *The End of Economic Man: Custom and Competition in the Labour Market* (Brighton: Wheatsheaf).

Marshall, A. (1920) *Principles of Economics* (London: Macmillan, eighth edition).

Marshall, R. (1974) 'The Economics of Racial Discrimination: a Survey', *Journal of Economic Literature*, vol. 12, pp. 849–71.

Marx, K. (1844) *Economic and Philosophical Manuscripts of 1844* (New York: International Publishers, 1964).

Marx, K. (1865) 'Wages, Price and Profit', in K. Marx and F. Engels, *Selected Works, Volume I*, pp. 398–447 (Moscow: Foreign Languages Publishing House, 1962).

Marx, K. (1867) *Capital, Volume I* (Moscow: Foreign Languages Publishing House, 1961).

Mayer, T. (1960) 'The Distribution of Ability and Earnings', *Review of Economics and Statistics*, vol. 42, pp. 189–95.

Mayhew, K. (1979) 'Economists and Strikes', *Oxford Bulletin of Economics and Statistics*, vol. 41, pp. 1–19.

Mayhew, K. and Rosewell, B. (1979) 'Labour Market Segmentation in Britain', *Oxford Bulletin of Economics and Statistics*, vol. 41, pp. 81–116.

McCallum, J. (1983) 'Inflation and Social Consensus in the Seventies', *Economic Journal*, vol. 93, pp. 784–805.

McCallum, J. (1985) 'Wage Gaps, Factor Shares and Real Wages', *Scandinavian Journal of Economics*, vol. 87, pp. 436–59.

McCallum, J. (1986) 'Unemployment in OECD Countries in the 1980s', *Economic Journal*, vol. 96, pp. 942–60.

McConnell, C. R. and Brue, S. L. (1986) *Contemporary Labor Economics* (New York: McGraw-Hill).

McCormick, B. (1986) 'Evidence About the Comparative Earnings of Asian and West Indian Workers in Great Britain', *Scottish Journal of Political Economy*, vol. 33, pp. 97–110.

MacDonald, I. M. and Solow, R. M. (1981) 'Wage Bargaining and Employment', *American Economic Review*, vol. 71, pp. 896–908.

MacKay, D. I. *et al.* (1971) *Labour Markets Under Different Employment Conditions* (London: Allen & Unwin).

McLellan, D. (1969) 'Marx's View of Unalienated Society', *Review of Politics*, vol. 31, pp. 459–65.

McNabb, R. and Psacharopoulos, G. (1981a) 'Racial Earnings Differentials in the U.K.', *Oxford Economic Papers*, vol. 33, pp. 413–25.

McNabb, R. and Psacharopoulos, G. (1981b) 'Further Evidence on the Relevance of the Dual Labor Market Hypothesis for the United Kingdom', *Journal of Human Resources*, vol. 16, pp. 442–8.

McRobie, G. (1981) *Small is Possible* (New York: Harper and Row).

Meade, J. E. (1982) *Wage-Fixing* (London: Allen & Unwin).

Medoff, J. L. and Abraham, K. G. (1980) 'Experience, Performance and Earnings', *Quarterly Journal of Economics*, vol. 95, pp. 703–36.

Mellow, W. (1982) 'Employer Size and Wages', *Review of Economics and Statistics*, vol. 64, pp. 495–501.

Meszaros, I. (1972) *Marx's Theory of Alienation* (London: Merlin).

Miller, P. W. (1984) 'Education and the Distribution of Income', in R. Blandy and O. Covick (eds), *Understanding Labour Markets in Australia*, pp. 16–36 (London: Allen & Unwin).

Miller, P. W. (1987) 'The Wage Effect of the Occupational Segregation of Women in Britain', *Economic Journal*, vol. 97, pp. 885–96.

Mincer, J. (1962) 'Labor Force Participation of Married Women: a Study of Labor Supply', in National Bureau of Economic Research, *Aspects of Labor Economics* (Princeton: Princeton University Press).

Mincer, J. (1974) *Schooling, Experience and Earnings* (New York: National Bureau of Economic Research).

Minford, P. (1983) *Unemployment: Cause and Cure* (Oxford: Martin Robertson).

Minford, P. (1984) 'Response to Nickell', *Economic Journal*, vol. 94, pp. 954–9.

Mitchell, B. R. (1962) *Abstract of British Historical Statistics* (Cambridge: Cambridge University Press).

Mitchell, D. J. B. (1985) 'Comment', *Industrial and Labor Relations Review* 38, pp. 253–6.

Molho, I. (1986) 'Theories of Migration: a Review', *Scottish Journal of Political Economy*, vol. 33, pp. 396–419.

Moore, B. J. (1988) *Horizontalists and Verticalists: the Macroeconomics of Credit Money* (Cambridge: Cambridge University Press).

Morley, R. (1979) 'Profit, Relative Prices and Unemployment', *Economic Journal*, vol. 89, pp. 582–600.

Mueller, D. C. (1979) *Public Choice* (Cambridge: Cambridge University Press).

Mulvey, C., Norris, K., Karmel, T., Aungles, P. and Maclauchlan, M. (1985) *Labour Market Efficiency in Australia* (Canberra: Australian Government Publishing Service, BLMR Monograph Series No. 9).

Newell, A. and Symons, J. (1987) 'Corporatism, Laissez-Faire and the Rise in Unemployment', *European Economic Review*, vol. 31, pp. 567–614.

Nickell, S. J. (1984) 'A Review of "*Unemployment: Cause and Cure*" by P. Minford *et al.*', *Economic Journal*, vol. 94, pp, 946–53.

Nickell, S. (1987) 'Why is Wage-Inflation in Britain So High?', *Oxford Bulletin of Economics and Statistics*, vol. 49, pp. 103–28.

Nissim, J. (1984a) 'The Price Responsiveness of the Demand for

Labour By Skill: British Mechanical Engineering: 1963–1978', *Economic Journal*, vol. 94, pp. 812–25.

Nissim, J. (1984b) 'An Examination of the Differential Patterns in the Cyclical Behaviour of the Employment, Hours and Wages of Labour of Different Skills: British Mechanical Engineering, 1963–1978', *Economica* n.s., vol. 51, pp. 423–36.

Nolan, B. (1987) 'Cyclical Fluctuations in Factor Shares and the Size Distribution of Income', *Review of Income and Wealth*, vol. 33, pp. 193–210.

Nolan, P. and Brown, W. (1983) 'Competition and Workplace Wage Determination', *Oxford Bulletin of Economics and Statistics*, vol. 45, pp. 269–87.

Norris, K. (1984) 'Job Durations in Australia', *Journal of Industrial Relations*, vol. 26, pp. 188–99.

OECD (1988) *Labour Force Statistics 1966–1986* (Paris).

OECD (1989) *Main Economic Indicators April 1989* (Paris).

Oi, W. (1962) 'Labor as a Quasi-Fixed Factor', *Journal of Political Economy*, vol. 70, pp. 538–55.

Okun, A. (1981) *Prices and Quantities: a Macroeconomic Analysis* (Washington, DC: Brookings Institution).

Olson, M. Jr. (1965) *The Logic of Collective Action* (Cambridge, Mass.: Harvard University Press).

Oswald, A. J. (1985) 'The Economic Theory of Trade Unions: an Introductory Survey', *Scandinavian Journal of Economics*, vol. 87, pp. 160–93.

Oswald, A. J. (1986) 'Wage Determination and Recession: a Report on Recent Work', *British Journal of Industrial Relations*, vol. 24, pp. 181–94.

Ozanne, R. (1968) *Wages in Practice and Theory: McCormick and International Harvester 1860–1960* (Madison: University of Wisconsin Press).

Paci, P. (1988) 'Tax-based Incomes Policies: Will They Work? Have They Worked?', *Fiscal Studies*, vol. 9, pp. 82–93.

Parsley, C. J. (1980) 'Labor Union Effects on Wage Gains: a Survey of Recent Literature', *Journal of Economic Literature*, vol. 18, pp. 1–31.

Peirson, J. (1988) 'The Importance of Being Unimportant: Marshall's Third Rule of Derived Demand', *Scottish Journal of Political Economy*, vol. 35, pp. 105–14.

Pencavel, J. and Hartsog, C. (1984) 'A Reconsideration of the Effects of Unionism on Relative Wages and Employment in the United States, 1920–1980', *Journal of Labor Economics*, vol. 2, pp. 193–232.

Penn, R. (1983) 'The Course of Wage Differentials Between Skilled and Nonskilled Manual Workers in Britain Between 1856 and 1964', *British Journal of Industrial Relations*, vol. 21, pp. 69–90.

Perlman, R. (1969) *Labor Theory* (New York: Wiley).

Perry, G. L. (1986) 'Policy Lessons from the Post-war Period', in W. Beckerman (ed.), *Wage Rigidity and Unemployment*, pp. 127–52 (London: Duckworth).

Phillips, A. W. (1958) 'The Relation Between Unemployment and the Rate of Change of Money Wage Rates in the United Kingdom, 1861–1957', *Economica* n.s., vol. 25, pp. 283–99.

Piachaud, D. (1982) *The Distribution and Redistribution of Incomes* (London: Bedford Square Press).

Piore, M. J. (1968) 'The Impact of the Labor Market on the Design and Selection of Productive Techniques Within the Manufacturing Plant', *Quarterly Journal of Economics*, vol. 82, pp. 602–20.

Piore, M. J. (1973) 'Fragments of a "Sociological" Theory of Wages', *American Economic Review*, vol. 63 (Papers and Proceedings), pp. 377–84.

Piore, M. J. (1983) 'Labor Market Segmentation: to What Paradigm Does it Belong?', *American Economic Review*, vol. 73 (Papers and Proceedings), pp. 249–53.

Piore, M. J. (1987) 'Historical Perspectives and the Interpretation of Unemployment', *Journal of Economic Literature*, vol. 25, pp. 1834–50.

Piore, M. J. and Sabel, C. F. (1984) *The Second Industrial Divide: Possibilities for Prosperity* (New York: Basic Books).

Popper, K. (1959) *The Logic of Scientific Discovery* (London: Hutchinson).

Purdy, D. (1988) *Social Power and the Labour Market* (London: Macmillan).

Reder, M. W. (1952) 'The Theory of Trade Union Wage Policy', *Review of Economics and Statistics*, vol. 34, pp. 34–45.

Reder, M. W. (1955) 'The Theory of Occupational Wage Differentials', *American Economic Review*, vol. 45, pp. 833–52.

Reder, M. W. (1962) 'Wage Differentials: Theory and Measurement', in National Bureau of Economic Research, *Aspects of Labor Economics*, pp. 257–317 (Princeton: Princeton University Press).

Rees, A. (1963) 'The Effects of Unions on Resource Allocation', *Journal of Law and Economics*, vol. 6, pp. 69–78.

Rees, A. (1978) 'New Policies to Fight Inflation: Sources of Skepticism', *Brookings Papers in Economic Analysis*, part 2, pp. 453–77.

Rees, A. and Schultz, G. P. (1970) *Workers and Wages in an Urban Labor Market* (Chicago: Chicago University Press).

Reich, M. (1981) *Racial Inequality: a Political-Economic Analysis* (Princeton: Princeton University Press, 1981).

Reich, M. (1984) 'Segmented Labour: Time Series Hypothesis and Evidence', *Cambridge Journal of Economics*, vol. 8, pp. 63–81.

Reich, M. and Devine, J. (1981) 'The Microeconomics of Conflict and Hierarchy in Capitalist Production', *Review of Radical Political Economics*, vol. 12, pp. 27–45.

Reynolds, L. G. (1951) *The Structure of Labor Markets: Wages and Labor Mobility in Theory and Practice* (New York: Harper).

Reynolds, L. G. and Taft, C. M. (1956) *The Evolution of Wage Structure* (New Haven: Yale University Press).

Reynolds, L. G. and Gregory, P. (1965) *Wages, Productivity and Industrialisation in Puerto Rico* (Homewood, Ill.: Irwin).

Robinson, D. (ed.) (1970) *Local Labour Markets and Wage Structures* (London: Gower Press).

Robinson, J. (1933) *The Economics of Imperfect Competition* (London: Macmillan).

Robinson, J. (1934) 'Euler's Theorem and the Problem of Distribution', *Economic Journal*, vol. 44, pp. 398–414.

Robinson, J. (1956) *The Accumulation of Capital* (London: Macmillan).

Robinson, J. (1965) 'The General Theory After 25 Years', in Robinson, *Collected Economic Papers*, volume III, pp. 100–2 (Oxford: Blackwell).

Roche, W. K. (1987) 'Leisure, Insecurity and Union Policy in Britain: a Critical Extension of Bienefeld's Theory of Hours Rounds', *British Journal of Industrial Relations*, vol. 25, pp. 1–17.

Roemer, J. E. (1979) 'Divide and Conquer: Microfoundations of a Marxian Theory of Wage Discrimination', *Bell Journal of Economics*, vol. 10, pp. 695–705.

Rosen, S. (1985) 'Implicit Contracts: a Survey', *Journal of Economic Literature*, vol. 23, pp. 1144–75.

Ross, A. M. (1953) *Trade Union Wage Policy* (Berkeley: University of California Press).

Ross, A. M. (1958) 'Do We Have a New Industrial Feudalism?', *American Economic Review*, vol. 48, pp. 903–20.

Routh, G. (1980) *Occupation and Pay in Great Britain 1906–79* (London: Macmillan).

Rowe, J. W. F. (1969) *Wages in Practice and Theory* (London: Routledge & Kegan Paul: first published 1928).

Rowthorn, R. (1977) 'Conflict, Inflation and Money', *Cambridge Journal of Economics*, vol. 1, pp. 215–39.

Rubin, P. H. (1973) 'A Paradox Regarding the Use of Time', *Indian Economic Journal*, vol. 20, pp. 469–71.

Sahota, G. S. (1980) 'Theories of Personal Income Distribution: a Survey', *Journal of Economic Literature*, vol. 16, pp. 1–55.

Samuelson, P. A. (1963) 'Discussion', *American Economic Review*, vol. 53, pp. 231–6.

Sawhill, I. V. (1988) 'Poverty in the United States: Why Is It So Persistent?', *Journal of Economic Literature*, vol. 26, pp. 1073–1119.

Sawyer, M. C. (1985) *The Economics of Michal Kalecki* (London: Macmillan).

Sawyer, M. C. (1988) 'Theories of Monopoly Capitalism', *Journal of Economic Surveys*, vol. 2, pp. 42–76.

Schor, J. B. (1985) 'Changes in the Cyclical Pattern of Real Wages: Evidence for Nine Countries, 1955–80', *Economic Journal*, vol. 95, pp. 452–68.

Schumacher, E. F. (1973) *Small is Beautiful* (London: Blond and Briggs).

Schumacher, E. F. (1974a) *People's Power* (London: National Council of Social Service).

Schumacher, E. F. (1974b) *The Age of Plenty: a Christian View* (Edinburgh: The Saint Andrews Press).

Schumacher, E. F. (1979) *Good Work* (London: Cape).

Scully, G. W. (1969) 'Interstate Wage Differentials: a Cross Section Analysis', *American Economic Review*, vol. 59, pp. 757–73.

Segal, M. (1986) 'Post-Institutionalism in Labor Economics: the Forties and Fifties Reconsidered', *Industrial and Labor Relations Review*, vol. 39, pp. 388–403.

Sen, A. K. (1979) 'Issues in the Measurement of Poverty', *Scandinavian Journal of Economics*, vol. 81, pp. 285–307.

Sen, A. K. (1979) 'Personal Utilities and Public Judgements: or

What's Wrong With Welfare Economics', *Economic Journal*, vol. 89, pp. 537–58.

Shah, A. and Walker, M. (1983) 'The Distribution of Regional Earnings in the United Kingdom', *Applied Economics*, vol. 15, pp. 507–19.

Shapiro, C. and Stiglitz, J. E. (1984) 'Equilibrium Unemployment as a Worker Discipline Device', *American Economic Review*, vol. 74, pp. 433–44.

Siebert, W. S. (1985) 'Development in the Economics of Human Capital', in D. Carline *et al.* (eds), *Labour Economics*, pp. 5–77 (Harlow: Longman).

Siebert, W. S. and Addison, J. T. (1981) 'Are Strikes Accidental?', *Economic Journal*, vol. 91, pp. 389–404.

Siebert, W. S. and Sloane, P. J. (1981) 'The Measurement of Sex and Marital Status Discrimination at the Workplace', *Economica*, n.s., vol. 48, pp. 125–41.

Simon, H. A. (1951) 'A Formal Theory of the Employment Relationship', *Econometrica*, vol. 19, pp. 293–305.

Simon, H. A. (1957) 'The Compensation of Executives', *Sociometry*, vol. 20, pp. 32–5.

Simon, H. A. (1982) *Models of Bounded Rationality* (Cambridge, Mass.: MIT Press).

Simons, H. C. (1944) 'Some Reflections on Syndicalism', *Journal of Political Economy*, vol. 52, pp. 1–25.

Sinclair, P. (1987) *Unemployment: Economic Theory and Evidence* (Oxford: Blackwell).

Sjaastad, L. A. (1962) 'The Costs and Returns of Human Migration', *Journal of Political Economy*, vol. 70 (Supplement), pp. 80–93.

Slichter, S. H. (1950) 'Notes on the Structure of Wages', *Review of Economics and Statistics*, vol. 32, pp. 80–91.

Sloane, P. J. (1985) 'Discrimination in the Labour Market', in D. Carline *et al.* (eds), *Labour Economics*, pp. 78–158 (Harlow: Longman).

Smith, A. (1776) *The Wealth of Nations* (London: Methuen, 1961).

Smith, E. (1988) 'Vacancies and Recruitment in Great Britain', *Employment Gazette*, April, pp. 211–3.

Solow, R. M. (1958) 'A Sceptical Note on the Constancy of Relative Shares', *American Economic Review*, vol. 48, pp. 618–31.

Solow, R. M. (1980) 'On Theories of Unemployment', *American Economic Review*, vol. 70, pp. 1–11.

Solow, R. M. (1986) 'Unemployment: Getting the Questions Right', *Economica* n.s., vol. 53, pp. S23–S34.

Southall, H. R. (1988) 'The Origins of the Depressed Areas: Unemployment, Growth and Regional Economic Structure in Britain Before 1914', *Economic History Review n.s.*, vol. 41, pp. 236–58.

Steindl, J. (1952) *Maturity and Stagnation in American Capitalism* (Oxford: Blackwell; second edition; New York, Monthly Review Press, 1976).

Stewart, M. B. (1983a) 'Relative Earnings and Individual Union Membership in the United Kingdom', *Economica* n.s., vol. 50, pp. 111–25.

Stewart, M. B. (1983b) 'Racial Discrimination and Occupational Attainment in Britain', *Economic Journal*, vol. 93, pp. 521–41.

Stewart, M. B. and Greenhalgh, C. A. (1984) 'Work History Patterns and the Occupational Attainment of Women', *Economic Journal*, vol. 94, pp. 493–519.

Stigler, G. J. (1962) 'Information in the Labor Market', *Journal of Political Economy*, vol. 70 (Supplement), pp. 94–105.

Stiglitz, J. E. (1987) 'The Causes and Consequences of the Dependence of Quality on Price', *Journal of Economic Literature*, vol. 25, pp. 1–48.

Stone, K. (1974) 'The Origins of Job Structures in the Steel Industry', *Review of Radical Political Economics*, vol. 6, pp. 113–73.

Sweezy, P. M. (1939) 'Demand Under Conditions of Oligopoly', *Journal of Political Economy*, vol. 47, pp. 568–73.

Symons, J. S. V. (1985) 'Relative Prices and the Demand for Labour in British Manufacturing', *Economica* n.s., vol. 52, pp. 37–49.

Symons, J. and Layard, R. (1984) 'Neoclassical Demand for Labour Functions for Six Major Economies', *Economic Journal*, vol. 94, pp. 788–99.

Taylor, D. (1986) 'Measuring Unemployment', *Unemployment Bulletin*, vol. 22, pp. 16–17.

Taylor, J. (1974) *Unemployment and Wage Inflation* (Harlow: Longman).

Taylor, J. (1986) 'The Use of Unemployment and Vacancy Data in Analyzing Unemployment', *Recherches Economiques de Louvain*, vol. 52, pp. 257–82.

Therborn, G. (1986) *Why Some Peoples Are More Unemployed Than Others: the Strange Paradox of Growth and Unemployment* (London: Verso).

260   *Bibliography*

Thurow, L. C. (1969) *Poverty and Discrimination* (Washington, DC: Brookings Institution).
Thurow, L. C. (1970) *Investment in Human Capital* (Belmont, Cal.: Wadsworth).
Thurow, L. C. (1976) *Generating Inequality* (London: Macmillan).
Todaro, M. P. (1976) *Internal Migration in Developing Countries* (Geneva: International Labour Office).
Treble, J. G. (1984) 'Does the Union/Non-Union Differential Exist?', *Manchester School*, vol. 52, pp. 160–70.
Turk, J. (1983) 'Work and Unemployment', in D. Shepherd, J. Turk and A. Silberston (eds), *Microeconomic Efficiency and Macroeconomic Performance*, pp. 40–76 (Deddington: Philip Allan).
Unemployment Unit (1986) 'The Count Controversy', *Unemployment Bulletin*, vol. 22, pp. 14–15.
US Bureau of the Census (1988) *Current Population Reports*, 'Income of Families and Persons in the United States', P-60 series.
Wachtel, H. M. and Betsey, C. (1972) 'Employment at Low Wages', *Review of Economics and Statistics*, vol. 54, pp. 121–9.
Wallich, H. C. and Weintraub, S. (1971) 'A Tax-Based Incomes Policy', *Journal of Economic Issues*, vol. 5, pp. 1–19.
Webb, S. and Webb, B. (1897) *Industrial Democracy* (London: Longmans, Green).
Weisskopf, T. E. (1979) 'Marxian Crisis Theory and the Rate of Profit in the Postwar U.S. Economy', *Cambridge Journal of Economics*, vol. 3, pp. 341–78.
Weisskopf, T. E., Bowles, S. and Gordon, D. M. (1983) 'Hearts and Minds: a Social Model of U.S. Productivity Growth', *Brookings Papers on Economic Activity*, pp. 381–441.
Whitehead, D. W. (1973) *Stagflation and Wages Policy in Australia* (Camberwell, Victoria: Longman).
Wiles, P. (1974) 'The Correlation Between Education and Earnings: The External-Test-Not-Content Hypothesis (ETNC)', *Higher Education*, vol. 3, pp. 43–58.
Wilkinson, F. (ed.) (1981) *The Dynamics of Labour Market Segmentation* (London: Academic Press).
Williamson, O. E. (1964) *The Economics of Discretionary Behaviour: Managerial Objectives in a Theory of the Firm* (Englewood Cliffs, NJ: Prentice-Hall).
Williamson, O. E. (1975) *Markets and Hierarchies: Analysis and Antitrust Implications* (New York: The Free Press).

Williamson, J. G. (1985) *Did British Capitalism Breed Inequality?* (London: Allen & Unwin).

Willis, R. J. (1986) 'Wage Determinants: a Survey and Reinterpretation of Human Capital Earnings Functions', in O. Ashenfelter and R. Layard (eds), *Handbook of Labor Economics*, volume I, pp. 525–602 (Amsterdam: North-Holland).

Withers, G., Pitman, D. and Whittingham, B. (1986) 'Wage Adjustments and Labour Market Systems: a Cross-Country Analysis', *Economic Record*, vol. 62, pp. 415–26.

Wolff, E. N. (1987) *Growth, Accumulation, and Unproductive Activity: an Analysis of the U.S. Economy* (Cambridge: Cambridge University Press).

Wood, B. (1984) *Alias Papa: a Life of E. F. Schumacher* (London: Cape).

Woodbury, S. A. (1979) 'Methodological Controversy in Labor Economics', *Journal of Economic Issues*, vol. 13, pp. 933–55.

Wootton, B. (1955) *The Social Foundations of Wages Theory* (London: Allen & Unwin).

Yellen, J. L. (1984) 'Efficiency Wage Models of Unemployment', *American Economic Review*, vol. 74 (Papers and Proceedings), pp. 200–5.

Zabalza, A. and Tzannatos, Z. (1985) 'The Effect of Britain's Anti-Discriminatory Legislation on Relative Pay and Employment', *Economic Journal*, vol. 95, pp. 679–99.

Index